PRAISE FOR
LOSERS AND WINNERS,
SAINTS AND SINNERS

"LOSERS AND WINNERS, SAINTS AND SINNERS will challenge and encourage you . . . As [Greg] points out, there will be many who have the opportunity of finishing life's race strong but don't. As you read through these pages, take these biblical insights to heart and ensure you finish strong."

—Franklin Graham, president and CEO,
Billy Graham Evangelistic Association
and Samaritan's Purse

"Greg Laurie understands the hard realities faced by everyday people in today's world. He also grasps—and marvelously communicates—the timeless ultimate reality that provides workable answers for people like us."

—Dr. Jack W. Hayford, president,
International Church of the Foursquare Gospel,
and chancellor, The King's College and Seminary

"Greg Laurie . . . creatively tells the riveting, real-life stories of both saints and sinners who have run the race of life . . . If you want to win in life and develop a strong, vibrant faith, this book is for you."

—Dr. Jack Graham, pastor,
Prestonwood Baptist Church, Plano, Texas

LOSERS
AND
WINNERS,
SAINTS
AND
SINNERS

*How to Finish Strong in
the Spiritual Race*

GREG LAURIE

WARNER
Faith®

NEW YORK   BOSTON   NASHVILLE

Warner Faith
1271 Avenue of the Americas
New York, NY 10020

The Warner Faith name and logo are registered trademarks.

Printed in the United States of America
Originally published in hardcover by Warner Books
First Trade Edition: June 2006
10 9 8 7 6 5 4 3 2 1

The Library of Congress has cataloged the hardcover edition as follows:
Laurie, Greg.
    Losers and winners, saints and sinners : how to finish strong in the spiritual race / Greg Laurie.
        p. cm.
    Summary: "Pastor Greg Laurie uses biblical examples to show that everyone faces adversity, but how one handles it is what sets people apart"—Provided by the publisher.
    Includes bibliographical references.
    ISBN 0-446-50015-1
    1. Christian life—Biblical teaching. 2. Bible—Criticism, interpretation, etc. I. Title.
BS680.C47L38 2005
248.4—dc22   2004030837

Cover design by David Koechel

ISBN-13: 978-0-446-69175-8 (pbk.)
ISBN-10: 0-446-69175-5 (pbk.)

This book is dedicated to Billy Graham,
a man who has been a friend to me personally
and who has given us all an example of
personal integrity lived out.
Billy started and is finishing his race well.
I am confident the Lord will say to him in that final day,
"Well done, thou good and faithful servant."

CONTENTS

Special thanks to . . .

Chuck Fromm, for giving me the original idea for a message called "Finish Well" that ultimately became this book.

Mark Ferjulian, for his hard work and behind-the-scenes efforts to help make this project a reality.

Leslie Peterson, for her vision, patience, and encouragement.

Rolf Zettersten, for still believing, and finally to

The congregation of Harvest Christian Fellowship, the church I have had the privilege of pastoring for thirty-one years. It was to them I originally gave these messages.

INTRODUCTION

I am a runner.

I can't believe I just wrote those words because I fought it for years, even decades. Sure, as a kid I loved to run and even went out for track and field in high school. But as the years passed and the waistline grew, running became less appealing. For years I sat in wonder as I listened to those who spoke almost euphorically of the endorphins their brains released as they ran.

I had never experienced any endorphin release. Just pain and more pain.

But I had to acknowledge that those who did jog regularly dropped quite a few pounds. So I decided to start again.

Someone watched me run a bit and told me that I "pronated."

"Pro-what?"

In other words, I ran on the inside edges of my feet, causing more strain on shins, knees, and so on. This was surprising to me, as I had the ultimate running shoes—or so I thought. I ended up with a less expensive, but firmer, pair of shoes.

Other runners told me music helped them as they jogged.

So I loaded up my ipod and was ready to go. My first time out was more walking than running. After a while it became about equal periods of both. Soon it was primarily running. And that is what I am doing as of this writing. It takes discipline to run, but the results are worth it.

There's another kind of running that requires discipline. But the results are worth it in that race too. If you are a Christian, you are in a spiritual race, as Paul made clear in his epistles. No doubt you've felt the occasional strained muscle, days when the track seemed too long and the sun too hot, and moments of victory that made all the pain worthwhile.

What's great about being in a race is that you are a participant, not a spectator. You have something to say about how you are going to do spiritually. Make no mistake about it: people fall away from their faith and quit the spiritual race only because they choose to do so. It's up to you.

It's a well-proven truth that we can learn from one another's mistakes as well as each other's successes. You may be wondering, *What is the secret to spiritual longevity? What steps can I take to assure I will make it across the finishing line? How can I know I will hear the Lord say to me, "Well done, good and faithful servant"?*

We should all be asking these questions because one day every one of us will complete this race we are running. And each of us will be either a winner or a loser. One day, we all are going to die. (The statistics on death are quite impressive: one out of every one person will die!)

Let me ask you this: what would you like written on your tombstone? How about something that would tell us a bit about you, what you believed and stood for? Larry King authored a book called *Remember Me When I'm Gone*. It contains the epitaphs the rich and famous have written for themselves—things for which they want to be remembered.

Some are humorous, some bizarre, some touching. Here are a few samples.

> Here lies Stacy Keach.
> A Georgia peach.
> Lived at the beach.
> Now out of reach.
> —ACTOR STACY KEACH

> I am speechless. Trust me.
> —FILMMAKER AND DIRECTOR MILOS FORMAN

> I seem to have run out of tomorrows.
> —COMEDIAN ARTE JOHNSON

> Calvin Klein by Eternity
> —CLOTHING DESIGNER CALVIN KLEIN

Hugh Hefner, founder and publisher of *Playboy* magazine, noted in King's book, "I'd like to be remembered as someone who played some part in changing our hurtful and hypocritical views on sex—and had a lot of fun doing it."[1]

Sometimes tombstones describe how the person died. In memory of an accident in a Uniontown, Pennsylvania, cemetery one tombstone read:

> Here lies the body of Jonathan Blake
> Stepped on the gas instead of the brake.

Sometimes tombstones are painfully blunt. I read about one for a man named John Starkweather. It says:

Here is where friend Starkweather lies.
Nobody laughs.
Nobody cries.
Where he goes, how he fares,
nobody knows. Nobody cares.

A tombstone in a Thurmont, Maryland, cemetery contains a more telling statement:

Here lies an atheist
All dressed up
And no place to go.

What would your friends or family write on your tombstone? What statement could they make to sum up your life? Would you like what it says?

When we finish this race of life, we will stand at the judgment seat of Jesus Christ. There we will receive our rewards, if we have run well. Some of us have acquired the great awards this world has to offer over the years. Perhaps you excelled in sports, and your shelves were lined with trophies and plaques. Personally, I always had a lot of those Honorable Mention ribbons (which means I showed up but came in last place). But in heaven there will be many rewards for those who have been faithful to God over the years. The Lord doesn't overlook even the smallest and most insignificant gesture on behalf of His kingdom. Jesus said that our service to God, though not seen by people, is seen by God: "Your Father who sees in secret will Himself reward you openly" (Matt. 6:4). Speaking of this day in the future of all believers, the Bible says, "For we must all appear before the judgment seat of Christ, that each one may receive what is due him for the things done while in the body, whether good or bad" (2 Cor. 5:10 NIV).

Paul further developed this concept:

> For no one can lay any foundation other than the one already laid, which is Jesus Christ. If any man builds on this foundation using gold, silver, costly stones, wood, hay or straw, his work will be shown for what it is, because the Day will bring it to light. It will be revealed with fire, and the fire will test the quality of each man's work. If what he has built survives, he will receive his reward. If it is burned up, he will suffer loss; he himself will be saved, but only as one escaping through the flames. (1 CORINTHIANS 3:11–15 NIV)

According to this and other passages, the promises of God guarantee our presence in the kingdom. But the quality of service we render here and now will determine what *position* we will have in the kingdom. Salvation is a gift through faith in Jesus Christ. Honor is a reward for service to Jesus Christ.

When Paul wrote of "wood, hay or straw," he was basically speaking not of gross sin as much as putting more importance on the passing things of this world than on the things of God. It might be a career, some sport or hobby, endless hours spent in front of a TV, and so on. I've heard more than once that the average American spends somewhere around fifteen years of his or her life in front of the TV set! What a waste. Things such as these will pass.

On that final day, God will want to know what you did with your gifts (talents and abilities) and your time. He will want to know what you did with the sacred charge of spreading the gospel, which He entrusted to you. I can't tell you how important this is. When a person dies, and I am asked to speak at the memorial service, I always try to find out as much as I can about the person. Sometimes, the person was a friend, or someone I knew, so I can talk about what I personally observed. But when I do not know the person, I ask family members and friends to tell me about him or her. I never point out how successful the person was in business because at a funeral, frankly, nobody cares. I don't talk about how handsome or beautiful he or she may have been. I try to find the enduring qualities of such people's lives: acts of kindness, sacrificial acts, a story that might sum up what really mattered to them.

I can't tell how grieving it is to find nothing of this kind. Then I realize I am dealing with a person who largely wasted his or her life, and that is just pathetic!

But it happens far too often.

This reminds me of the Prophet Daniel's words to the irreverent King Belshazzar: "You have been weighed in [God's] balances, and found wanting" (Dan. 5:27). In other words, Daniel was saying "Belshazzar, you are a spiritual lightweight. You have no substance. And guess what? Your life is required of you!"

Let me ask you this: if someone were to honestly sum up your life at your funeral service, for what would he or she remember you?

It's sad for us when someone dies. But if that person dies in the Lord, and if he has served him for his whole life, it is really a glorious thing in many ways. The Bible says, "Precious in the sight of the LORD / Is the death of His saints" (Ps. 116:15). We all know death is going to come. What we need to do—what we need to focus on—is finishing well and making every single day count. We all want a life that is worth living. The tragedy of life is not that it ends so soon, but that we wait so long to begin it. Or that we live our lives in a way that seems to go nowhere fast.

In Florence, Italy, a young artist labored long and hard over a marble statue of an angel. When finished, he asked the great artist Michelangelo to examine it. No master looked over the work more carefully than Michelangelo. It appeared perfect in every way.

The young artist waited for Michelangelo's response. His heart nearly broke when he heard, "It lacks only one thing."

But the great artist didn't tell him what it lacked. For days the artist could not eat or sleep, until finally a friend called on Michelangelo at his studio and asked him to please tell what he thought it lacked.

He said, "It lacks only life."

That could be said of so many today. They have everything they should to supposedly be "happy"—a good job, a family, a beautiful home—but "it lacks life."

Most of us could well say somewhere down the road of life, "If I had known what I know now, I would have lived differently. I would have done things differently in order to have a better life." Remember, some die earlier than expected. Somehow we think we are all going to make it into our eighties or nineties. We may, we may not. Some of us may have shorter courses to run. That makes every minute count—for all of us.

One man who lived his life well was Jim Elliot. He was in his early twenties when he felt called to take the gospel to the Auca Indians in Ecuador. He, along with some friends and his new bride, Elisabeth, followed God's leading. Jim paid with his life when the very people he'd been trying to teach turned on him. He and his missionary colleagues died from spear wounds. Wrapped around one spear was a gospel tract they had given the Aucas.

Jim gave his life for the gospel. It seems like a tragic thing, but he lived for the glory of God. He did what he was supposed to do. And he finished well. He understood the importance of that; in fact, he wrote in his journal before his death: "I seek not a long life but a full one, like Yours, Lord Jesus." He lived that full life.

Time is passing by, and we don't want to squander this precious thing God has given us called *life*. And we don't want anything less than a spectacular finish.

In this book I'd like to share some examples of Godly people who managed to lead not just blessed and productive lives, but who finished victoriously as well—people like the martyr Jim Elliot. In contrast, I will also share stories of people who failed in life, death, or both. We can learn from them as well.

I'm sure that for you, as for me, life both physical and spiritual has been filled with surprises. Some people I thought were going to do great things for God started out tremendously but then veered off course. They have actually fallen away. Some people I thought would never even make it as Christians are not only making it but also serving the Lord gloriously and with great effectiveness.

We can take the mystery out of running and finishing well. Those who look as though they are going to make it across the finish line with flying colors—I want to be one of those people. Don't you? Let's take a run together and find out how.

LOSERS *AND* WINNERS, SAINTS *AND* SINNERS

Princes and paupers, sons and daughters
Kneel at the throne of grace
Losers and winners, saints and sinners
One day will see His face
And we all bow down
Kings will surrender their crowns
And worship Jesus
For He is the love, unfailing love
He is the love of God

1
RUNNING UP
A MOUNTAIN

Caleb is one of the unsung heroes of the Bible. He stands as a shining example of one who never lost his edge spiritually. He was faithful to the very end. He himself said at age eighty-five, "I am as strong this day as on the day that Moses sent me; just as my strength was then, so now is my strength for war, both for going out and coming in" (Josh. 14:11).

Let's try to identify where he got this true grit, this spiritual chutzpah to live so strong for so long. His story is in Joshua 14. At that point in the history of God's people, the Israelites had finally made it to the long-awaited promised land, and Joshua was dispersing portions of it to the various tribes. Caleb suddenly spoke up, saying,

You know the word which the LORD said to Moses the man of God concerning you and me in Kadesh Barnea. I was forty years old when Moses the servant of the LORD sent me from Kadesh Barnea to spy out the land, and I brought back word to him as it was in my heart. Nevertheless my brethren who went up with me made the heart of the people melt, but I wholly followed the LORD my God.
(JOSHUA 14:6–8)

1

In response, Joshua granted faithful Caleb what he asked: Caleb would inherit the land he had surveyed. Yet the old man proved he had not yet exhausted his courage, for then he said:

> Here I am this day, eighty-five years old. As yet I am as strong this day as on the day that Moses sent me...Now therefore, give me this mountain [the land of Hebron] of which the LORD spoke in that day; for you heard in that day how the Anakim were there, and that the cities were great and fortified. It may be that the LORD will be with me, and I shall be able to drive them out as the LORD has said. (JOSHUA 14:10–12)

The other guys must have thought old Caleb was senile. Hebron was not some beautiful green pasture; it was one of the most treacherous mountainous areas of the promised land. Worse, formidable adversaries, identified as the three sons of Anak, lived there. They would have to be routed before the old man could take possession. No one wanted to take them on except eighty-five-year-old Caleb, holding up that muscular old arm, saying, "Give me this mountain."

I love his boldness. Caleb ran up the mountain. He slew his adversaries. He was victorious. He had been strong all those years, and he finished well.

....

A Strategy for Strength—Courtesy of Caleb

Let me share some principles with you from Caleb's life that can give us this spiritual stamina we all need to run and indeed finish in the race of life.

1. Follow the Lord 100 Percent

Scripture says again and again that Caleb "wholly followed the LORD." It's in Joshua 14:8–9 and verse 14 too: Joshua blessed

Caleb and gave the old man what he asked because "he wholly followed the LORD God of Israel."

This is clearly a key to Caleb's spiritual success. But what does it mean to "wholly follow the Lord"? It means that you must fully follow our Lord not halfheartedly, but completely. One hundred percent.

What does that mean? It means that you give everything to God. Many people don't do this—the way they live provides the evidence. It all starts with priorities; when crisis hits, they expect God to drop everything and get them out of the mess they are in. But when it comes to honoring Him by just going to church on Sunday, they are too busy: "I don't know if we should go to church. The weatherman said it might rain today. There is no rain out there right now, but we don't want to risk our lives and tempt the Lord. We'd better not go. How about the mall or the movies?"

The real problem here is lack of total commitment. There will always be a hundred convenient excuses to hide behind, but the fact is you will make time for what matters to you.

We see the priority problem in their resources and giving as well. They ask God to provide for them and take care of their needs. Even though He does, they don't even think about giving when the offering plate passes.

What is wrong with these pictures? Are you wholly following the Lord your God? Are you fully following Him?

Let me tell you something. If you are not, you will be picked off eventually. It is only a matter of time until you become a casualty in the race of life. You can see this in the lives of the Israelites.

Caleb mentioned a very important place in his little speech called Kadesh Barnea. Forty-five years earlier, Caleb, Joshua, and Moses, along with the children of Israel, had come to the brink of the promised land, a point of entry known as Kadesh Barnea. You remember God had gloriously delivered the Israelites from their slave masters in Egypt, in answer to their prayers. He had opened up the Red Sea for them to cross through, then drowned the Egyptian army as it pursued them. When the Israelites arrived at the new land God had promised them that was flowing with milk and honey, God instructed Moses to send twelve representatives to check it out.

After forty days, the spies returned and gave their report. It happened that they had divided into two groups. The majority—ten of them—said, "There are these huge, walled cities and giant adversaries." They exaggerated, saying, "We were like grasshoppers in their sight." Then the spies showed their people the bounty they had found in that dangerous land: a bunch of grapes so large two men had to carry it on a pole between them. The consensus: "There is no way we should go in."

Joshua and Caleb gave the minority report: "It is true things are big there, but the Lord will be with us. Let's go for it." But the Israelites were so upset with Joshua and Caleb for suggesting this that they clamored about heading back to Egypt.

The Lord was angry with the Israelites for failing to honor Him. He had brought them that far, had done great things to deliver them, yet they didn't believe He would preserve them in the new land. So God declared, "Of those that have come this far, only Joshua and Caleb are going into the land. The rest of you are not going in."

In other words, those who followed the Lord wholeheartedly won the race; the others were disqualified.

I guess it's all in how you look at things. You could say two were optimists and the others were pessimists. It is more than that. Joshua and Caleb looked at the promised land—remembering it was the "promised" land—through the eyes of faith.

I once heard the story of an American shoe salesman sent to a foreign country. He had been there just a week when he e-mailed the company for money to come home. They asked why. He said, "Nobody here wears shoes."

That man returned. They quickly sent another salesman in his place. After a couple of days, he e-mailed back, saying, "Send me all of the shoes you have. Absolutely no one here has shoes. There are unlimited opportunities!"

Caleb saw God's promise where others saw only trouble and defeat. It isn't that Caleb had great faith in God as much as he had faith in a great God. He knew God had delivered them from one enemy, and He would deliver them from others as well.

2. Don't Compromise—Stand Your Ground

How easy it would have been for Caleb to go along with the crowd, not ruffle anybody's feathers. But he knew what was right, and so he stood his ground. At the risk of being personally ostracized, he took a stand for what he knew was true. He knew he needed to be more concerned with God's approval than man's. And he was rewarded.

As you walk with the Lord, you will face many temptations to cave in to peer pressure, to do what everybody else does. I know what you're thinking: if you take a stand with your family, neighbors, or coworkers, they may ostracize you. They may mock you. They might even harm you physically. But if you are going to fully follow the Lord, then, like Caleb, you must make this principle operative in your life. Stand firm—seek God's pleasure, no one else's.

3. Take God at His Word

Caleb didn't win immediate entrance to the promised land. First he had to wander around with those ungrateful, complaining Israelites for forty years. They said things like "We remember the good old days back in Egypt, where we had garlic, leeks, and onions." Now, when you read about life for the

Israelites in Egypt, you don't see anything about their having great food. You read about their being miserable slaves who cried out to God, day and night, to be delivered. The Israelites conveniently forgot all that.

Isn't it interesting how the devil helps us exaggerate our pasts when he wants to pull us back? The devil will whisper in our ears, "Remember the good old days." *Yeah. That* was *good,* we think.

The devil is clever. He doesn't say, "Remember when you were so miserable that you actually considered suicide? Remember the times you were so drunk you didn't even know where you were when you woke up? Remember when your marriage almost fell apart?" He will remind you only of the few "good times" you had in order to draw you back. He did exactly this to the Israelites, and they went right along with it.

Except for Caleb. Despite the Israelites' childish clinging to fictitious memories, Caleb hung on to the promises of God. It didn't matter to him that he had to wait forty years. He knew God would be faithful, regardless of the time frame.

We need to do the same. Some who have been walking with us will turn away and go back to the old life. Crises will hit. Hardship falls on everyone. But like Caleb, we have to believe God's promise that we are going to make it across that finishing line.

Fortunately, we don't have to do this in our own strength. Jude referred to "Him who is able to keep you from stumbling / And to present you faultless / Before the presence of His glory with exceeding joy" (1:24). Scripture reminds us that the Lord is "the author and finisher of our faith" (Heb. 12:2).

Caleb trusted God's word to him. We can do the same.

4. Long for Fellowship with Your God

Caleb asked for a place in the promised land called Hebron.

There is something interesting about the name *Hebron,*

which, in the original language, means "fellowship, love, and communion." Hebron is where Abraham met with God face-to-face and received the promise of the new land in the first place.

Here is my point: Caleb yearned for fellowship with God. While the other Israelites longed for Egypt, Caleb longed for Hebron. While the others looked back, Caleb looked forward. While others wanted to please themselves, Caleb wanted to please God. Of Caleb, Chuck Swindoll once said: "Caleb? Every new sunrise introduced another reminder that his body and rocking chair weren't made for each other. While his peers were yawning, Caleb was yearning."

This is an essential key to spiritual longevity. You must always move forward. You must always seek to grow spiritually and never look back. That's what will keep you going. You have to follow the Lord even if your friends aren't there with you. As the song says, "Though none go with me, still I will follow."[1] If you are living this Christian life for others' applause, you won't make it. People are going to let you down. Circumstances are going to challenge you. You have to run empowered by your love for God.

Is that why you're running the race right now?

I already told you that in high school, I ran track and field. I found a little secret back then about running faster.

Whenever a pretty girl was watching, I somehow had a new burst of energy to run a bit longer and faster.

I have a better motivation for you than pretty girls: the Lord Himself is watching you. He is the only One for whom you need to run the race. That is what kept Caleb going. And that longing for fellowship and communion with God resulted in his finishing well. We need to apply Caleb's principles in our lives.

The author of Hebrews reminded us of this motive in running the race of life well in the twelfth chapter of the book:

Therefore we also, since we are surrounded by so great a cloud of witnesses, let us lay aside every weight, and the sin which so easily ensnares us, and let us run with endurance the race that is set before us, looking unto Jesus, the author and finisher of our faith, who for the joy that was set before Him endured the cross, despising the shame, and has sat down at the right hand of the throne of God. (HEBREWS 12:1–2)

. . . .

Another Who Finished Well

Let me share with you a contemporary story about a man who operated on these principles. On September 11, 2001, flight attendant Al Marchand hugged his wife, Rebecca, in Boston's Logan Airport before heading off to a plane bound for Los Angeles. "I guess this is good-bye," he said, kissing her. "I love you."

"See you in four days," she answered.

Marchand, 44, had retired from the police force only eight months prior and landed a new job with United Airlines. Rebecca had questioned a career change that pulled him away from the family, but Al insisted that God wanted him to take the job for a reason. Sixty-four minutes after take-off, Al Marchand's plane, flight 175, plowed into the World Trade Center's South Tower... "I know it was no mistake that he was on flight 175," Rebecca said. "You can see a lifetime of planning on God's part."

Just four years earlier, Al Marchand had first heard about having a personal relationship with God—at a pub. When he wasn't working as a policeman, he moonlighted as a brewer. The people who cleaned the pub listened to my messages on tape while they worked. Al tried to avoid hearing the tapes, but some of what I was saying caught his ear anyway. Eventually Al left his office door open just a bit so he could hear more.

Al enjoyed a lively drinking relationship with his girl-friend, Rebecca, and they visited club after club every night. But when Rebecca found Jesus, she gave Al an ultimatum: follow Jesus with me, or let me go.

Al resisted, but the words he heard me say haunted him, and he found himself visiting a church the next weekend. A week later, he gave his life to Jesus. A week after that, he and Rebecca married.

The couple became enthusiastic believers. Al made a point of talking about Jesus to everyone he met. He loved to share this life-giving relationship.

Then Al received a new call from God, and it beckoned from an Internet advertisement: "Become a flight attendant." Al was certain he'd found God's plan for his life, saying to Rebecca, "What if there is a time when a flight is going down? What if I am the only one who can share the gospel?" In fact, when a passenger once asked him if he ever feared flying, Al answered, "I became a flight attendant so if a plane went down I could have 30 to 40 seconds to speak the gospel so people could receive Christ."

Then came September 11. The night before he'd been asked to take the place of another flight attendant who had become ill. For her part, Rebecca believes Al was supposed to be on that fatal flight: "At some point," she says, "I am sure he shared the gospel with the other passengers."

Though now in heaven, Al is still impacting people with his relationship with Jesus. Said one passenger who flew with him on an earlier flight, "He encouraged me to speak about Christ more. You don't know how your life is going to affect another person's. Al made me realize we don't know how much time we have."[2]

When you read a story like that, you say, "How tragic." On one hand, it is. But on the other hand, I think it is glorious! I am confident Al did what he loved to do: share the gospel.

Who knows how many came into eternity as a result of his being in the right place at the right time and finishing the course that God had set for him?

This man finished well. We need to do the same.

. . . .

Kept, Preserved, Protected

Though you are the only person who can run your spiritual race, you don't have to run alone. The Bible says God will keep you and preserve you. Jude addressed his letter "to those who are called, sanctified by God the Father and preserved in Jesus Christ" (1:1). How secure is that? The original language uses the perfect tense. The nearest equivalent of that is "continually kept by Jesus Christ." It is a continuing result of a past action.

You need to know that whatever difficulties you face today as a believer, you are being watched over and protected by Christ.

God will always protect His own, because He loves us.

Even we careless humans don't lose something we love. We keep our eyes on it. If I have a cheap pair of sunglasses, I may not be all that concerned about their whereabouts. But if I have a more expensive pair, I will tend to know where they are. We protect that which is dear to us.

Look at it this way: you are loved by God. He is going to protect his investment. Imagine: if it were not for God's intervention on our behalf, every one of us would vapor lock on the spot. None of us would make it across the finishing line.

Fortunately for all of us, Jesus Christ is in heaven, loving, preserving, and interceding for us before the Father. Hebrews 7:25 says, "He is able to save completely those who come to God through him, because he always lives to intercede for them" (NIV). We are preserved. We are protected. And we are being kept by the power of God. That is good—no, great—news!

What is our part in this powerful equation? The Bible says we are to keep ourselves in the love of God (Jude 1:21). Is that a contradiction? On one hand, the Bible says God will keep us. On the other hand, it says we need to keep ourselves. But, no, it's not a contradiction at all—these two verses complement one another. They merely show us that there is God's part, and then there is ours. We don't keep ourselves saved, but we can keep ourselves safe.

That is why Jude reminded us to keep ourselves in the love of God. God's love is unconditional. It is undeserved. But we are capable of stepping out of harmony with his love. Jude was saying to keep ourselves away from all that is spiritually destructive. In other words: consciously avoid any influence that would violate God's love and bring sorrow to His heart. Maintain a position where God can actively show His love to you. Keep yourself in the love of God.

We all know of situations, activities, places where we would find ourselves more vulnerable to the devil's enticements. Now that we have been delivered from his power, we don't want to put ourselves in a position of vulnerability again. Right?

Why do I bring this up? Because Scripture tells us that "some will turn away from the faith, giving attention to deluding and seducing spirits and doctrines that demons teach" (1 Tim. 4:1 AMP). In these critical days, the devil is walking about "like a roaring lion," looking for people he can pull down (1 Pet. 5:8).

The book of Hebrews warns us of the perils of throwing in the towel and turning back spiritually. Hebrews 3:12 says, "Beware, brethren, lest there be in any of you an evil heart of unbelief in departing from the living God." Notice that the writer did not direct this admonition to nonbelievers. He said, "Beware, *brothers*." Christian, be careful—you *can* depart from the living God.

. . . .

Don't Stop Short of the Goal

Then the writer added, "[So] exhort one another daily, while it is called 'Today,' lest any of you be hardened through the deceitfulness of sin. For we have become partakers of Christ if we hold fast the beginning of our confidence steadfast to the end" (Heb. 3:13). Did you catch that? You become a *partaker of Christ* if you hold your confidence all the way to the end. In other words, you have to cross the finishing line.

It's not enough to do well for the first five years or the next twenty. You have to cross the finishing line in order to *finish* well.

That is why Paul, when he was leaving the elders of Ephesus, said:

> None of these things [such as the threat of imprisonment] move me; neither do I esteem my life dear to myself, if only I may I want to *finish my course with joy* and the ministry which I have obtained from the Lord Jesus, faithfully to attest to the good news...of God's grace. (ACTS 20:24 AMP)

My question to you is this: are you doing what God has called you to do? Are you finishing the course? Like Caleb, like Al, let's keep moving forward spiritually: maintain our love for God, take Him at His word, seek His approval alone. If indeed we wholly follow Him, we will, without doubt, finish well.

That's what we all should be hoping for right now. This is not the time for slowing down. This is not the time for easing up. This is not the time for resting on your laurels. This is the time to pour it on! Keep yourself in the love of God. Pick up the pace!

2
WALK LIKE
A MAN

I am glad the Bible not only compares the Christian life to running a race but also to walking a walk. Isaiah 40:31 pulls it together:

> Those who wait upon the LORD
>   Shall renew their strength;
> They shall mount up with wings as eagles,
>   They shall run and not be weary,
> They shall walk and not faint.

Different levels of movement, same strength in God.

In Genesis is a man who walked—not ran—with God. In his story we will discover more secrets for winning the spiritual race of life. We will discover how we can learn to endure—and not do what athletes call "bonking." That's when you are running and you just don't feel as though you can go any farther. It's as if you have hit a wall.

Certainly this happens in the spiritual race. We think, *I can't make it another inch. I'm worn out. I'm stopping here.* But we need to learn how to press on and endure, because in our relationship with God, we are in it for the long haul. We want to finish this race well. It is more than a journey of feeling. It is a journey of faith.

....

The Longest Day

Let's look at the story of a man who took that journey. Talk about taking a long walk: this man's was the longest possible. It lasted three hundred years. His name was Enoch. He walked with God for—that's right—three centuries.

It is interesting how in the whole Bible, only five passages refer to Enoch. One is in Hebrews 11: "By faith Enoch was taken from this life, so that he did not experience death; he could not be found, because God had taken him away. For before he was taken, he was commended as one who pleased God" (v. 5 NIV).

Though the Bible contains little information about Enoch, what we do have is significant. His story appears in Genesis 5:21–24:

> Enoch lived sixty-five years, and begot Methuselah. After he begot Methuselah, Enoch walked with God three hundred years, and had sons and daughters. So all the days of Enoch were three hundred and sixty-five years. And Enoch walked with God; and he was not, for God took him.

It is a short passage of Scripture for such an interesting character. Understand that Enoch lived in a very dark time in human history. It was just before God's judgment, which was coming in the form of the Flood. The twin sins of violence and sexual perversion characterized mankind. Man was so wicked that God said, "I am sorry that I even made him because the thoughts and intents of his heart are wicked continually" (see

Gen. 6:6). Judgment was on its way to cleanse the earth. It was a miserable era in the history of our world.

In the midst of all of this stood a man who walked with God. This was no small feat. The people of this day were largely wicked, and Enoch walked *alone* with his God. Consider the spiritual and moral climate he confronted—and overcame— every day.

It's clear Enoch was a Godly man, but what about him so touched God that He "took" him so he would not see death? Certainly he was a man of passions like all other humans. He didn't live in a monastery. Yet he managed to walk with God for three hundred years in an extremely wicked time in human history. How? He was not perfect, but he gave us a model to live by.

. . . .
How to Finish the Race, by Enoch

I want to identify for you three principles of Enoch's life. These are three keys that will help us finish the race as winners, not losers.

1. Enoch Walked with God

In short, Enoch *continued on.* "Walking" speaks of making progress. You are headed toward a destination, and you are moving toward it, slowly but surely. There is no mention of stopping or giving up.

The idea of walking with God appears constantly in the Bible. Some examples:

- As you received Christ Jesus the Lord, *so walk in him,* rooted and built up in him and established in the faith. (Colossians 2:6 ESV)
- *Walk in the Spirit,* and you shall not fulfill the lust of the flesh. (Galatians 5:16)

- *Let us walk properly as in the daytime,* not in...sexual immorality and sensuality, not in quarreling and jealousy. (Romans 13 esv)
- *And walk in love,* as Christ loved us and gave himself up for us, a fragrant offering and sacrifice to God. (Ephesians 5:2 esv)

Over and over again, the Bible tells us to walk with God, walk in love, walk in the light. What does it mean practically to "walk with God"? Let me tell you what it doesn't mean: it is not merely living by rules, regulations, and daily resolutions that you quickly break. It is more than that. Much more.

Malachi 2:6 gives us *God's* description of one who walks with Him: "True instruction was in his mouth, and no wrong was found on his lips. He walked with me in peace and uprightness, and he turned many from iniquity" (esv).

Think about this. God Himself says, "True instruction was in his mouth...He walked...in peace and uprightness...turned many away from sin." Let me ask you: are you walking with God?

What does it mean for us to be walking with God? Let's take a look at some of the elements.

Walk as a single unit. Amos 3:3 is another key verse for unlocking the principles of walking with God. It is a short passage, but it is action-packed: "Can two walk together, except they are agreed?" All sorts of subtle nuances and shades of meaning from the original language help us to flesh out what it means to walk with God. The original meaning spoke of God and man walking as a single unit, as though they were one.

We could compare it to riding a tandem bicycle. Let's say that you and I went out for a ride. You were in the front, pedaling away. I was in the back, hitting the brakes. Is that going to help you? No. It's going to slow you down and impede your performance. We need to ride in tandem. We need to ride with the same rhythm and pacing so we can make progress. The two of us together can go even faster than one can.

We could compare it with rowing a boat. If everybody is rowing a large boat, people are paddling on the left and the right, and somebody's in the back barking out the commands. If one guy in the back is digging his paddle in on the wrong side, it's going to impede the performance of the vessel.

We could compare it to singing. When we all sing together, the sound is beautiful. But there's always someone who has no rhythm or pitch whatsoever. He sings out of harmony, and people cringe (because you know people who are off-key usually sing louder than everyone else!). The beauty of the song is marred by one person's jarring notes.

The idea is to get into harmony with God. You are moving in tandem with God. You are paddling in the direction God wants you to take, you are singing in harmony with Him.

Live in communion with God. When that happens, the Christian life starts firing on all cylinders. That's also the secret to getting prayers answered. How many times have you been frustrated because you pray consistently for something, yet your prayers seem to reach only to the ceiling? God never seems to answer your prayers in the affirmative. Why? Maybe because you are praying outside of His will. Maybe you are praying for something God does not want you to have.

We need to tap into Jesus' promise in John 15: "If you abide in Me, and My words abide in you, you will ask what you desire, and it shall be done for you" (v. 7). Another translation says, "If you maintain a living communion with me and my words are at home with you, you can ask at once for yourself whatever your heart desires and it is yours" (WUEST). I really like that translation. It makes the conditions clear: "*If* you maintain a living communion with me and my words are at home with you." When you live in communion with God, your desires will change.

So will your prayers. You will get into sync with the will of God. You will discover the important truth that prayer is not getting him to do what you want Him to do; prayer is getting you to do what God wants you to do. It's not bending God your way. It's bending you God's way. It's not getting your will in heaven. It's getting God's will on earth.

If you want to see your prayers answered in the affirmative, you need to get into harmony with God. Or, as we have said, you need to be like Enoch and walk with God.

Keep your appointment with God. Amos 3:3 is also translated, "Do two men walk together unless they have made an appointment?" The original language implies that meaning: you have an *appointment* with God.

Some people are late for everything. One guy I know, no matter when I tell him to be somewhere, is always fifteen to twenty minutes late. I try to help him; I tell him to leave early because the last time (and the time before) he was late. Nothing changes. He is consistently inconsistent.

It's one thing to be late for an appointment with a friend. It's another thing to be late for an appointment with God Himself.

Adam had an appointment with God every day. After the sun set, the Lord God and Adam met and conversed. One day Adam didn't show up for his appointment. Why? Because he had sinned. He was hiding. The Lord God walked through the garden "in the cool of the day," asking, "Adam, where are you?" (Gen. 3:8–9 NIV).

I wonder if the Lord is saying that to some of us: "Where are you? I wanted to speak with you this morning. You didn't have time for Me. You had time for newspapers...for telephone calls...for TV...for e-mails. You had no time for prayer. You had no time for Bible study. I wanted to talk to you at lunch, but your prayer was so fast. Later on I wanted to speak to you, but you didn't have the antenna up. Where are you? We had an appointment."

Make time for God each and every day.

Pool your resources. Finally, walking with God means pooling your resources. That, too, the original text of Amos 3:3 implies. Think of it this way: Maybe you want to start a business, but you don't have investment capital. You call a friend and ask him to go into business with you. If you do this together, the business is a go. You draw up a contract and get started.

God says He wants to go into business with you, but He needs you to bring your resources to the table. If you do that, He will bring His as well. Do you understand what a great deal this is? This is like Bill Gates wanting to go into business with someone who has only a dollar to invest.

Bill says, "We will be equal partners."

You say, "That sounds good."

"How much do you have?"

"One hundred pennies."

"You have one dollar. Put it on the table."

"There it is, Mr. Gates. How much do you have?"

"Billions. I may be worth a billion dollars more than I was an hour ago. I am the richest man in the world. And when we go into business together, I am going to bring my resources, and you bring yours."

Sound like a good deal?

God says, "I want to go into business with you. Let's pool our resources. What do you have?"

"I have my talents. They aren't many, but here they are."

"What else do you have?"

"I have my life."

"What else do you have?"

"I have these resources and a few problems."

"Put it all there. Is that it?"

"That is it."

"Let me bring all of My power and glory and resources to this as well, and let's go into business together."

Walking in harmony with God, keeping your appointment with God, and pooling your resources with God are what it means to walk with God.

I ask you today: are you walking with God?

Late bloomers are welcome. Exactly when did Enoch start walking with God? Look at Genesis 5:21: "Enoch lived sixty-five years, and begot Methuselah." It appears that the birth of Methuselah brought about the conversion of Enoch; that is when his walk with God began. This should give hope to late bloomers. There are a lot of them. For instance, we all know Ronald Reagan was sixty-nine years old when he was elected the president of the United States and seventy-seven when he left office. That's blooming late!

I heard about a late bloomer named Jim Ward. He was one of the best-known triathletes in the world. What's unusual about Jim is that he started triathlons at the age of sixty-eight. He recently died at the age of eighty-three; he was five miles into a bike race at the time. It was Jim's goal to complete the Iron man Triathlon as an octogenarian, and he almost made it.

Do you know what the Ironman is? It's a contest held in Hawaii once a year. The challenge includes these sports in this order: a 2.4-hour swim in the ocean; a 112-mile bicycle race; and a 26.2-mile run. You don't do these over a week. You do them in a seventeen-hour span. One is right after the other.

Jim Ward was a ten-time triathlete world champion in his age group. In his seventies, he became the oldest athlete to finish the Ironman; he was planning on doing the same in his eighties.

Jim Ward was quoted as saying, "I am just not going to quit." It reminds me of Caleb who said, at age eighty-five,

"Give me this mountain." It reminds me of Enoch, who hung in there for three hundred years.

Enoch didn't start walking with God until Methuselah, his son, was born. The name *Methuselah* has a profound meaning: "When he is dead, it shall be sent." God revealed to Enoch, because he walked with the Lord, that when the child Methuselah died, judgment would come upon the earth—He would send it. This was fair warning to Enoch. In other words, "Neither you nor your son will face this judgment. I will initiate it after you both are gone."

That speaks volumes about the grace of God.

As we look at our world today, we might wonder why the Lord hasn't come back and established His kingdom. Why does He allow wicked people to prosper? God's answer is in 2 Peter 3:

> Knowing this first: that scoffers will come in the last days, walking according to their own lusts, and saying, "Where is the promise of His coming? For since the fathers fell asleep [the beginning of time], all things continue as they were from the beginning of creation."
>
> ...With the Lord, a day is as a thousand years, and a thousand years as one day. The Lord is not slack concerning His promise, as some count slackness, but is longsuffering toward us, not willing that any should perish but that all should come to repentance. (VV. 3-4, 8-9)

God has not brought judgment upon the earth yet because He is waiting for more people to believe. He wants more people to come into His kingdom.

Imagine being Enoch. You had this child, Methuselah. You knew when he died, judgment would come. Every time that kid got the sniffles, you would think, *This is it. Judgment is coming!*

What would this do to you practically? It would cause you always to be ready. You would live in recognition of life on earth's temporary nature and the nearness of eternity. That is exactly what Methuselah did. It was his birth that got Enoch right with the Lord.

2. Enoch Was Well Pleasing to God

Jesus said, "I always do the things that are pleasing to [God]" (see John 5:30). Can you imagine making such a statement? That you *always* please God? I certainly couldn't claim that. Neither could you. Yet Hebrews 11:5 says, Enoch "had this testimony, that he pleased God."

Enoch was a man who walked with God. He lived a life that was well pleasing to him. What are those things that God specifically says are pleasing to Him? Let's take a look.

Patient endurance. First Peter 2:19–20 says,

> God is pleased with you when, for the sake of your conscience, you patiently endure unfair treatment. Of course, you get no credit for being patient if you are beaten for doing wrong. But if you suffer for doing right and are patient beneath the blows, God is pleased with you. (NLT)

Have you ever been misrepresented? Have you ever been mistreated? Has anyone ever told a lie about you, and you just endured it? That pleases God. You need to know that.

Worship and helping others. Hebrews 13:15–16 says, "By Him let us continually offer the sacrifice of praise to God, that is, the fruit of our lips, giving thanks to His name. But do not forget to do good and to share, for with such sacrifices God is well pleased."

Don't you know that when you engage your heart and lift up your voice to praise the name of the Lord, it pleases Him? Notice that this verse says it is the "sacrifice of praise." Sometimes offering our praise to God is indeed a sacrifice. We may not be in the mood because we are having trouble of some kind. But that is the best time to worship God—not because we necessarily feel like it, but because He is worthy.

The Bible says "Oh, give thanks to the LORD, / for He is good! / For His mercy endures forever" (1 Chron. 16:34). That verse does not say, "Give thanks unto the Lord when you feel good," but rather because He is good.

Giving to the work of the kingdom of God. In Philippians 4:17–18, Paul wrote,

> Not that I am looking for a gift, but I am looking for what may be credited to your account. I have received full payment and even more; I am amply supplied, now that I have received from Epaphroditus the gifts you sent. They are a fragrant offering, an acceptable sacrifice, *pleasing to God.* (NIV)

Paul was saying to those believers, "This gift you sent for the work of the kingdom—I know it was hard. I know you sacrificed. But this pleases God."

When you invest your financial resources into the work of the kingdom, you delight the Lord. When you lift your voice in praise, you honor the Lord. When you are mistreated but you take it, you please God. These instructions are so clear that we have no excuse for not following them.

Enoch walked with God. He was well pleasing to God.

3. Enoch Was a Witness for God

Hebrews 11:5 says, "Enoch was taken away so that he did not see death, 'and was not found,' because God had taken him; for before he was taken he had this testimony, that he pleased God."

Do you have a good testimony? Are you being an effective

witness? When you get down to it, every Christian is a witness in some way, shape, or form. Even if you never open your lips and speak about your faith, you have a testimony. The question is, is that testimony a good one or is it a poor one?

Believe me, people do say something about you and your faith after observing you. It's up to you to affect what they say. When you walk with God and Jesus overflows from you and someone asks, "What makes you different? What makes you joyful and peaceful? I want to know more," you can say, "Let me tell you about my faith in Jesus Christ." What a glorious thing that is. As Augustine once said, "Preach the Gospel, and when necessary, use words."

Maybe sometimes we aren't good witnesses because we don't walk with God. We don't enjoy fellowship with Him. We don't live in communion with Him. We don't move in harmony, in tandem, with Him. God wants to change us so we will be pleasing to Him and be witnesses for Him.

What is the end result of our good testimony and witness? Genesis 5:24 says, "Enoch walked with God; and he was not; for God took him." The phrase "took him" could be translated "carried over or across." God carried Enoch over death. The Bible says, "It is appointed for men to die once, but after this the judgment" (Heb. 9:27). In the case of Enoch, God made an exception and took him straight to heaven. He picked him off of one shore and put him on the other.

The fact of the matter is that when you walk with God on earth, you will also walk with Him in heaven. Revelation 3:4 says, "They will walk with me, dressed in white" (NIV). Enoch is representative of those believers who will not die but be caught up to heaven, as mentioned in 1 Corinthians 15:51–52 where Paul said, "I tell you a mystery. We shall not all sleep [die], but we shall all be changed, in a moment, in the twinkling of an eye" (ESV).

Let me ask you this: if the Lord were to come back today,

would He take you along? He took Enoch. Why? Enoch walked with God. He was well pleasing to God. He was a witness for God.

. . . .
Keep Your Eyes on the Prize

We see from Enoch's life that in the spiritual race, speed doesn't matter nearly as much as distance does. Sure, run fast if you want, but definitely run (or walk) long. Finish it. That is the objective. Paul said as much in Philippians:

> Not that I have already attained all this, or have already been made perfect, but I press on to take hold of that for which Christ Jesus took hold of me. Brothers,... one thing I do: Forgetting what is behind and straining toward what is ahead, I press on toward the goal to win the prize for which God has called me heavenward in Christ Jesus. (3:12–14 NIV)

Nowhere did Paul say to sprint. He said to keep pressing on: hang in there, and finish what you have begun.

Paul concluded that statement by saying, "All of us who are mature should take a view of such things. And if on some point you think differently, that too God will make clear to you" (Phil. 3:15 NIV). In other words, Paul was saying if we want to grow up spiritually, we need to pace ourselves—we are in this for the long haul.

Are you walking with God? Are you well pleasing to God? Are you a witness for God? God wants you to come into harmony with Him. He wants to reveal His plan and purposes to you. He wants you to walk with Him—even if it is for less than three hundred years.

By imitating Enoch, you can guarantee you'll survive the long haul and finish well: you will win the race.

3

TRIPPING UP
IN THE RACE
OF LIFE

We've all heard it so many times it has basically become a cliché: "God loves you and has a wonderful plan for your life!" Supposed cliché or not, this is an absolutely true statement. It's true for all of humanity, true for me, and, yes, true for you.

People often ask what my favorite Bible passage is, and I have to say that's a tough call. But if you allow me to say what some of my favorite passages are, one comes to mind quickly: Jeremiah 29:11–12: "For I know the thoughts that I think toward you, says the LORD, thoughts of peace and not of evil, to give you a future and a hope. Then you will call upon Me and go and pray to Me, and I will listen to you."

Isn't that encouraging?

It's true.

God loves you. God has a good plan for you. God has a future and hope for you.

God wants to use you. God wants you to make your mark in some way. You may be known to millions, thousands, hundreds, or maybe only a handful, but God has a purpose for your life. You are significant.

The question is, do you want to reach your potential as a

Christian? Do you want to cross the finish line in the spiritual race, or are you going to self-destruct? You might be surprised to know that you have everything to say about that. In the spiritual race, we can see many who started with such great promise but somehow crashed and burned.

Paul wrote to the believers in Galatians 5:7, "You were running a good race. Who cut in on you and kept you from obeying the truth?" (NIV). We can all do better in this race of life. Much better.

The Bible offers us a story of a man who had incredible potential, but who largely wasted it. God gave him amazing physical strength, and this man had God's blessing and anointing on his life. The fact is that he could have been one of the greatest leaders in the history of Israel.

Instead his life became a proverb; it became an example of how not to live. His was a life of squandered resources and dissipated potential and ability. He threw it all away because of some subtle but serious mistakes—something we are all capable of doing. His name was Samson, and this is his story.

. . . .
Lotsa Hair, Little Sense

The life of Samson illustrates the ancient truth that a good beginning does not necessarily guarantee a good ending. That is why Solomon wrote in Ecclesiastes 7:8, "The end of a matter is better than its beginning" (NIV). American poet Henry Wadsworth Longfellow said, "Great is the art of beginning, but greater is the art of ending."

When we think of Samson, our minds immediately race to his compromised involvement with the wicked Delilah. The truth is a number of smaller compromises ultimately led to his fall with that woman.

It's a fact that seemingly insignificant choices can create disaster and destruction. Remember the horrific explosion of the space shuttle in January 1986? You might have been watching the takeoff live on television when the shuttle exploded on its ascent.

NASA's extensive research finally concluded that the explosion was the result of a faulty O-ring. When this ring failed to seal in hot gases, they escaped, caught fire, and blew up the spacecraft. This incredible vessel, on which we had spent millions of dollars and put well-trained astronauts as well as a civilian, completely self-destructed because of something as small and seemingly insignificant as a defective ten-dollar O-ring.

In the same way, it is the little things in life that often bring us down. This is certainly what happened with Samson. He had all the potential to be someone great for God and lead the people of Israel out of their backslidden state. Humanly speaking, no one was stronger than Samson. He also had spiritual sharpness and mental ability. An angel of the Lord predicted of Samson before he was born, "He will *begin* the deliverance of Israel from the hands of the Philistines" (Judg. 13:5 NIV).

Note the word "begin." The angel didn't say Samson would complete the task. God knew he would never reach his full potential.

As in Enoch's day, this was a dark era in Israel's history. The Bible says that in the time prior to Samson's ascent, "Israel did evil in the eyes of the LORD" (Judg. 13:1 NIV), and he consequently turned them over to their enemies, the Philistines. God's people did what they wanted without regard for the One who made them. Then God raised one man, Samson, up to make a difference.

This is often how the Lord works. When times are especially dark, God brings forth a leader. He designates someone to turn the light on...someone to stand in the gap...someone to turn the tide. Someone like you.

The angel of the Lord declared Samson was to live a life separated from the sinful compromise of Israel; he would be a Nazarite. This meant, among other things, that he would never partake of fermented drink—never come under the influence of alcohol. As well, no one could ever cut his hair. Some wrongly think Samson's strength was a result of his long hair, but the reality is that his strength came from God; the long hair symbolized his being set apart by God.

....

Immediate Enemies

In the beginning, it was clear God's hand was upon Samson. Scripture tells us, "The LORD blessed him, and the Spirit of the LORD began to stir him" (Judg. 13:24–25 NIV). No sooner did this happen than we find Samson marrying a Philistine woman—against the wishes of his parents, I might add. Samson's marriage led to a series of conflicts with the Philistines in which he came up victorious because of the superhuman strength God gave him. But the Philistines bore a grudge.

And all was not well with God's hero. Look at Judges 16:

Now Samson went to Gaza and saw a harlot there, and went into her. When the Gazites were told, "Samson has come here!" they surrounded the place and lay in wait for him all night at the gate of the city. They were quiet all night, saying, "In the morning, when it is daylight, we will kill him." And Samson lay low till midnight; then he arose at midnight, took hold of the doors of the gate of the city and the two gateposts, pulled them up, bar and all, put them on his shoulders, and carried them to the top of the hill that faces Hebron. (vv. 1–3)

Samson made a choice. Gaza was an enemy city with un-Godly people in it. Samson was self-confident, thinking, *I have gotten myself out of messes before. I can get myself out of another if one arises.*

While Samson spent time with the prostitute, his enemies found out that the famous strongman was in their little city. They thought, *We are going to take this guy out once and for all. We have had enough of him.* Then they figured, *Why do it at night? Let's wait until the sunrise.*

They posted a guard by the house and set an ambush. His enemies went to sleep that night thinking that annihilating their enemy would be like shooting fish in a barrel.

But around midnight, Samson decided to skip town. He walked to the gates of the city and looked at them for a minute. We know from archaeological studies that these massive gates were covered with studded nails as well as metal to make them fireproof. They weighed thousands of pounds.

To any normal man this would have been an insurmountable obstacle. For Samson, it was a mere inconvenience. The mighty Judge of Israel reached down and ripped them out of their foundation, and then he toted them along as he left town. It would have been enough to lift them up and simply drop them. But I guess old Samson decided to get a little cardiovascular with his weight-training that day as he carried these incredibly heavy gates some twenty miles from where he found them.

Needless to say, when his enemies woke and saw that, no one went after him. Samson was far too intimidating. The incredible strength God had given him made him a formidable opponent, to say the least. This is what makes the story tragic. Samson had power without purity. He had strength without self-control.

God extended His grace to Samson for twenty long years, and Samson experienced the thrill of victory time after time. Whenever his enemies came against him, he handily destroyed them. On one occasion he killed one thousand Philistines with a donkey's jawbone he randomly picked up. They just couldn't stop this man so blessed and empowered by God Himself. He seemed indestructible.

....

A Fatal Flaw

After observing Samson's weakness for sexual lust the Philistines decided there was only one way to subdue this powerhouse: with a woman. Samson was a he-man with a she-weakness.

If the Philistines could not prevail on the battlefield, they would do so in the bedroom. And the Philistines took full advantage. Let's read about it.

> Afterward it happened that he loved a woman in the Valley of Sorek, whose name was Delilah. And the lords of the Philistines came up to her and said to her, "Entice him, and find out where his great strength lies, and by what means we may overpower him, that we may bind him to afflict him; and every one of us will give you eleven hundred pieces of silver."
>
> So Delilah said to Samson, "Please tell me where your great strength lies, and with what you may be bound to afflict you." And Samson said to her, "If they bind me with seven fresh bowstrings, not yet dried, then I shall become weak, and be like any other man."
>
> So the lords of the Philistines brought up to her seven fresh bowstrings, not yet dried, and she bound him with them. Now men were lying in wait, staying with her in the room. And she said to him, "The Philistines are upon you, Samson!" But he broke the bowstrings as a strand of yarn breaks when it touches fire. So the secret of his strength was not known. (JUDGES 16:4–9)

The Philistines enlisted Delilah to do their dirty work: find out the secret of Samson's strength so they could overpower him. They offered her fifty thousand dollars to do this. The deck was stacked against the unsuspecting he-man. There is no question but that Delilah was a very attractive and enticing woman. For temptation to be tempting, it has to be appealing. That's the rub. Temptation will promise you life, but it will ultimately bring you death. It will promise you fulfillment, but it will ultimately result in emptiness. It promises freedom, but it will ultimately bring you bondage.

Delilah began her strategic attack. Samson had shown his vulnerability—women—and the devil exploited it. He had a willing victim in Samson.

This is important. Sometimes we think the devil can pretty much pick us off at will. I remember once hearing a preacher who had fallen into sin say, "The reason I fell is because the devil did it to me. I was being so used of God that Satan just pulled me down." That's partially true. Of course the devil wants to pull you down—especially if God is using you—but he needs your cooperation.

Satan cannot take you against your will. You have to give into the temptation. As James wrote, "Each one is tempted when he is drawn away by his own desires and enticed. Then when desire has conceived, it gives birth to sin; and sin, when it is full-grown, brings forth death" (James 1:14–15). For Satan to succeed we must listen, desire what he offers, and yield. The devil is no fool. He will vary his bait depending on whom he is tempting. As those of you who fish know, you use different kinds of bait for different kinds of fish. Keep this in mind: it is not the bait that constitutes sin. It is the bite. It is not a sin to be tempted. It is a sin to give into that temptation.

Samson took it hook, line, and sinker and paid the price.

. . . .
The Games People Play—to Death

Why didn't Samson realize what was going on? Look at how crazy it was. Delilah was pretty explicit in declaring her objectives to the foolish Samson: "Please tell me where your great strength lies," she cooed into his ear, "and with what you may be bound to *afflict you*" (Judg. 16:6). This is the first clue that this was not a healthy relationship; the woman was saying, "I want to afflict you."

For Samson it was a game. He was probably thinking, *As if you could afflict me. I am Samson, who kills Philistines for entertainment. I rip huge gates out of their foundations and carry them for sport. I am the Samson whom no one can stop, and you, this little girl named Delilah, are going to afflict me?* I think he found it humorous and toyed with her. He started telling lies—this is important—but he got closer and closer to the truth as she continued to press him.

Sometimes we think, *I can handle this. I am not going to fall. I am stronger than that.* You have all heard the rationalizations and maybe even used them. "I'll go only so far, and then I'll stop. I promise." Or how about this one: "I'll return it. I'm only borrowing it." Here's another: "Just one time. We'll never do it again." How many people have ended up in a pit of bondage because they took the bait of temptations like those? The Bible says, "Can a man scoop fire into his lap / without his clothes being burned?" (Prov. 6:27 NIV).

Really, Samson should have realized Delilah offered a trap from the devil. The fact that she said, "The Philistines are upon you" and his enemies lurched at him from the shadows should have clued him in.

But he was not thinking clearly. People never do when under the intoxicating effects of lust. Delilah leaned in for the kill.

Then she said to him, "How can you say, 'I love you,' when your heart is not with me? You have mocked me these three

times, and have not told me where your great strength lies."
And it came to pass, when she pestered him daily with her
words and pressed him, so that his soul was vexed to death,
that he told her all his heart, and said to her, "No razor has
ever come upon my head, for I have been a Nazarite to God
from my mother's womb. If I am shaven, then my strength
will leave me, and I shall become weak, and be like any
other man." (JUDGES 16:15–17)

When Delilah realized she'd finally gleaned the essential
information, she sent for the Philistines. They paid her, and
she finished the job:

Then she lulled him to sleep on her knees, and called for
a man and had him shave off the seven locks of his head.
Then she began to torment him, and his strength left him.
And she said, "The Philistines are upon you, Samson!" So
he awoke from his sleep, and said, "I will go out as before,
at other times, and shake myself free!" But he did not know
that the LORD had departed from him. Then the Philistines
took him and put out his eyes, and brought him down to
Gaza. They bound him with bronze fetters, and he became
a grinder in the prison. (JUDGES 16:19–21)

This is such a sad story. If Samson were a runner in a race, we
would say he fell and fell hard—so hard it looked as though he
would never get up again. Ironically, if anyone had the ability
to win the gold, it was Samson. But instead he was disqualified. Certainly he is one of the losers in the spiritual race.

Delilah said to him, "If you love me, you will do this."
Warning: if you are ever in a relationship with someone who
asks you to compromise your values as a believer to prove your
love, that is not a good relationship. That's exactly what Delilah did, and Samson took a one-way trip to Delilah's barber-
shop.

Talk about sleeping with the enemy! This woman had posi-
tively declared she wanted to destroy him, yet he felt comfortable enough to doze off in her lap.

Here is the truly tragic part: "He did not know that the
LORD had departed from him" (Judg. 16:20). Samson had lost
touch with God. This happens. When someone starts compromising with sin, other believers may warn him, "Brother,
you are doing this thing, the Bible says is wrong. You really
shouldn't." But how does this person often respond? "Hey
man, don't judge me. The Bible says, 'Judge not lest you be
judged.' Who are you to judge me? You have no right to do
that."

The fact of the matter is we are to make evaluations and,
yes, judgments as believers on our own lives and on the lives of
fellow Christians. How else are we to heed biblical warnings to
beware of false prophets or not "cast our pearls before swine"
(See Matt.7:15 and 7:6)? I obviously need to make some judgment or evaluation to determine if a person is teaching false
doctrine or is not open to the gospel. Now, the word Jesus used
for *judge* means "condemn"(See Matt.7:1). I am not to condemn a fellow Christian, but if I observe or judge that he is
going in the wrong direction I need to warn him.

The Bible says, "Because the sentence against an evil work
is not executed speedily, therefore the heart of the sons of men
is fully set in them to do evil" (Eccl. 8:11). Allow me to loosely
paraphrase that: because we don't get busted immediately, we
think we can get away with sin forever. The Bible warns, "Be
sure your sin will find you out" (Num. 32:23).

. . . .
Sin Blinds, Finds, and Grinds

Samson was about to find out the truth of that. The Philistines captured him. That time his supernatural strength was
not there. The Lord was no longer with him as He once was,

so Samson could no longer shake them off like rag dolls. They pinned the mighty warrior to the ground and heartlessly gouged out his eyes. The Philistines then put Samson to work as a grinder in prison. It was a cruel and tragic end to a brilliant reign.

This shows us that sin blinds us, it finds us, and it grinds us. Let's take a closer look at how this happens.

1. Sin Blinds Us

Sometimes we do completely irrational things. We all know of men and women who have great families, loving spouses and children. They are blessed by the Lord. Then they go and have a fling with a coworker. They are blinded. They deceive themselves into thinking that it is somehow okay. This kind of immorality usually starts with a fantasy: *I would never do this, but what would it be like if I did?* Then you take it to the next level and start flirting with that person. After that you start having intimate conversations, maybe sharing some of your marital problems. You become very close friends. Too close. The next thing you know, you are embroiled in an affair. "Adultery" is what the Bible calls it. It blinds you. You have been deceived by sin.

2. Sin Finds Us

Sure, there is that euphoric excitement when you get away with sin. You've made your decision, you've followed through, and you think you've gotten away with it. You feel unrestrained by rules. But in the end, sin will bind you. As we saw earlier, the Bible says, "Your sin will find you out." We can't escape it or its consequences. Samson couldn't. You won't.

3. Sin Grinds Us

You will pay the miserable price: The broken marriage. The betrayed trust. The damaged witness and reputation. The devastated children with deep wounds they often carry for the rest of their lives. Not to mention other problems such as HIV, venereal disease, and—depending on what you have done—maybe even jail time. Your sin will find you out, and it will grind you down. And you will be left with nothing.

Or will you be?

. . . .

Hope Among the Ashes

Samson found out the hard way what a horrible and devastating thing sin could be. Yet even in his mess, there was hope. Look at Judges 16:22: "However, the hair of his head began to grow again after it had been shaven." Do you know what this verse is about? It tells us that God gives second chances.

You might be thinking, *Greg, you are warning us about divorce, adultery, and other things, but it's too late. I am a divorced man [or woman]. I have had the affair. I have been caught. I feel horrible. You are hitting me so hard, and I am already overwhelmed with guilt.*

But look at this: *the hair on Samson's head began to grow again.* Yes, I am warning those who have not done it to not do it. But I am also saying to you, if you have fallen into sin, learn from it and know God gives you another opportunity to serve him.

Maybe now you're in another marriage; make this one work. Don't let it fall apart. If you are estranged from your children, try to reconnect with them. Try to make up for the wrongs you have done. Make the best of what you have. God has given you a second chance. Try to *fail forward.*

Aren't you glad God gives second chances? I am. Samson was as well. As his hair grew, his strength began to return. While Samson helped push the grinding rock, day in and day out, the Philistines laughed at him. They felt powerful. The mighty man was a blind mouse.

Then one day the Philistines had a big feast. Everybody was in town—about three thousand in number—to celebrate their god, Dagon, for giving them victory over Samson. They said, "Let's bring Samson out. Let's have a laugh at his expense. Let him perform for us."

They led the former mighty man of Israel out. They deemed him harmless enough that a little boy held his hand. Samson asked the boy to put his hands on the foundational pillars of the pagan temple, so he could "lean on them." Then Samson prayed: "O LORD God, remember me, I pray! Strengthen me, I pray, just this once, O God, that I may with one blow take vengeance on the Philistines for my two eyes!" (Judg. 16:28).

With all of his might he pushed, and those pillars gave way and the roof collapsed. All of those Philistines, blaspheming and worshiping their false god, were killed that day. In fact, Samson "killed many more when he died than while he lived" (Judg. 16:30 NIV).

Maybe you're being tempted right now. Maybe you've already acted on it. Learn the lesson of Samson. Look at what can happen to you! Heed the warnings God is giving you. And remember, if you have already failed, God will forgive you if you will repent. Acknowledge that you have done wrong, and God will give you a second chance. You may not be allowed to win the gold, but continuing on with God's redeeming grace is better than giving up completely.

4
DISQUALIFIED *IN* THE RACE *OF* LIFE

The moment we put our faith in Jesus Christ, we were enrolled in a spiritual race. One of the mandates of any competition is that we play by the rules or we will be disqualified. This is true in every race, but perhaps especially in the spiritual one.

I base this on 1 Corinthians 9:24–27, where Paul said,

Remember that in a race everyone runs, but only one person gets the prize. You also must run in such a way that you will win. All athletes practice strict self-control. They do it for a prize that will fade away, but we do it to win an eternal prize. So I run straight to the goal with purpose in every step. I am not like a boxer who misses his punches. I discipline my body like an athlete, training it to do what it should. Otherwise, I fear that after preaching to others I myself might be disqualified. (NLT)

First Samuel gives us the story of a man who did not play by the rules. Ironically, he could have done very well. He had all the makings to be someone great for God. Like Samson, this man before us might have succeeded incredibly, but because he did not play by God's rules, he was disqualified. His name was Saul.

. . . .
Another Great Start, Tragic Ending

The life of King Saul, the first king for the nation Israel, is a study in contrasts. He began his reign in victory and ended in humiliating defeat. He lost his character, power, crown, and in the end, his very life.

Saul's life stands as a warning, much as Samson's does, that you cannot rebel against God and get away with it. It will catch up with you. It may not be today or tomorrow. But as we saw in the last chapter, sin will blind you, find you, and grind you.

Saul's life was a tragic waste.

I mentioned what you might want written on your tombstone in the beginning of this book. King Saul's epitaph would have been: "I have played the fool and erred exceedingly" (1 Sam. 26:21).

Those were his actual words.

Tragically, it didn't have to be that way. But it was. He had so much potential.

It all started when Israel demanded a king. Judges such as Samson had been ruling God's people, and God spoke to the Israelites through such prophets as Samuel. The judges and prophets revealed the will of God to the nation. It was a glorious arrangement, because God Himself directed them.

However, the Israelites, as was often the case, were not content: they wanted to be like the other nations and thus have their own king. They approached the prophet Samuel and made their request. Samuel took it to the Lord. The Lord said He would give Israel exactly what it requested.

This is a reminder to be careful what you ask for; God just

might answer your prayer with a yes. As we are going to see, Israel's request was fraught with peril. This is one reason Jesus taught us in the Lord's Prayer to say, "Your kingdom come, Your will be done." In other words, "Lord, if what I am about to pray is in any way outside of Your will, overrule it. Your will be done. Your kingdom come. I want Your will more than I want my own."

God gave the Israelites a man named Saul. They got what they deserved. You have heard of the People's Choice Awards—Saul was the people's choice. But he wasn't necessarily God's.

Don't get me wrong. At first, Saul had many fine qualities, traits that were admirable in a leader for a nation. He was an obedient son from a good family; he was humble enough to tackle the little as well as the large tasks. He looked to be someone great who would do wonderful things for the nation of Israel. But as we will see, he squandered his resources and opportunities. He ignored the rules. He played the fool, and, because of that, he was disqualified. He was a man who had a tremendous beginning but a tragic ending.

....

A Promising Start

Let's look at his story. The son of a rich man, Saul was doubly blessed; the Bible calls him "the most handsome man in Israel" (1 Sam. 9:2 NLT). That was important then. Maybe it is even more important now. I think back to the debate between John F. Kennedy and Richard Nixon for the presidency. People who listened to that debate on the radio felt Nixon won, and people who watched it on television felt Kennedy won. It was all because of how telegenic Kennedy was. Presidential debates have not been the same since then.

That is typical of our culture. We celebrate attractive people. We prefer style over substance.

For instance, *People* magazine does not publish an annual issue called "The Most Ordinary People." It is called "The World's Most Beautiful People." Certainly Saul would have been included. He might even have made the cover of *People*'s "Sexiest King Alive." He was an attractive man.

Even good-looking people have to do chores. One day Kish's donkeys ran off, so he told Saul to find them and bring them home. Saul enlisted a servant's help, and the two set out. They searched everywhere with no success. But while they were out on this errand, they walked right into the middle of the will of God. Saul's servant said, "I have heard that there is a man of God around here. It is the prophet Samuel. Maybe he will know where the donkeys went."

They found the legendary Samuel. When the men met, the Lord suddenly spoke to the prophet, "This is the king I have selected for Israel." Imagine Saul's surprise when "Samuel took a flask of olive oil and poured it over Saul's head. He kissed Saul on the cheek and said, 'I am doing this because the LORD has appointed you to be the leader of his people Israel'" (1 Sam. 10:1 NLT).

Saul was just out looking for a donkey, and he ended up being anointed as the king of Israel!

There is an important lesson for us to learn from this story. It is simply this: we need to be willing to do the small, seemingly insignificant things before God will call us to do the larger ones. You can never be too small for God to use—only too big.

As Saul was faithful in the little things, God opened a great door for him. It's worth noting that God often selects people for His service who are going about the ordinary, the mundane, the everyday activities of life.

Consider the fact that the great Moses was tending sheep when God spoke to him through the burning bush and told him to deliver the people of Israel. He was just going about his business when he found out the course of his life was to change forever.

Elisha was plowing a field when the prophet Elijah called him to be his successor. David was running an errand for his father when the Lord used him to conquer the mighty Goliath. Peter, James, and John were fishing when Jesus came to them and said, "Follow Me, and I will make you fishers of men." You never know what great doors may turn upon small hinges.

Look at what happened next: the Spirit of the Lord came upon Saul and "gave him another heart" (1 Sam. 10:9). God took this young man who had so much natural potential—a striking appearance, a strong background, an obedient heart—and He anointed him. Then he had everything he needed to be a great leader. He had the whole package. Everything was going Saul's way.

The Bible says God then raised up some good men to assist Saul. First Samuel 10:26 says, "When Saul returned to his home at Gibeah, a band of men whose hearts God had touched became his constant companions" (NLT).

In his race, Saul was off of the blocks with a bang. So far so good.

. . . .

Failing the Test

Then the first test came. One of Israel's enemies, the Ammonites, had surrounded an Israeli city. The enemy's wicked king, Nahash, ordered the occupants to surrender. Israel asked for a peace agreement instead: "We will be your servants." Nahash agreed but added, "I will gouge out the right eye of every one of you as a disgrace to all Israel!" (1 Sam. 11:2 NLT).

The Israelites wisely said, "Can we get back to you on that?" Amongst themselves they reasoned, "Let's see if anyone will come and back us up. If not, we'll surrender." They sent word to the other tribes.

Saul heard what was happening. He was outraged. He was righteously indignant. He said, "Now is the time for the tribes of Israel to come together." He rallied an army of more than three hundred thousand men. He sent word back to the little Israeli city: "Help is on the way." When Saul and his army showed up, they completely wiped out the Ammonites. Israel had a new hero. Saul more than rose to the occasion.

Saul was not only brave, he was compassionate. After his triumph over the enemy, he refused to put to death those who questioned whether he should be king (because, of course, some did). Again, it was a very good beginning.

The prophet Samuel them reaffirmed Saul as the king of Israel. He called the people and said:

> All right, here is the king you have chosen. Look him over. You asked for him, and the LORD has granted your request.
>
> Now if you will fear and worship the LORD and listen to his voice, and if you do not rebel against the LORD's commands, and if you and your king follow the LORD your God, then all will be well. But if you rebel against the LORD's commands and refuse to listen to him, then his hand will be as heavy upon you as it was upon your ancestors. (1 SAMUEL 12:13–15 NLT)

There was the condition: worship and honor God. Do what He tells you to, follow Him, and everything will be fine. Samuel warned that if they rebelled and disobeyed, they would reap what they sowed.

Isn't the same true for us today? God tells us how to live our lives. He tells how to have successful marriages. He tells us how to conduct ourselves in business, how to live life to its fullest. He says, "Here are My rules and standards. Here is My power to help you live them. If you go this way, all will be well. If you disregard what I say, you will regret it." It is true.

Essentially, God was giving Saul fair warning: "Listen to Me: you have the potential. You have the power. I have given it all to you. Now the ball is in your court. If you follow Me, all will be well. If you rebel, you will have trouble."

You know the rest of this story. Saul started immediately to rebel. He went into a free fall, starting with one error that eventually led to his complete decline.

Another enemy of Israel, the Philistines, mounted an attack. The Philistine armies were huge. Israel was paralyzed with panic. Saul tried to rally the troops to go into battle, but the Lord told him, through Samuel, to wait until the prophet showed up and offered a burnt offering. Saul grew impatient, and "his men were trembling with fear" (1 Sam. 13:7 NLT).

Saul thought, *Why do I have to wait for some prophet? I know how to present a burnt offering. I have watched him do it so many times I will just do it myself. Surely God will make an exception under such circumstances.* He proceeded to directly disobey the Lord.

Samuel appeared as Saul was finishing the offering and confronted him: "What is this you have done?" Saul explained his need to proceed. "'How foolish!' Samuel exclaimed. 'You have disobeyed the command of the LORD your God. Had you obeyed, the LORD would have established your kingdom over Israel forever. But now your dynasty must end'" (1 Sam. 13:11, 13–14 NLT). In fact, he said, the Lord had already chosen Saul's successor.

I know that at first blush, this may seem a bit extreme on God's part, but the Lord could see Saul's heart had already turned away. Saul had determined to follow his own rules, not God's.

. . . .
Giving in to "Little" Sins

We may not like some of the rules God sets forth in his Word. "Why can't I do thus and so? I still have to live in the real world. Why does God say I can't do that? It doesn't seem fair. What is wrong with a little bit? Just a few drinks. A little flirting. A small white lie. I will know when to stop." Famous last words. What you need to realize is it's always the "little" sins that lead to the big ones.

I read a bizarre story in the paper some years ago about an eighteen-year-old young man in London. The article said he was hospitalized after his pet scorpion stung him on the tongue. It turns out this young man kissed the scorpion (its name was Twiggy) good night every evening before bed. One night Twiggy pinched him on the lip. He opened his mouth in pain, and Twiggy jumped inside and pinched him on the tongue. The young man had to be hospitalized as a result.

In the same way, some of us are giving sin a little good-night kiss. We think, *It is just a little thing. How much harm could this do?* We should know better.

. . . .
Partial Obedience Is No Obedience

Let's get back to Saul. What happened after he disobeyed God with the sacrifice is even sadder. God commanded King Saul to settle accounts with an old enemy, the Amalekites. God said to completely destroy them. Instead Saul partially obeyed the Lord; he defeated the enemy in battle but kept some livestock (he also only captured, didn't kill, the king).

Again Samuel confronted Saul, and Saul lied: "I really

planned on giving it all to the Lord anyway. That is why I kept it." Samuel replied:

> What is more pleasing to the LORD: your burnt offerings and sacrifices or your obedience to his voice? Obedience is far better than sacrifice... Rebellion is as bad as the sin of witchcraft, and stubbornness is as bad as worshiping idols. So because you have rejected the word of the LORD, he has rejected you from being king. (1 SAMUEL 15:22–23 NLT)

Saul confessed, "Yes, I have sinned. I have disobeyed your instructions and the LORD's command, for I was afraid of the people and did what they demanded. Oh, please, forgive my sin now and go with me to worship the LORD" (1 Sam. 15:24–25 NLT). Samuel refused.

. . . .
Repentance Must Be Real

Let's say you have a friend who betrays your confidence. You tell him something in secret, and the next thing you know, Larry King is talking about it on his show. How did this happen?

You confront him: "I shared with you a struggle I was having. I asked you to pray, and instead you told everyone. That offends me."

He says, "I am so sorry. Can you find it in your heart to forgive me? I'll never do it again."

Okay—you forgive him. A little time passes. It turns out your friend proceeds to go out and tell complete lies about you. You confront him again. He says, "I am so sorry. I don't know why I did it. I'll take you out to a nice dinner. Will that even the score?"

You go to dinner. But another day passes, and it gets even worse. He says, "I'm sorry. But look, I bought you a new shirt."

So, you are discovering something about your so-called friend. He is not a friend at all. The fact of that matter is you don't want him to take you to dinner or buy you a new shirt. What you want is for him to keep your confidence and be what he claimed to be: a true friend.

In the same way, many of us today say we are friends of Jesus. We claim to be Christians. But if we don't do what He tells us to do, we really have no right to call ourselves His friend. We may lift our hands in praise at Church and proclaim "Lord, I love You so much. You are so good. I will do whatever you want me to do!" Then we go out and break His commandments left and right. Then we pray, "God, I am so sorry. Let me make up for it. I'll put more money in the offering. I'll go to a couple of midweek Bible studies. Here, Lord, let Me show you my love in some way."

News flash: God does not want your money or your attendance at another service if it is all for the wrong reason. God wants your heart. Jesus said in John 15:14, "You are My friends if you do whatever I command you." That means we need to do it.

. . . .
Off-Key Worship

Worship music has become very popular today. It's not uncommon to see commercials on TV offering the latest collection of songs of praise to God, and in many ways I applaud that. But at the same time, true worship is not about how catchy the tune may be, or even how well it is performed. It's all about the heart.

Did you know that if your lifestyle contradicts what you believe, your worship can actually be offensive to God? Amos

5:23–24 says, "Away with your hymns of praise! They are only noise to my ears. I will not listen to your music, no matter how lovely it is. Instead, I want to see a mighty flood of justice, a river of righteous living that will never run dry" (NLT).

I bring this up because I know people who have a yo-yo-like relationship with God. They're either really up or really down. They're either fully backslidden or passionate to the point of being obnoxious. One day all they can talk about is how much Christ means to them. The next day they're engaged in something that is clearly sinful. What happened? A week later they're back in church, singing louder than anyone else. A week after that, they're back in sin again.

It is ridiculous.

This is why David prayed in Psalm 51, "Create in me a clean heart, O God, / And renew a steadfast spirit within me" (v. 10). The word David used for *steadfast* means to be consistent. This is more important than your roller-coaster spiritual highs and lows.

You might see someone singing beautifully to the Lord. *What a voice,* you think. *How that must please God.* If the singer's heart is in the right place, it does honor God. (Let me add that if someone has the worst voice you ever heard, but she loves the Lord, her singing honors Him as well.) But if that person with a beautiful voice is contradicting what she sings by the way she lives, her song offends God. Again, God looks on the heart.

God looked in Saul's heart. Spiritually speaking, his songs were off-key.

. . . .
The Torment of Disobedience

Tragically, Saul went from bad to worse. It wasn't long before David emerged on the scene to take over, by God's command. Saul began to hunt him relentlessly. Paranoia and jealousy filled the wicked king. Saul even tried to murder David on more than one occasion. After Samuel's death, Saul was so desperate that he consulted a witch to try to make contact with the departed prophet. Ultimately he died a pathetic death on the battlefield—realizing he was defeated, Saul committed suicide.

His life had so much promise, potential, and talent, and it ended like that. God had blessed him. He had everything he needed, but he threw it all away.

If Samson was defeated in the race of life by lust, then Saul was defeated in the race of life by pride.

Saul is great proof of the fact that you never know how someone is going to turn out. Think of when you were in school: certain kids you knew would never amount to anything. They weren't the star athletes, the great quarterbacks, the brilliant scholars, the cheerleaders, or the most popular persons on campus. Maybe for all practical purposes, they were nobodies. They may have had a few too many pens in their shirt pockets or wore their pants a bit too short. We laughed at them, calling them "geeks" or "nerds."

It's quite possible that today we call them "Boss," isn't it? People can come out from nowhere and suddenly make their mark.

Then there were those we expected to be great successes in life, whatever their fields of endeavor, and none of them ever made a name for themselves.

The spiritual life carries the same kinds of surprises. I think of those I knew as a younger believer, people God was so mightily using. They were impacting others. I was so excited that I could say I knew them! I knew they would make their mark on the world for the Lord Jesus Christ. Some of those people, though, self-destructed; they got tripped up in the race of life. You probably know some people like that too.

Epitaph for a Fool

I've mentioned that Saul himself summed up his life with these words: "I have played the fool and erred exceedingly." That would have been a fitting epitaph for this man.

As I asked in the introduction, if you were to create a phrase that summed up your own life, what would you say? Let me ask you this: what *should* be said? What you would like may be different from what ought to be said about you.

Could you imagine if we told the truth on tombstones? We always see things like "Loving father and wonderful husband." What if really he was a failure as a man? What if it should've said, "Total screw-up"? But we don't want to put things like that on a tombstone.

I wonder what someone will write on your tombstone. Or what someone will write on mine.

Saul played the fool. He started the race well but once he fell, he never got up again. At least in the end, Samson made a comeback. Saul never did. He was disqualified in the race of life. He foolishly threw his life away. And in the end he knew it.

Let me share a few principles Saul might have written based on his life. These are things to do if you want to fail and lose the race of life:

1. Ignore the Little Things

Spiritual decline is gradual. Saul's failure was not immediate. At first he was humble, but pride soon set in. Then pride turned into envy, and he took matters into his own hands. He ignored what God had plainly told him to do.

It is not for us to pick and choose what parts of the Bible we like and dispense with the others. We are to obey God even in the smallest matters, because "small" sins turn into big sins. They certainly did for Saul.

2. Never Take Responsibility for Your Actions

More than once Saul blamed others for his own bad choices. When Samuel confronted Saul about the burnt offering, the king answered, "I saw my men scattering, and you didn't arrive when you said you would, and the Philistines are...ready for battle...So I felt obliged to offer the burnt offering myself" (1 Sam. 13:11–12 NLT). In other words, "It is my men's fault. It is your fault." Saul just wanted to save face. He forgot that no matter what we try to say about ourselves and our motives, God knows the truth.

3. Don't Just Get Mad, Get Even

Saul's animosity ultimately destroyed him. He was jealous when God placed His anointing upon the young shepherd boy, David, and began to use him. We need to understand there are always going to be people who will do better than we will. We will meet people who are smarter, more attractive, more talented, younger. The Lord God may raise up a certain person, and we will say, "Why him [or her]? Obviously I am the right choice. I am better looking, gifted, dedicated, and *so humble*." Maybe it is because you think so much of yourself that He does not choose you. God gets to choose whom He will use. Don't let hatred make you a victim.

. . . .

The Rules Work for Everyone

God has given you, like Saul, potential. God has given you certain talents. God has made you able to perform certain tasks well. He has put his hand upon you. The call of God is the enabling of God; He has not asked you to do anything that He will not give you the strength to do.

Maybe as you read Saul's story, you felt as though you were reading your own. You feel you are on your way down. If you can heed his example, you can change your ways. If you continue in the way you are going, you will find it a slippery slope. One day you may end up like Saul, saying, "I have played the fool and erred exceedingly." Don't let that happen. Make a recommitment if you need to.

It is up to us to run the race well and play by the rules. Don't be disqualified. Don't be prideful. Don't play the fool. Don't crash and burn. It is such a waste of life.

5

OVERCOMING OBSTACLES *IN* *THE* SPIRITUAL RACE

Have you ever felt underappreciated and unloved? Have you ever felt as though your work was always going to go unnoticed in life? Have you ever faced a problem so large it seemed impossible to overcome?

If you answer yes to any of those questions, you will find encouragement in the next story.

Remember, the Bible compares the Christian life to running a race. If it is a race, it is a long-distance run. We have discovered some important truths together about running the race of life, such as: we must not only start well but finish well; we must follow the rules or be disqualified.

We saw that Samson did not play by the rules and was disqualified in the race of life. The same was true of the first king of Israel, Saul. But now we come to the story of a man who ran very well in the race of life. Though he faced many hurdles and obstacles, he overcame most of them very well.

. . . .

A Heart Like God's

He came from the most humble of beginnings and rose to be the greatest king in the history of the nation Israel. In battle he was fearless. In wisdom and ruling, he was without peer. Yet he was not some macho dude; he was a guy who had a tender, even sensitive, heart. He was both a warrior and a poet. A clear-thinking ruler and talented musician. He was someone God described uniquely as being a man after his own heart. Of course, you know I'm talking about David.

In the last chapter, we saw that the Lord ruled Israel through the various judges, and He spoke to them through the prophets. But because the other nations had human kings, Israel wanted one too. For all practical purposes, God gave them exactly what they asked for: a man after *their* own heart. Saul was the first king of Israel. We saw that on one hand, he had many wonderful attributes. He started off very well, but then he began to unravel and self-destruct. What seemed to be relatively small sins led to very large sins. Saul crashed and burned.

The Lord chose someone to take his place. With David, it was as though the Lord was saying to Israel, "You have had your turn. I gave you the man with all of the characteristics and attributes you wanted in a leader. Now let me give you a man I want." Saul was the man after "man's own heart." David was the man after "God's own heart."

God's selection was so unexpected that we need to pay careful attention to it. In David, the Lord is showing us the kind of person He is looking for today.

. . . .

God's Eyes versus Man's

As our story begins, Saul's failures have devastated the prophet Samuel. Yet the Lord said to him, "You have mourned enough for Saul. I have rejected him as king of Israel. Now fill your horn with olive oil and go to Bethlehem. Find a man named

Jesse who lives there, for I have selected one of his sons to be my new king" (1 Sam. 16:1 NLT).

It is interesting that the Lord did not tell Samuel who was to be the king—*yet.* He did not say which son of Jesse He had chosen. This is typical of the Lord—He leads us one step at a time. Just take that step the Lord has told you to take.

When a man of the magnitude and stature of the prophet Samuel showed up in Bethlehem, the people were understandably concerned and even alarmed. "Do you come in peace?" they asked (1 Sam. 16:4 NLT). The prophet reassured them and invited them to attend the sacrifice he was about to make to the Lord. He wanted to scope out the crowd and see if he could identify God's anointed.

> When they arrived, Samuel took one look at Eliab and thought, "Surely this is the LORD's anointed!" But the LORD said to Samuel, "Don't judge by his appearance or height, for I have rejected him. The LORD doesn't make decisions the way you do! People judge by outward appearance, but the LORD looks at a person's thoughts and intentions."
> (1 SAMUEL 16:6–7 NLT)

A man named Jesse instructed his sons, one by one, to step forward and walk before Samuel. The aged prophet was taken with Eliab, most likely because he reminded him of Saul. But he was not the one. Seven times, Samuel said, "This is not the one the LORD has chosen." Then the prophet asked if Jesse had any more sons. Jesse replied that his youngest was tending sheep. Samuel ordered that the boy be brought to him, stating this imperative: "We will not sit down to eat until he arrives" (1 Sam. 16:8, 11 NLT).

> So Jesse sent for him. He was ruddy and handsome, with pleasant eyes. And the Lord said, "This is the one; anoint him."

So as David stood there among his brothers, Samuel took the olive oil he had brought and poured it on David's head. And the Spirit of the LORD came mightily upon him from that day on. (1 SAMUEL 16:12–13 NLT)

. . . .

God's Choice

When Jesse said David, "the youngest," was out in the fields, he used an interesting phrase. "The youngest" meant not just that David was younger in years than the others, but that he was least in his father's estimation—so much so that Jesse would not have even acknowledged David's existence had the prophet not persisted.

Fortunately, God the Father had more sense than Jesse the father. Maybe you can relate to David on this point. Maybe your parents didn't appreciate you or show you affection. They may have foolishly favored your siblings over you, heaping praise on them and little to none on you. Know this: those whom man rejects often become beloved of the Lord. You need to know that in spite of your parents' lack of love for you, you have always had a heavenly Father who cares for you.

Alan Redpath wrote in his wonderful book on David, *The Making of a Man of God,* "The thought of God toward you began before He even flung a star into space. Then He wrote your name on His heart. It was graven in the palm of His hands before the sky was stretched out in the heavens."[1] God has always been thinking about you.

God chose David in spite of the fact that his father did not show much love toward him. David later wrote, "Even if my mother and father abandon me, / the LORD will hold me close" (Ps. 27:10 NLT).

. . . .

Him?

The Lord rejected all of the magnificent seven, and Jesse called David. Picture it: he came bounding in, a young kid, a teenager. A good-looking boy, but still wet behind the ears. He had reddish hair, maybe some freckles on his face. No doubt he smelled like the sheep he faithfully attended.

In biblical days, no one admired shepherds. People looked down on them. In fact, a court of law did not allow the testimony of a shepherd. They were at the bottom of the social ladder. So whom did God select as His man?

A young boy who had the lowliest profession and whose father did not appreciate him. I am sure the brothers were thinking, *What is our little brother doing in here? This has nothing to do with him.*

Then, to their shock and surprise, the prophet took out oil and poured it on David's head and said he was the new king of Israel. I think the brothers suspected that aged Samuel had gone senile. You can be sure they felt resentment and anger. *How could he possibly say our little brother, David, is the new king of Israel? There must be some mistake here.*

David took it so well. He didn't boast about it. He just went back to watching his sheep. As Chuck Swindoll points out in his great little book on David:

> He didn't go down to the nearest department store and try on crowns. He didn't order a new set of business cards telling the printer to change it from shepherd to king elect. He didn't have a badge that said I am the new man. He didn't shine up a chariot and race through the streets of Bethlehem yelling I am God's choice.

David just went back to doing what he had been doing before and waited for further direction.

The Person God Will Use

Let's look a bit more closely at the account of David's rise to the throne. From it we can identify some principles about the man or the woman God will use.

1. God Uses Ordinary People

David was in many ways the opposite of King Saul. Saul came from a family who loved him; David came from a family who neglected him. Saul was the most handsome man in all Israel; David was a handsome enough guy, but relatively ordinary. Saul was attractive on the outside, but on the inside he was vain, shallow, and devoid of true integrity. In contrast, David had a deep spiritual life and an intense devotion to God. (If you want to know about David's spirituality profile, just read some of the Psalms. They are like windows into his soul.) Saul's problem was that he was full of himself. The Lord rejected him. David was full of the Lord, and God accepted him.

This reminds us of the truth of the Scripture in 1 Corinthians 1:26–29:

> Brothers, think of what you were when you were called. Not many of you were wise by human standards; not many were influential; not many were of noble birth. But God chose the foolish things of the world to shame the wise. God chose the weak things of the world to shame the strong. He chose the lowly things of this world and the despised things—and the things that are not—to nullify the things that are, so no one may boast before him. (NIV)

The Lord seems to go out of His way to use ordinary people to do extraordinary things; then people give credit to the Lord rather than to human beings. Just as surely as God plucked David from obscurity, He is looking for men and women He can use in these critical days in which we are living. God is looking for people to touch this generation. He is looking for people to change this world. Second Chronicles 16:9 says, "The eyes of the LORD run to and fro throughout the whole earth, to show Himself strong on behalf of those whose heart is loyal to Him."

What kind of person does He look for? Someone strong? No. The previous passage says He is looking for someone He can show *His* strength through—someone whose heart is turned toward Him. Is your heart totally turned toward God?

One of the men God used mightily in his generation was D. L. Moody. Moody was the Billy Graham of his day. Dwight Moody was a shoe salesman when he came to faith. You might say that Moody went from selling soles to saving souls. He was just a run-of-the-mill guy.

Do you know what got Moody pointed in the right direction after his conversion? A man went up to him once and said, "Moody, the world has yet to see what God can do in and through and with a man who is totally committed to Him." Moody said, "When I heard that, I said to the Lord, 'I want to be that man.'"

Do you know what Billy Graham was when God called him? He was a farm boy living in North Carolina. He came to faith at a meeting held by a traveling evangelist. Young Billy Frank, as they called him, dedicated his life to the Lord. Who could have imagined what God would do with that young man?

The most Godly people I know are also the most down-to-earth. God is looking for ordinary people to use. David was an ordinary man.

2. God Uses Spiritually Focused People

David had a real insight into who God was and set his heart to follow him. In Psalm 57:7, he wrote, "My heart is fixed, O God, my heart is steadfast and confident!" (AMP). This means that David's heart was totally focused on who God was. He was locked in to what was right. He was not fickle. He was meditative. Yet he was brave and courageous.

In Psalm 27:4, David laid out the focus of his life:

One thing I have desired of the LORD,
That will I seek:
That I may dwell in the house of the LORD
All the days of my life,
And behold the beauty of the LORD,
And to inquire in His temple.

Paul made a similar statement in the book of Philippians: "One thing I do, forgetting the things which are behind and reaching forward to those things which are ahead, I press toward the goal for the prize of the upward call of God in Christ Jesus" (3:13–14).

One thing. Everybody has the one thing in his or her life. I ask you: what is that one thing for you. What is your clear focus in life? Our greatest danger in life is permitting the urgent things to crowd out the important; to fail to live by a clear set of priorities. David said, "This is my heart. It is my one thing." Everybody is living for something. The main thing is to keep the main thing the main thing.

Many of us, if we're honest, could say the one thing we are most focused on right now is a career: "I want to get established. I want to make a good living. I want to provide for my family." The other thing many of us might say is, "My main priority is my family. I want to be a good husband [or wife]. I want my family to stay strong." I am not criticizing either of these. It's fine to want to have a good career and family. These are worthy goals.

But neither of these should be the *one thing*. The one thing should be Christ.

In Matthew 6:33, Jesus said, "Seek first the kingdom of God and His righteousness, and all of these things shall be added to you." Let me translate that into the modern vernacular: put the things of God number one in your life, and everything else will work out just fine. Seek first the rule and reign of Christ in your life.

God may not give you everything you hoped for in life. Then again, He may give you more. You just leave that up to Him and put Him first.

That is what David did.

3. God Uses People Who Are Willing to Act in Faith

At that particular time in his life, David's primary responsibility was to watch sheep. If lions or boars attacked his sheep, he fought to the death to protect them. He spent hours insuring their safety. No doubt that's when he came up with Psalm 23. He was probably watching the sheep munching contentedly in a lush green field one day when he thought, *The Lord is my shepherd, I shall not want.*

David figured if that was what God wanted him to do, then those were going to be the best-fed and most protected sheep around. In fact, he would, if necessary, lay his life down for them.

Did the young shepherd boy dream of one day doing great things for God? Did he ever think he would be crowned as the King of Israel. We can't know for sure. But one thing we do know is David had a clear focus and proper sense of what his priorities should be in life.

. . . .
What God Can Do Through the Willing

Divine opportunity usually, if not always, comes unexpectedly. The Lord was about to open a big door for David. Faithfulness on an errand for his father would result in David's greatest victory. Big doors swing on small hinges.

His brothers were all away, fighting for the Israeli army. They were facing off with the Philistines at the Valley of Elah. The Philistines had a warrior known as Goliath. This guy was big. He was nine feet, six inches tall. A wall of a man, all muscle. The Bible tells us that his armor alone weighed two hundred pounds. He carried a javelin that weighed more than twenty-five pounds.

This oversized Philistine challenged the Israelites every day: he would growl "Who is going to come and fight me? Who has the courage to face off with me?" He did this for forty days.

Then the redheaded youth showed up in town. He was on an errand for Dad, taking bread and cheese to his brothers. (Though announced king, David had yet to take his throne. Saul was still in power.) He heard all the commotion. He scurried down to the front to see for himself who was making all this noise. And there in the Valley of Elah was this frightening, over-sized man bellowing his threats.

David was amazed—not at Goliath's incredible size but that the man was blatantly and openly blaspheming God and no one was lifting a finger to stop him. David's blood began to boil with righteous indignation. He asked for an audience with King Saul. When he came into Saul's presence he confidently said, "Don't worry; *I* will kill the Philistine."

Can you imagine? Everyone probably had a good laugh at David's expense.

Amazingly, Saul agreed to let the boy try. What did he have to lose? Perhaps the giant would laugh himself to death. Little did he realize he was preparing the way for David's ultimate ascent to the throne of Israel.

Saul clothed David with his massive coat of armor. It was so heavy and cumbersome, David couldn't even move. He left it behind, choosing instead his staff and his slingshot.

David was ready if necessary to lay it all on the line.

If you want to play it safe—keep everything predictable, maintain your routine—have a nice time on Easy Street. You will never be a man or a woman God will use. If you are going to make a difference, you are going to have to take some steps of faith.

David risked everything he had to honor God. Look at 1 Samuel 17:

> He picked up five smooth stones from a stream and put them in his shepherd's bag. Then armed only with his shepherd's staff and sling, he started across to fight Goliath.
>
> Goliath ... sneer[ed] in contempt at this ruddy-faced boy. "Am I a dog," he roared at David, "that you come at me with a stick?" And he cursed David by the names of his gods. "Come over here, and I'll give your flesh to the birds and wild animals!" Goliath yelled.
>
> David shouted in reply, "You come to me with sword, spear, and javelin, but I come to you in the name of the LORD Almighty—the God of the armies of Israel, whom you have defied. Today the LORD will conquer you, and I will kill you and cut off your head. And then I will give the dead bodies of your men to the birds and wild animals, and the whole world will know that there is a God in Israel! And everyone will know that the LORD does not need weapons to rescue his people. It is his battle, not ours. The LORD will give you to us!" (VV. 40–47 NLT)

Talk about going for broke. There was now no turning back for the shepherd-boy-anointed-king. If God didn't come through, he was dead.

Look at what happened in verse 48—this is important: "As Goliath moved closer to attack, David *quickly ran* out to meet him." You would expect David to perhaps hold his ground, or, at the most, take some cautious steps in the direction of his adversary. But instead he sprinted full speed at Goliath.

Talk about running a race!

Reaching into his shepherd's bag and taking out a stone, David placed it in his sling. He no doubt shot up a silent prayer. Then he hurled that stone with all the might a young shepherd boy could muster. Like a guided missile, the stone found its target: the forehead of the rapidly approaching Goliath.

The giant was stopped in his tracks, and, like a massive redwood, he went crashing to the ground with a mighty thud.

Victory was David's!

Since he had no sword, he ran over and pulled Goliath's from its sheath. He cut off Goliath's head, and fear shot through the ranks of the Philistines as quickly as David's stone had felled the giant.

When the Philistines saw that their champion was dead, they turned tail and ran.

. . . .
Strategy for Giant-Killing

We all face giants in life. You might be facing one right now—something that looms so large, something so frightening or so powerful that you don't think you can ever win against it. Maybe it's the giant of addiction. You find yourself under the power of a drug habit or alcohol dependency or you are hooked on pornography. Then again, it could be the giant of fear and worry, or the giant of jealousy. You have tried to overcome and conquer it, but it smacks you down again and again. This giant lords its power over you. It terrifies you. It taunts and terrifies you.

You might face a different kind of giant altogether: an incurable illness, a lawsuit, a marriage that seems doomed for failure, a prodigal son or daughter. David gives us a four-step model for slaying giants and running the spiritual race.

1. Remember the Battle Is the Lord's

Look at verse 47: "It is his battle, not ours. The LORD will give you to us!" (NLT). We sometimes forget, when circumstances fill us with fear, that we are fighting a spiritual battle. Ephesians 6:12 says, "We are not struggling against flesh and blood, but against the rulers, against the authorities, against the powers of this dark world and against the spiritual forces of evil in the heavenly realms" (NIV). You need to fight fire with fire. Fight a spiritual battle with spiritual weapons.

Utilize the spiritual weaponry that God has made available to you. As Paul wrote in 2 Corinthians 10:4, "The weapons we fight with are not weapons of the world. On the contrary, they have divine power to demolish strongholds" (NIV).

What are those weapons? One of them is prayer. When we pray, we remind ourselves of who God is. In the Lord's Prayer, Jesus taught us: "In this manner, therefore, pray: / Our Father in heaven, / Hallowed be Your name" (Matt. 6:9). Before personal petition, just contemplate the fact that you are talking to God Almighty. He is all-powerful. He is all-knowing. He is present everywhere. There is nothing God cannot do. If you seek God for who He is, you will see your giants for what they are. Suddenly your giants will be transformed to midgets. God is more powerful than anyone or anything else.

David said to Goliath, "You come to me with sword, spear, and javelin, but I come to you in the name of the LORD Almighty—the God of the armies of Israel" (v. 45 NLT). He put his enemy into perspective.

You are on the winning side. God is stronger than the devil. Your God is mightier than any vice, addiction, or problem. Your God is greater. First John 4:4: "You are of God, little children, and have overcome them, because He who is in you is greater than he who is in the world."

2. Attack!

Earlier in the story the Israelites said, "Have you seen this man who has come up?" (1 Sam. 17:25). Goliath had crossed the ravine and was climbing up Israel's side. If you tolerate a Goliath, he will take over your territory. He will come right up on your doorstep. That is why you can't make any deals with the devil. Of course you try, right? You say, "I can control this. I can handle this. I can manage this. I can keep this under control." Yeah, right. It's like a wildfire—it gets out of control. It will run over your life. You won't know how it ever happened.

That's why you don't run from giants. You attack them. You don't negotiate with them, you eradicate them. You don't yell at them, you kill them. You go after them.

Verse 48 says, "As Goliath moved closer to attack, David quickly ran out to meet him" (NLT). As the enemy grew closer, David raced right at the guy. You need to do the same with your giant.

3. Get Your Giant Out of Hiding

You need to force your giant out into the light of day. Stop allowing this sin to enjoy the comfort of darkness. Stop rationalizing it. Stop blaming other people for it. Admit it, not only to God but to someone else—a responsible Christian, such as a pastor or a spouse. Or a close Christian friend. Come right out and say it: "I have a problem. I have never revealed this to anyone before. I am sick of it. I want to slay my giant. I need your help. I am asking you to keep me accountable. Call me every day, and ask me what steps I am taking to deal with this. I want you to confront me about it. I need prayer. I need help."

4. Trust Only God

David put no trust in Saul's armor. This is a temptation we all face: trusting in our own resources. Sometimes the Lord will reduce us to nothing so He, and He alone, will get the glory. Has that happened to you? That is good. Then God can get the glory and show you what He is really capable of.

That is what David did. Don't wear Saul's armor.

. . . .

Are You Ready for God to Use You?

Are you ready to go for it? You are just an ordinary person. No matter. Are you a person who is willing to be faithful in what God has set before you today, no matter how small and insignificant? Are you willing to take chances and leaps of faith? Are you willing to run toward your giants in this spiritual race?

I am telling you that God can and will use you. Just make yourself available and say, "Lord, here I am." You can be like David: an ordinary man God used to do extraordinary things. The power was all God's; the courage was all David's. Like David, you can, with God's help, overcome every hurdle and begin to run well the race of life.

We've seen how David handled the early laps of his race. In the next chapter we'll see how he fared as he settled into his pace.

6

YOUR CHOICE: FORGIVE OR FALL

In 2 Samuel 9 we find one of the most beautiful messages on forgiveness in the pages of the Bible. David extended it toward a potential enemy, a man he could have eliminated had he chosen to do so. Instead David graciously forgave.

The obstacle before David on the track of life could have ultimately destroyed him. The same obstacle certainly destroyed David's predecessor, King Saul, who harbored a grudge like nobody's business. One of the reasons God described David as a man after His own heart is because he forgave.

If you want to be a man or woman after God's own heart and run this spiritual race well, you have to learn how to forgive others. Why? Because as fatally flawed people, we are going to sin against people, and people are going to sin against us. We are going to hurt one another, whether it is intentional or not. Husbands are going to hurt wives, and wives are going to hurt husbands. Children are going to hurt their parents, and parents are going to hurt their children. Family members will offend one another. Friends will hurt friends. That is why we need to learn how to forgive.

Only as forgiving people can we run instead of limp through our race.

Let's pick up where we left off looking at David. We will see how he demonstrated that he was indeed a man after God's own heart.

. . . .

God's People Forgive

You recall that God had rejected Saul as king over Israel because of repeated disobedience. The Lord told the prophet Samuel to go to Bethlehem, where God identified David as the next king of Israel.

In the battle that had broken out between the Israelis and the Philistines, you'll recall that King Saul should have faced off with Goliath. Instead he hid in his tent. David told King Saul, "Don't worry about anything. I'll take care of that guy for you."

Saul and the members of his court had a good chuckle. "You and what army? You are just a boy." But when David succeeded in killing the giant, Israel had a new hero. A hit song on Israeli radio: "Saul has slain his thousands / And David his ten thousands" (1 Sam. 18:7). He was the man.

Needless to say, King Saul wasn't happy to hear that. It was a potential threat to his throne. "Therefore Saul eyed David from that day forward" (v. 9).

In the interim David forged a very strong relationship with Saul's son, Jonathan, and it lasted a lifetime. Jonathan, in contrast to his wicked father, understood David was a good and a Godly man. He knew David would one day become the king of Israel. Back in that culture, when one king took over for another, he often destroyed all that king's descendants, because they might try to take the throne. So Jonathan asked David to make a deal with him: to pledge himself to looking out for Jonathan's offspring.

David agreed. Meanwhile, Saul hunted David like a wild dog. He was determined to kill his replacement. David had to hide in caves. It was a difficult life. He might have said, "Lord, what's this all about? I choose to follow You. I respond to Your call, and yet here I am living like a hunted animal. I thought I was supposed to be the king. Why do I have to live this way?" Instead, David hung in there and trusted God.

He had a couple of shots himself at killing King Saul. One time David was hiding in a cave and King Saul walked in to relieve himself. Some of David's men said, "God is giving you an opportunity. Kill him right now." David said no. He would not harm the Lord's anointed, but he "arose and secretly cut off a corner of Saul's robe" (1 Sam. 24:4).

Saul left the cave, and David called out from a distance, saying, "I just wondered if you were feeling a draft, King Saul. I cut a little bit of your robe off. I could have killed you, but I didn't do it." Then he threw in a holy promise: "May the Lord avenge the wrongs you have done to me, but my hand will not touch you." Evidently this moved Saul, who wept and said, "You are more righteous than I. You have treated me well, but I have treated you badly ... I know that you will surely be king" (1 Sam. 24:12, 17, 20 NIV).

Of course, we know he still pursued David. But he failed. Ultimately Saul and his son Jonathan died on the battlefield, and David ascended to the throne.

This would have been the time to strike out all potential enemies. Any offspring of Saul or Jonathan, David could have destroyed justifiably. But David would have none of that. Imagine what you would have done if you had been in David's shoes. Would you have extended kindness to the relatives of one who had abused—in fact, tried to kill—you, not once but many times?

Let's read about it in 2 Samuel 9:1: "One day David began wondering if anyone in Saul's family was still alive, for he had promised Jonathan he would show kindness to them" (v. 13 NLT). When David learned that Jonathan had left a crippled son, David sent for the boy. His name was Mephibosheth.

> When he came to David, he bowed low in great fear and said, "I am your servant."
> But David said, "Don't be afraid! I've asked you to come so that I can be kind to you because of my vow to your father, Jonathan. I will give you all the land that once belonged to your grandfather Saul, and you may live here with me at the palace!" (2 SAMUEL 9:6–7 NLT)

. . . .

God's Love for the Down-and-Out

This is not just a story of David extending grace to a young boy named Mephibosheth; it is a picture of God extending grace to us as well.

In 1 Samuel 4:1, the word "kindness" is important; a better translation would be *grace*. *Grace* is a very important word to us as Christians. One definition of grace is "God's unmerited favor." Let me further define grace by contrasting it with a couple of other words: justice and mercy. Justice is getting what you deserve. Mercy is not getting what you deserve. Grace is getting what you don't deserve.

Let's say you try to steal a car and you are arrested. Justice is meted out. That means you serve a sentence. You got what you deserved. Let's say the judge decided to show you mercy; instead of prosecuting you to the full extent of the law, maybe he put you on probation and told you to never steal another car again. That was mercy. Grace means that not only were you not charged with the crime, but the judge gave you the keys to his car and told you it was now yours!

This is what David wanted to do for Mephibosheth. He wanted to show grace to a member of Saul's household.

When David sent for Saul's former servant, Ziba, the servant said, "One of Jonathan's sons is still alive, but he is crippled" (2 Sam. 9:3 NLT). Ziba seemed to be saying, "There is someone, but you might not want him because he is defective. He may not be worth the trouble. I don't know if this young man would fit into your beautiful palace. Maybe you ought to rethink it."

David's response was beautiful. He said only, "Where is he?" (2 Sam. 9:4 NLT). He wasn't taken aback. He didn't ask for details. He just wanted to know where the man was that he might show grace to him.

In the same way, God does not base His grace and love on the recipient's worthiness.

Ziba answered that Mephibosheth was living in Lo-debar. Lo-debar looked the way it sounds: dry and dead. Its name means "the name of no pasture." It was barren. It was a place where no one wanted to live. It certainly was not an appropriate hometown for a grandchild of the former king.

Why was Mephibosheth there? He was in hiding. He was by then an adult, and he had a son himself. He lived in fear of King David's reprisal. To make matters worse, he was isolated and separated from the tabernacle where God's people met. He was living apart from fellowship, in a barren place, unable to walk.

What a perfect picture of all of us living in Lo-debar, feeling unloved, unwanted, unneeded, undeserving. Just as David reached out to Mephibosheth, God reaches out to us. Romans 5:8 says, "While we were still sinners, Christ died for us."

. . . .
Active Compassion

Remember the story of those four men who brought their friend to Jesus? Jesus was teaching in a room that was tightly packed with people. Those guys were so determined that they climbed up on the roof and dug away. They lowered the guy down on a cot right in front of the Lord. All four worked together so the Lord could deal with the man's need. He rewarded their persistence and touched the man. I love that.

We need that kind of persistence. We need to reach out. Right now we know people who are living in Lo-debar. By that I mean we know Mephibosheths out there who are hurt. They are perhaps angry with God. They feel they have been mistreated. They live in isolation and fear. They need someone to reach out to them with the love of Jesus Christ.

Some think God is just out to get them. This reminds me of a story I heard about a thief who broke into a house. He was looking around in the dark with his flashlight. Suddenly he heard a voice in the darkness say, "Jesus is watching you." The thief just about jumped out of his skin as he thought, *Where did that come from?*

Again he heard it. "Jesus is watching you!" The thief was absolutely terrified. He followed the sound of the voice with his flashlight and heaved a sigh of relief when he saw a parrot on a perch, who once again said, "Jesus is watching you!"

The thief laughed. Then he looked down, and at the foot of the parrot's perch was a very large Doberman pinscher, baring his teeth.

Then the parrot looked down at the Doberman and said, "Sic 'im, Jesus."

That is how a lot of people see God today: *Jesus is against me.* As Mephibosheth might have thought, they think, *All that has gone wrong in my life is God's fault. Why did God let this happen?* It's a lie of Satan that persuades people to keep their distance from God. Satan doesn't want us to know God's love. Mephibosheth kept his distance from David, which is exactly what Satan wanted. But David listened to what God wanted, and it was he who ended up seeking out Mephibosheth.

In the same way, it is God who makes the first move in our lives. I know we as Christians like to refer to "the day I found the Lord." The truth is He wasn't lost, we were. Certainly one day we discovered a God who loved us. But God found us before we found Him. He chose us before we chose Him. Jesus sought us out as a shepherd looks for a lost sheep.

This was what David was doing: "You tell Mephibosheth that the king wants him to come into the palace."

. . . .

A Kindly King, a Good God

Imagine how Mephibosheth felt when that knock came on his door and he heard, "We are from the palace, representing King David." A sense of dread must have washed over him. His heart sank. He had feared this day, and now it had finally come.

"The king wants you to show grace to you," they said.

No, he wants to kill me. Mephibosheth was probably filled with doubt. But the moment he met David, this man after God's own heart, he was stunned to see a heart full of love and compassion.

David said, "I want you to come here. All of the land that belonged to your grandfather Saul I want to give to you. I want you to live in the palace with me. I want you to eat at my table and be like a member of my own family. Let me show kindness to you." That is exactly what God does for us. He extends kindness to us. Our relationship with God is based 100 percent on what Jesus Christ did for us. That doesn't mean we should not to seek to live Godly lives. But a Godly life does not bring the blessing of God; it is the blessing of God that produces the Godly life. God loves you. He accepts you not because of who you are but because of Jesus.

I heard a story about something that happened in the 1800s in London. A little boy wanted to hear the great American evangelist D. L. Moody, whom I referenced earlier. Moody had come to town to preach. This little street urchin made his way across the entire city of London, risking his very life, with no food or proper shoes. After a long journey, he finally came to the great church where Moody was scheduled to speak.

It was overflowing with people. He could hear the singing through the opened windows. The little guy was so excited. As he made his way up to the door, an old usher scowled at him and asked, "What are you doing, young man?"

The boy said, "I am going to go hear the great evangelist D. L. Moody."

"Not looking like that! You are filthy. Go away!"

The little boy was crushed. He was sitting on the steps, crying, when a black carriage pulled up in front of the church. Out of it stepped a large man. He saw the sad little boy on the steps and asked, "Young man, what is wrong?"

The boy answered, "I came here to hear the great preacher D. L. Moody, but they won't let me in the church."

"Is that so?" the big man said. "You just put your hand in my hand, and I will see what I can do to help you."

The little boy put his dirty little hand into the man's big clean hand. The man led him right down the middle aisle, past the usher who wouldn't let him in, to the front row. The big guy sat him in a front-row seat. Then the man stepped up to the pulpit.

That man was, of course, D. L. Moody. That young boy couldn't get in on his own, but when he held Moody's hand, he walked through the front door.

So it is with us—because of Jesus. We are filthy in sin, but he takes our dirty hands in his clean one and leads us to the front-row seats in the palace.

David provided a marvelous and practical example of this in 2 Samuel.

. . . .

Table for Two

Note that four times in thirteen verses, the writer of 2 Samuel 9 mentions that Mephibosheth sat at David's table. That may not seem significant to us, but in biblical times, dinner was the big event of the day. People then didn't have all of the entertainment and distractions we have today. Dinner was it. Not only did they have a great feast in the palace, but afterward they spent time talking and having fellowship.

Think about Mephibosheth. He had been living in that barren place called Lo-debar. The next thing he knew, he was in the palace in Jerusalem, sitting at the table of the king, just like a member of the royal family.

David's commitment to his friend Jonathan was what brought Mephibosheth to the king's table. We can glean several important principles from this.

1. We Need to Extend Forgiveness to Others

I don't care if they have wronged you or needlessly hurt you. I don't care if you would love to get them back. God commands you to forgive, and that is what you ought to do. Don't let a root of bitterness ruin your life.

2. We Need to Reach Out to the Mephibosheths of the World

These are people we know who may seem hostile to God or opposed to the gospel. We need to show them God's love and not give up on them.

David did both these things. He listened to the will of God, and he determined that he would hold true to how he knew God wanted him to act. He showed forgiveness and compassion. And because of this he prospered. Remember: Saul harbored unforgiveness, and he fell. David did not. He not only started the race well, but he bounded into the lead.

In the next chapter, let's take a final look at just how David finished his race.

7

HE TRIPS, HE FALLS, HE GETS BACK UP

I don't know about you, but I love to read biographies. And the Bible is, among other things, a biographical book. It tells us stories of some very great and some very wicked people. The authors added no "spin" to what we read in its pages. God's Word is just unvarnished truth, telling us what different persons were really like—flesh-and-blood people like you and me. That is why I have called this book *Losers and Winners, Saints and Sinners*.

The Bible always gives us a hero, warts and all. God arranged this so we could learn from others' failures and successes. First Corinthians 10:11 says, "All these events happened to them as examples for us" (NLT).

We are going to take a third look at the life of a man who certainly made his mistakes. As you recall, David was a young man whom God plucked out of obscurity to become the greatest king in Israel's history. It's worth noting the New Testament mentions David more than any other Old Testament character. Truly he made his mark.

In his biography, we look at how David ruled: his wisdom, his compassion, his great courage on the battlefield, his keeping a promise to an old friend to extend kindness to his son. We see such a beautiful example of a man after God's own heart.

Yet in the spiritual race, even the strongest runners sometimes fall. An easy stretch of track can lull a champion into relaxing the pace—so much so that he takes a disastrous tumble.

. . . .

David Trips over a Bathing Beauty

As he was running the race of life, David was doing so well he thought he could slow down a little bit: take a breather, relax a bit. He didn't have to run with as much commitment. He got sloppy.

It started with a lustful look, and it ended up as a nationwide scandal. Though the sin we are about to read about in David's life lasted only minutes, the repercussions of it lasted for the rest of his life.

I am speaking, of course, of the story of David and Bathsheba. This sin was so devastating to David's life, you might think that he could never survive such a fall. Amazingly, he did, though it cast a shadow over his life from which he never fully recovered.

Let's not forget, as sordid as the details are, that David was still a man after God's own heart. That is not to justify what he did in any way, but we should remember David was a Godly man who made a big mistake. (Which, by the way, could happen to any one of us. If David had the potential to fall into sin like this, then you or I can fall as well.)

The story begins in 2 Samuel 11:

The following spring, the time of year when kings go to war, David sent Joab and the Israelite army to destroy the

Ammonites. In the process they laid siege to the city of Rabbah. But David stayed behind in Jerusalem.

Late one afternoon David got out of bed after taking a nap and went for a stroll on the roof of the palace. As he looked out over the city, he noticed a woman of unusual beauty taking a bath. He sent someone to find out who she was, and he was told, "She is Bathsheba, the daughter of Eliam and the wife of Uriah the Hittite." Then David sent for her; and when she had come to the palace, he slept with her...Then she returned home. Later, when Bathsheba discovered that she was pregnant, she sent a message to inform David. (VV. 1–5 NLT)

David was around fifty years old at that point in his life. He had been ruling successfully for about two decades. He had distinguished himself as a man of God, a great musician, a poet, a writer, a warrior, and of course, a ruler. No doubt about it, David was on a roll. That's always the time to put up your guard. When things are going reasonably or even unreasonably well, when we are moving from glory to glory, we often find ourselves in a danger zone. That is exactly what David did.

He got lazy. Note the Bible says that when the time had come for kings to battle, David sent Joab instead. Instead of fighting the good fight, the king was sleeping in his bed. Instead of moving forward, he appeared to be moving backward.

There is no vacation from the spiritual battle. I wish there were. I wish we could kick back for a month or so. But the Christian life is not a playground—it is a battleground. The moment you begin to slow down or relax your grip spiritually, you are going to start having some serious problems.

David had set the scene for his own failure. He had compromised his duties as king not only by avoiding battle, but by gathering concubines (See 2 Sam. 6:13, 11:1). He was not only lazy, he was lustful. At that point in David's life, we don't read of his singing beautiful songs of praise to God. We don't read of his playing his stringed instrument. We don't read of his treasuring close fellowship and intimacy with God as he had done before. This fact made him far more vulnerable on the day he saw the beautiful Bathsheba bathing.

The sight of a lovely woman without her clothes would be a temptation for any man, but for David it was more intense than that. Why? He had been feeding the fire of lust. So he took one look, and he crumbled; he swiftly took action to have the woman.

Again, we don't see David growing in his relationship with God at that time. This is what usually happens when we give into temptation. We don't cease to believe in God—we just forget about Him. As Dietrich Bonhoeffer wrote, "At this moment when lust takes control, God loses all reality, and Satan does not fill us with a hatred of God but with a forgetfulness of God."

When David sent his servant to find out who she was, the servant returned and reported, "She is Bathsheba...the wife of Uriah the Hittite" (2 Sam. 11:3 NLT). Apparently the servant understood why David inquired after the woman. He was warning the king: "Sire, she is a married woman. That means she's off limits." You have to admire this servant for his boldness. Through him, the Lord was trying to warn David: "Go over—not under—this hurdle."

· ·
Caution Thrown to the Wind

Now, as you know, when a person comes under the power of sin, he does the most insane, irrational things. I've seen it many times. Often the person who commits the sin is the last to see how far he has fallen. In the same way David, under the power of sin, wasn't thinking clearly. The man after God's own heart wasn't behaving as such.

Before we go farther, let's talk a little about Bathsheba. You might think of her as an innocent victim in this story. I disagree. Certainly the lion's share of guilt falls upon David, but we don't read of Bathsheba's necessarily protesting his request. It's true that if the king of the nation summoned you into his presence, you might submit out of fear of losing your life. On the other hand, one must ask if Bathsheba intentionally put herself in a place where she knew the king would see her. A Jewish woman given to modesty, as she should have been, would not normally have bathed herself in a place where others could see her. It is possible that Bathsheba was trying to entice the king. Perhaps she, too, allowed her sin to make her irrational.

Soon Bathsheba was brought into the king's chamber. They had sex. They probably had some passionate pleasure that night. The Bible acknowledges there is pleasure in sin. If we deny that, we are fools. Would any of us sin if it were miserable? Let's be honest about it—sin can be enjoyable. The Bible even speaks of the "pleasures of sin" but says it lasts only a few moments (Heb. 11:25). And it comes with a hefty price tag. David found this out.

. . . .

A Trickle Becomes a Flood

David at first must have thought he'd gotten away with it. Maybe he assumed, *It was just a one-night stand. No one will ever know.* A little time passed. Then a message came to David from Bathsheba that said, "Tell the king I am pregnant."

David had a problem on his hands. What should he do? What he should have done was realize he had sinned. He should have repented before God. Instead, David did what most of us do when we are caught in sin: he tried to cover it up.

David formulated an evil plan. He sent word to have Uriah, the husband of Bathsheba, come to the palace.

Imagine Uriah for a moment. He seems to have been a pretty low-ranking soldier in the army. Suddenly he got a message that the king of Israel had summoned him to the palace. Imagine how exciting that must have been. It would be like getting a call from the White House saying the president wanted to see you immediately.

Imagine Uriah's anticipation as he made his way from the misery of the battlefield to the splendor of the palace. *I'm going to meet the man after God's own heart. What a great king I have heard he is. I admire him so. I'm so proud to be in his army and fight for him.*

When they met, David said, "Uriah, how are you? I wanted to hear how things are going out there in the battle."

"It is tough out there, but it is an honor to fight for you, King."

"I just thought you would like a nice meal and a night home with your wife." We read, "Then he told Uriah, 'Go home and relax'" (2 Sam. 11:8 NLT). We know, of course, his motives were completely impure. He was thinking that if Uriah slept with Bathsheba, Uriah would think the child she had already conceived with David was his.

Uriah was such a committed soldier he wouldn't go to his wife; the humble man stayed that night at the palace entrance "with some of the king's other servants" (v. 9 NLT).

The king's response? He called him back to the palace and got him good and drunk. Still, honorable Uriah refused to go home to his wife, saying, "Joab and his officers are camping in the open fields. How could I go home to wine and dine and sleep with my wife?" (v. 11 NLT).

This was a man of integrity. He could not bear the thought of reveling in pleasure when his fellow soldiers were risking their lives for the king.

Again, David should have taken heed and repented. Again, he persisted in his sin. He put his murderous intentions in writing: "Dear Joab, I want this man dead. You make sure it happens." He sent Uriah back to the battle with this letter. Little did Uriah realize he was carrying his death warrant.

Joab obeyed and sent a message back to the king. "Dear King: We led an attack against the city. We lost a few men, including Uriah the Hittite."

Again David thought he had pulled it off. After Bathsheba mourned her husband, David ordered her back to the palace. They were married. Ultimately, everything seemed to work out.

There was one small problem. The Bible says, "But the LORD was very displeased with what David had done" (2 Sam. 11:27 NLT).

. . . .

Time to Pay the Price

It took a while for David to realize this. Why? Because he'd shut God out. Once he had loved to worship God. He had loved to pray. He had loved to spend time in the presence of his God. During the time he was consumed with Bathsheba, however, it's as though he hung up on God. There was no communication, no communion. Granted, he was still in a relationship with God, but he wasn't living in fellowship with God.

When you live with unconfessed sin, your communication with God is shut down. Scripture says, "If I regard iniquity in my heart / The LORD will not hear" (Ps. 66:18). David experienced that. It broke his heart. He missed God. And God missed him. Do you know that when you are in sin, God misses fellowship with you?

The time finally came for David to come clean. Did he do so willingly and at his own initiation? No. The Lord had to direct the prophet Nathan to confront him.

This prophet was clever. He didn't play his hand with David right up front. He told a little story.

> There were two men in a certain town. One was rich, and one was poor. The rich man owned many sheep and cattle. The poor man owned nothing but a little lamb he had worked hard to buy. He raised that little lamb, and it grew up with his children. It ate from the man's own plate and drank from his cup. He cuddled it in his arms like a baby daughter. One day a guest arrived at the home of the rich man. But instead of killing a lamb from his own flocks for food, he took the poor man's lamb and killed it and served it to his guest. (2 SAMUEL 12:1-4 NLT)

David's blood began to boil. His face was probably beet-red. He said, "That man should be put to death." That's pretty harsh. It's a bad thing to steal someone's lamb, but I don't think he deserved the death penalty.

Isn't it interesting how bad our sin can look in someone else's life? Isn't it amazing how people who are living in gross sin can be so judgmental of seemingly small sin in the lives of others?

Remember the illustration that Jesus used in the Sermon on the Mount; he said, "Why do you worry about picking a speck out of your brother's eye when you have a two-by-four in your own? Before you worry about that speck in your brother's eye, you had better get the telephone pole out of your own. Then you can see clearly." In other words, "How can you be so critical of others when you are guilty of worse?" That was the case with David. He wanted to kill a guy for stealing someone's sheep.

Then the prophet pointed his finger at the king and said, "You are the man." David realized he had stepped right into the trap. He had taken the noose and pulled it around his neck.

. . . .
Fellowship Restored—But at a Cost

David, at last, did the right thing. He said, "I have sinned against God." How do you think he felt? When you are living a sinful lifestyle and get busted, it's a horrible experience. But in some ways it's a relief. You can stop hiding. You can stop lying. You can just say, "I did it. Hopefully now I can change my behavior."

I think David was relieved. Look at something he wrote during that time in Psalm 51: "Create in me a clean heart, O God, / And renew a steadfast spirit within me. / . . . Restore to me the joy of Your salvation" (vv. 10, 12). In other words, "Lord, I have missed You. I want the joy back again. Give me a clean heart. Renew a right spirit."

. . . .
The Damage Done

The good news: God did forgive David in spite of the wickedness of his sin.

Still, the prophet Nathan reminded David, "By this deed you have given great occasion to the enemies of the LORD to blaspheme" (2 Sam. 12:14). Meaning, "David, you have given the enemy ammo to use against us. Couldn't you have thought about that?"

How I wish people would think about that before they sin: their reputations, the cause of Christ, the way their sin will affect others. I am amazed at what people who claim to be Christians will do. I have seen wives brazenly divorce their Christian husbands, though they had no scriptural grounds. I have seen husbands engaging in inappropriate, flirty relationships with women at the office.

I've seen Christian young people willingly put themselves in places of vulnerability sexually or dabble with drinking and drugs. I have confronted some of them, saying, "That is a sin against God."

They reply, "I know that."

"Why would you do something that is a sin against God?"

They say, "God will forgive me."

Technically, that is true. But every day a person continues in this attitude of disobedience, he is getting a harder heart. What about the cause of Christ? What about His reputation? What about His children? The sinner responds, "What about me?" How tragic this is. How often it happens in our selfish culture, and how foolish to assume there are no serious consequences.

Nathan said that because of David's actions, "The sword shall never depart from your house" (2 Sam. 12:10). Does that mean God did not forgive David? No. In spite of the wickedness of his sin, God forgave David. But he still paid a price for it. He saw his own sons behave exactly as he had. One son raped his half-sister. Another son killed the brother who raped his half-sister. The apples did not fall far from the tree.

In addition, Nathan said, "Your child will die" (2 Sam. 12:14 NLT). Bathsheba and David had to go through the excruciating experience of the death of a child.

And finally, God gave David's wives to another man, who slept with them in public. "You did it secretly, but I will do this to you openly in the sight of all Israel" (2 Sam. 12:12 NLT).

Thus David, for his actions, experienced violence, death, and public humiliation. David's story is an excellent reminder that though you can console yourself with the hope of God's forgiveness, you may still, to some degree, reap what you have sown.

To put a contemporary face on this issue, let's say you rob a bank. You get arrested. You say, "God, I am so sorry. Forgive me." Now you hope no one will press charges. You appear before the judge and say, "Your Honor, I know it was wrong to rob that bank. I want you to know I am sorry. I have asked

God to forgive me. I am asking you to forgive me. I would like to go home now for dinner."

The judge responds, "That is very touching, but you are going to prison."

You reap what you sowed. Look at the bright side: now you're going to have a prison ministry!

Just because you ask God to forgive you doesn't mean you won't face some repercussions for the sin you have committed. This story is a warning to us to avoid getting apathetic in our spiritual lives. Keep up the pace—don't slacken. It could very well cost you everything.

. . . .

Lessons for the Twenty-First Century

Let's rewind and see what we can learn from David's tragic mistake.

1. Learn to Look Away

I am sure David wished he had never seen Bathsheba. The original language implies that when David saw her, he looked *continuously*. Now, when your eyes catch something you are not supposed to see, you can turn and not look. Or you just keep looking ... drink it in ... commit it to memory. That is the way David looked: he locked in on her.

Jesus warned about that wrong look. In the Sermon on the Mount, the Lord told us how to deal with lust: "You have heard that it was said to those of old, 'You shall not commit adultery.' But I say to you whoever looks at a woman to lust for her has already committed adultery with her in his heart" (Matt. 5:27–28). Here is the solution:

> If your right eye causes you to sin, pluck it out and cast it from you; for it is more profitable for you that one of your members perish, than that your whole body be cast into

hell. And if your right hand causes you to sin, cut it off and cast it from you; for it is more profitable for you that one of your members perish than your whole body be cast into hell. (vv. 29–30)

Our Lord was not speaking literally, but figuratively. The heart of the matter is the matter of the heart: you can pluck out a right eye and still lust with the left one. You can cut off a right arm and still sin with the left. Jesus knew that. By using the phrases "right hand" and "right eye," He was making a point that the Jews listening immediately understood. In their culture, the right hand always represented a person's best skills and most precious faculties. The right eye, in their culture, represented one's best vision.

Jesus' point is that we should give up whatever is necessary to keep from falling into sin.

2. Take Heed

Look at your life and ask yourself, *Am I involved in anything that is feeding lust, impure thoughts, or setting the stage for sexual sin?* If David had practiced some careful and honest self-examination, he would not have fallen into this sin. Instead, he set himself up for the kill. Here is something to remember: don't feed lust, *starve* it.

Conduct a rigorous self-inventory. Ask yourself: *Am I involved in a relationship that could lead to adultery?* Maybe it's a flirty relationship with someone. On occasion I've had a woman say to me, "I am having marital problems with my husband, so I am getting counsel."

I ask, "From whom are you getting counsel? A pastor?"

"No."

"A Christian woman from church?"

"Not exactly. I am getting counsel from this guy I work with. He really understands."

Danger! You think nothing could ever happen between you. Stop that. You are setting yourself up. (And by the way, I've had men tell me the same thing about women in their lives.)

Let's say you're surfing the Internet, filling your mind with pornography, and you can't understand why you are always having lustful thoughts. What do you expect? Or you're listening to music that is incendiary and blatantly contrary to what you know God wants for you. Music is just a different kind of fuel that feeds uncontrolled fire.

As I said earlier, to kill lust, don't feed it—starve it. You have to recognize that it is a powerful force that can overtake you, regardless of whether you are a man or a woman, young or old, married two weeks or twenty-five years. *Anybody* can fall into devastating sin.

Remember, David was in his fifties. He had been walking with God for over twenty years when he succumbed to sin. It can happen to you if you don't keep your guard up. It could happen to me if I don't keep mine up. We have to learn from David. "Let him who thinks he stands take heed lest he fall" (1 Cor. 10:12). God has warned us.

....
Stumbling and Getting Back Up

In our spiritual race, if we want to win, we have to cope with failure. We have to get back up. We can't lie in the dirt, wallowing in guilt. We will be disqualified for quitting.

David recovered. He enjoyed many good years after his fiasco. Though he also faced the consequences of his sin, in the end, David made a beautiful comeback. He was like a runner who was sprinting, leaving everyone else in his dust—who then crashed. You would think he'd just admit defeat. But David got up and made it across the finish line.

If you want to run fast, you have to run light. Would you

run a 10K wearing scuba tanks? I don't think so. Hebrews 12 says,

> Let us strip off every weight that slows us down, especially the sin that so easily hinders our progress. And let us run with endurance the race that God has set before us. We do this by keeping our eyes on Jesus, on whom our faith depends from start to finish. (VV. 1–2 NLT)

As you run the race of life, you need to periodically ask yourself if the different things you are doing are weights or wings. Will they speed you on your way, or will they slow you down? Are they increasing your spiritual appetite or diminishing it? Are they making you stronger or weaker? If some activity is slowing you down, diminishing your hunger for God, or making you run slower, it is time to get rid of it. Jettison these things that pull you back, and run as lightly as you can.

Like David, you can get back in the race and make a beautiful finish.

8

A RACE THAT ENDED TOO SOON

I want to tell you the story of a man who pretty much tried it all. If ever a person could say, "Been there, done that, bought the T-shirt," it was this man. You might describe him as a wealthy hedonist extraordinaire who makes Hugh Hefner look like a lightweight in comparison.

He was highly educated, yet he went on unbelievable drinking binges. On one hand, he chased pleasure like there was no tomorrow. On the other hand, he was an architectural genius who masterminded the building of incredible structures, and a man known for his supernatural wisdom. On one hand, he was a skillful runner who had all the muscle for a win. On the other hand, he wasted his energy, and it cost him the race.

Who was it? I am not speaking of some contemporary billionaire. This man lived hundreds of years ago, yet the lessons and experiences of his life are as current as tomorrow's newspaper. His name was Solomon. This is his story.

A Bubble That Bursts

Solomon was the son of David and Bathsheba. After their first infant died, as Nathan the prophet had predicted, the couple produced another child. Solomon became the king of Israel after his father's death.

Like many of the biblical characters we have studied, he had such potential to do great things. God had given him supernatural wisdom, an unlimited power to do good. He had a Godly heritage (remember that in spite of David's lapse, he did make a strong spiritual recovery). In the beginning, Solomon ran the race of life powerfully and effectively.

Then, almost without warning, he chucked it all and crashed and burned. The book of Ecclesiastes is the story of his fall, backslide, and prodigal days. The first three verses introduce the theme of the book, which he wrote in retrospect: "'Vanity of vanities,' says the Preacher; / 'Vanity of vanities, all is vanity.' / What profit has a man from all his labor / In which he toils under the sun?'"

You see, Solomon had gone on a search for the meaning of life. It wasn't enough for him to hear from others what right and wrong were. Nor was it enough for him to see the consequences of sin in the life of his father, King David. It wasn't enough for God to tell him what right and wrong were. He wanted to know for himself.

You don't have to wait for the last chapter to see what the results of that search were. He laid it out in verse 2: "vanity of vanities."

Solomon liked the word "vanity." He used it thirty-eight times in the book of Ecclesiastes. When Solomon used this word, he was not describing a person who spends a lot of time primping in front of a mirror. The word "vanity," as used in the Bible, has different shades of meaning, such as "emptiness," "futility," "meaninglessness," "the wisp of a vapor," "a hollow, empty ring." One of my favorite translations is "a bubble that bursts."

In these opening verses, Solomon was saying: "I have looked at everything a person can experience in this life apart from

God. I am telling you it has an empty, hollow ring. It is a wisp of a vapor. It is empty. It is futile. It is like a bubble that bursts."

Solomon concluded that no possession, no relationship, no experience can satisfy the soul's deepest longing. He realized his quest had led him nowhere in life.

His pursuit of meaning was like riding a stationary bike. You pedal and pedal, but when you get off that thing you have gone nowhere. Solomon admitted, "I was just spinning my wheels. I was wasting my life."

. . . .

A Godly Heritage Abandoned

Ecclesiastes 1 continues:

> One generation passes away,
>   And another generation comes...
>   The wind whirls about continually,
> And comes again on its circuit.
>   All the rivers run into the sea,
> Yet the sea is not full...
>   The eye is not satisfied with seeing,
> Nor the ear filled with hearing.
>   That which has been is what will be,
> That which is done is what will be done,
>   And there is nothing new under the sun.
> Is there anything of which it may be said,
> "See, this is new"?
>   It has already been in ancient times before us. (vv. 4–11)

A phrase Solomon used many times is "under the sun." By using this phrase, Solomon was speaking of a horizontal, strictly human viewpoint of life. He was declaring there was no fulfillment in life under the sun—in other words, in life without God. He'd learned the hard way. Once he began his descent into human excess, Solomon rarely looked above the sun for answers. He proved that the attempt to meet the deepest needs of our lives, while leaving God out of the equation, will leave us empty.

This is ironic when you consider his life story. King David, the man after God's own heart, had raised Solomon in a Godly home. When David was on his deathbed, he had called young Solomon in to remind him of what really mattered in life.

And Solomon, my son, get to know the God of your ancestors. Worship and serve him with your whole heart and with a willing mind. For the LORD sees every heart and understands and knows every plan and thought. If you seek him, you will find him. But if you forsake him, he will reject you forever. (1 CHRONICLES 28:9 NLT)

In other words, David had been saying, "Son, you can't live off of your father's faith. You need to get your own. You need to serve God with an undivided heart. You need to completely commit yourself to Him. This is the secret I have learned about life."

Remember that David wrote,

One thing I have desired of the LORD,
That will I seek:
That I may dwell in the house of the LORD
All the days of my life,
And behold the beauty of the LORD,
And to inquire in His temple. (PSALM 24:7)

David had clear focus and purpose in life. He knew what he was living for. And at the end, he tried to pass this legacy on to his son.

For a time Solomon did follow the words that his father

gave him. Then he allowed his heart to be divided. He tried to love the Lord *and* the world. According to Scripture, that just won't wash. The Bible reminds us "friendship with the world is enmity with God" (James 4:4). If you are going to be the world's friend, you are going to be God's enemy.

. . . .

Tried Everything, Gained Nothing

Solomon did what most people only dream of: he personally tried everything that this world had to offer, including sex, drinking, partying, unlimited materialism, lavish entertainment, building huge estates, and more. And Solomon did far more than dabble in these things; he went after them, as they say in the South, "whole hog."

Again, the irony is that he really knew better. Not only did he have David's example and parting words, but in 1 Kings 3 we read:

> The LORD appeared to Solomon in a dream, and God said, "What do you want? Ask, and I will give it to you!"
>
> Solomon replied, "You were wonderfully kind to my father, David, because he was honest and true and faithful to you. And you have continued this great kindness to him today by giving him a son to succeed him. O LORD my God, now you have made me king instead of my father, David, but I am like a little child who doesn't know his way around. And here I am among your chosen people, a nation so great they are too numerous to count! Give me an understanding mind so that I can govern your people well and know the difference between right and wrong. For who by himself is able to govern this great nation of yours?"
>
> The Lord was pleased with Solomon's reply and was glad that he had asked for wisdom. So God replied, "Because you have asked for wisdom in governing my people and have not asked for a long life or riches for yourself or the death

of your enemies—I will give you what you asked for! I will
give you a wise and understanding mind such as no one else
has ever had or ever will have! And I will also give you what
you did not ask for—riches and honor! No other king in all
the world will be compared to you for the rest of your life!
And if you follow me and obey my commands as your father, David, did, I will give you a long life." (VV. 5–14 NLT)

That is such a beautiful story, and a perfect illustration of
what prayer is all about. Solomon had figured out that the
objective of prayer is to get one's will in alignment with God.
That is so important. We sometimes think that through prayer,
we are going to somehow cajole God into doing what we want
him to do. I have even heard people say, "I was wrestling with
God in prayer." Who won? I hope God did. If you're trying to
fight with God, you're going to lose, one way or the other. (I
wrote a small book on that very subject called *Wrestling with
God.*)

As I've pointed out, the purpose of prayer is not to move
God our way. It is to move us His way. It is to tap into what
His will is. Solomon said, "I need wisdom." That is exactly
what God wanted him to request. Thus the Lord gave him not
only what he prayed for but even more.

What would you say if God came to you tonight in a dream
and said, "I will give you whatever you want"? Your answer is
a real indication as to where you are spiritually—how you are
doing in the spiritual race.

We see that Solomon's heart was right with God because
he said, "Lord, I need wisdom. I am overwhelmed by my
responsibilities."

Have you ever felt that way? Are you overwhelmed by your
responsibilities as a father or a mother? Perhaps you're a CEO
of a corporation. You're a boss at a worksite. You oversee other
people in a ministry. You're a teacher in a classroom.

Everybody comes to you with problems. Often you feel you can't handle it all. You say, "Lord, give me wisdom." He will.

Maybe you're a parent. You're trying to create a Godly household while paying the bills and taking care of the children. You feel you're inadequate for the job. "Lord, give me wisdom." Again, He will.

The Bible tells us, "If you need wisdom—if you want to know what God wants you to do—ask him, and he will gladly tell you. He will not resent your asking" (James 1:5 NLT).

God told Solomon, "Because you have your priorities in order, I am going to bless you with a lot of other things as well." He did. Solomon possessed unparalleled wisdom. People came from all around the world to sit at his feet and drink in his words. An authority no less than the Queen of Sheba, after observing Solomon's accomplishments and wisdom first-hand, said, "The half was not told me" (1 Kings 10:7).

That is what made his downfall all the more shocking. Let's take a closer look at his fall from grace.

. . . .
Compromise Leads to a Painful Tumble

Solomon's fall and disillusionment began with a series of compromises, one of which was marrying the daughter of Pharaoh. This he did because he wanted to establish a political alliance. For all practical purposes, Solomon was "yoking" himself unequally with a nonbeliever. God told the Jewish people not to intermarry with the other nations. This was not a racial issue; it was a spiritual issue. God didn't want the Israelites aligning themselves with people who were worshipers of false gods. He knew their hearts would turn away. The same is true of us as Christians. You want to run this race with someone who loves the Lord as you do.

If you are a single person, you should pray for and wait on

the Godly man or woman that the Lord will bring into your life. You can be sure He would not want you romantically involved with a person who does not believe.

The Bible tells us, "Don't team up with those who are unbelievers. How can goodness be a partner with wickedness? How can light live with darkness? What harmony can there be between Christ and the Devil? How can a believer be a partner with an unbeliever?"(2 Cor. 6:14–15 NLT).

In the race of life, you want to run with someone who is going in the same direction that you are. And if you are Christians, both you and your mate will be running toward the Lord, and His plan and purpose for your lives.

But Solomon did not live by that principle. He teamed up with someone who did not share his faith or his God. More problems followed, and they always will.

After a while Solomon said—in spite of the fact that he had great wisdom, wealth, and power, and God had blessed in every way imaginable—"I am going to experience everything this world has to offer." In Ecclesiastes 1:13 he said, "I set my heart to seek and search out by wisdom concerning all that is done under heaven." The word that he used for "seek" could be translated "to investigate the roots of a matter." It is as though Solomon were doing a research paper. He wasn't going to just read about it. He was going to experience it.

In the process of doing so, Solomon ignored the affairs of state. He neglected his family. He set aside all spiritual principles and truth. Essentially, Solomon was saying, "I am not going to pass judgment and say that a thing is wrong until I have done it. Therefore, I am not going to read about getting drunk. I am going to get drunk—a lot. I am going to feel the burn of the alcohol as I take it in. I am going to commit acts of immorality. I am going to revel in unlimited possessions. I am going to try everything people do so I can speak with authority as to whether it is fulfilling or not."

That's a foolish way to do research, as we will see.

Here are some of the things he dabbled in.

1. Knowledge for Its Own Sake

He thought, *If I could get the finest education, surely that would satisfy the deepest needs of my soul.* Look at the outcome in Ecclesiastes 1:16–17:

> I said to myself, "Look, I am wiser than any of the kings who ruled in Jerusalem before me. I have greater wisdom and knowledge than any of them." So I worked hard to distinguish wisdom from foolishness. But now I realize that even this is like chasing the wind. For the greater my wisdom, the greater my grief. (NLT)

Solomon was trying to fill a void that only God could fill. Attaining knowledge is a good thing. But if you do it without God, it will leave you empty.

2. Solomon, the Party Animal

Then he shifted gears: "I am not going to pursue knowledge anymore. I am going to experience pleasure." He went from being an academic to being a party animal in a snap of the fingers.

He wrote about it in Ecclesiastes 2:1–2: "I said to myself, 'Come now, let's give pleasure a try. Let's look for the "good things" in life.' But I found that this, too, was meaningless. 'It is silly to be laughing all the time,' I said. 'What good does it do to seek only pleasure?'" (NLT).

There are people like that. They want to laugh. They want to have a good time. You can always tell in a restaurant which group is drinking. They get progressively louder and more obnoxious, and they laugh at everything. At some point they don't even know why they are laughing. You can see from their faces that they are trying so desperately to have a good time. It's clear they're thinking, *I want to escape from my problems—whatever it takes.*

These people often live a tragic existence all week long, looking forward to the weekend when they can get inebriated. Then they wake up the next morning with a numbing hangover, and it's back to the routine. Then Another week passes. Another month passes. Another year passes. Then you start seeing the effect all this sin brings into their lives, not only spiritually, but physically—their bodies start breaking down prematurely. The "good life" takes its pound of flesh.

Solomon tried that too. He thought maybe getting drunk would satisfy. In Ecclesiastes 2:3 he said, "After much thought, I decided to cheer myself with wine. While still seeking wisdom, I clutched at foolishness. In this way, I hoped to experience the only happiness most people find during their brief life in this world" (NLT).

After a few too many hangovers, and maybe waking up in bed with people he had never seen before, the king saw the emptiness of that as well.

3. Spectacular Possessions

Solomon shifted gears again. With unlimited resources at his disposal, he thought he would purchase all the luxurious goods that money could buy. Ecclesiastes 2 describes his further descent:

> I also tried to find meaning by building huge homes for myself and by planting beautiful vineyards...I made gardens and parks...I built reservoirs...I bought slaves...I also owned great herds and flocks...I collected great sums of silver and gold, the treasure of many kings and provinces. I hired wonderful singers, both men and women, and

had many beautiful concubines. I had everything a man could desire!

...But as I looked at everything I had worked so hard to accomplish, it was all so meaningless. It was like chasing the wind. There was nothing really worthwhile anywhere.

(VV. 4–8, 11 NLT)

Solomon experienced something over which you often hear lottery winners lament. I've read about it time and time again: Someone wins the lottery. For a while he enjoys the high life, buying cars, houses, boats, trips, everything he can think of. But after a while, it all begins to overwhelm. He becomes trapped by the very things he thought he wanted. People want to take advantage of him, and he find himself trapped by the very thing he thought would set him free. How many times have you heard of a lottery winner being quoted as saying, "I wish I'd never won"?

Solomon was saying the same thing. He tried to buy the world with money, but in the end, all he bought was misery.

. . . .
Raging Regret

Solomon was a man who threw his life away. He did it all. He learned that life without God is empty and futile. What can we learn from this? Two principles arise for us.

1. Don't Throw Your Youth Away

At the end of Ecclesiastes 12, Solomon summed up his lessons learned in pleasure without godliness. Among other things, we discover Solomon deeply regretted throwing his youth away as he chased after these things. Verse 1 says, "Remember now your Creator in the days of your youth, / Before the difficult days come, / And the years draw near when you say, / 'I have no pleasure in them.'" The New Living Translation puts it this way: "Don't let the excitement of youth cause you to forget your Creator. Honor him in your youth before you grow old and no longer enjoy living."

Youth is such an important time in life. It is there that we lay a foundation and establish our priorities. We set our course. We start the race.

In my thirty-plus years of ministry I have seen that most people make a commitment to Christ before the age of twenty-one. That is why it is so important to reach people when they are young. As John the apostle wrote, "I have no greater desire than to hear that my children walk in truth" (3 John 4). The decisions we make during our youth affect us for the rest of our lives. We sow the seeds of career and marriage, then reap their results in the years ahead.

When we are young, we are more flexible, more open to change, even embracing it. The one thing you hear from kids is "I'm bored!" (And this while they are watching TV, playing a video game, talking on the phone, and instant messaging—all at the same time.) In contrast, when you get older you find yourself liking a routine. You become more set in your ways. You go to the same restaurants and order the same things. You actually begin to take comfort in your routine.

Now, that is not necessarily a bad thing, if you have established good habits earlier. In the early years, the die is cast. The course charted. The path started. You decide what the evening of your life will be by the choices you make in the morning.

The stand you make today will determine what kind of stand you will make tomorrow. Solomon's conclusion was heartfelt: remember God when you are young. Don't throw your youth away. If you want to heed Solomon's wisdom and run a complete race, start good habits in your youth. Build a healthy foundation. Then you will have established something that will benefit you all your life—and all your race.

2. Don't Leave God Behind

Here, in a nutshell, is the lesson learned by a man who ran away from God. A man who was raised with a Godly heritage and given incredible wisdom from God. A man who had more wealth than any person could dream of. A man who had experienced everything this world has to offer.

Mark it well:

Let us hear the conclusion of the whole matter:

Fear God and keep His commandments,
For this is man's all.
For God will bring every work into judgment,
Including every secret thing,
Whether good or evil. (ECCLESIASTES 12:13–14)

Solomon was saying, "Take it from a seasoned pro. I know what I am talking about. If you leave God out of the picture, your life is going to be empty, meaningless, and futile. It is going to be like a bubble that burst."

Solomon said that if you want to live life to its fullest, "Fear God and keep His commandments." The phrase "fear God" means to reverence the Lord. It doesn't mean to cower in fear because you think God is going to hurt you. Rather, express a sense of awe and worship and praise to God. It is a healthy desire to want to please him in the way you live. Honor God. Glorify God. Hear God, and do what He tells you to do.

If we would just follow this little piece of wisdom from the Bible, so hard-won on Solomon's part, how it would change our lives. How many more people are going to say this doesn't apply to them and go out to try it all for themselves? How many more lives will be wasted? How many more marriages will be destroyed? How many more children will be deprived of a father and a mother to raise them? How many more people will be destroyed by substance abuse? How many more people will chase after materialism and living completely selfish lives? God knows.

Don't waste your life the way Solomon did. He was another who started well but stumbled. You think he would have learned from the example—both good and bad—of his father. He saw what happened when David followed the Lord and ruled well. He also saw what happened to David when he sinned against God and the repercussions he experienced. But Solomon had to find out for himself. He wasted a lot of years.

....
A Race Is All About the Finish

Let me liken Solomon's race to one I tried when my son Christopher ran track and field in high school. I had heard a rumor that after a certain meet, the dads could race. Just in case this was true, I bought myself the latest and lightest Nike Air shoes available; I had every intention of winning that race. I thought maybe I could relive some of my glory days from high school.

The fact is I was a pretty good sprinter. I had this burst of energy that kicked in and carried me to the finish line. I usually beat people in a race. I thought I would do it again, even though it had been many years since I had run like that.

Sure enough, after the track meet was over for the kids, the announcement came. All the dads made their way over. Surveying the competition, I thought, *This is going to be good.* I noticed a lot of potbellies. Not only was I going to win, I was going to win *big*.

They fired the starter pistol. I took off. I was shocked to see almost everybody dash ahead of me. Immediately I was behind. This concerned me. I thought it was time to call on that burst of energy that had always led me to victory. I reached down for that formidable strength. The burst had gone bust. I was already on empty.

I noticed the pack was even farther ahead of me. I quickly realized: not only was I going to lose the race, I was going to lose big. Not only would I be last, but I would probably be five minutes behind everybody else, if I even finished at all. I would get that courtesy applause that people give when you finish but you are pathetic.

I hadn't even finished the first lap, and I was in pain. Let me rephrase that: I was in total agony. I thought, *I have two choices. I can either try to finish this race and come in at the end, or I can quit.*

When I passed a certain tree, I just walked off. Someone said, "Greg, I thought you were running the race."

"No," I assured him. "I was just messing around."

Solomon might have said the same thing "Sure, I started the race, but I got off-track. I wasn't really in it for the prize; I was just messing around."

The spiritual race of life is nothing to mess around with. This is the race you must win.

Just as I got discouraged early and abandoned the race, Solomon got discouraged and quit his. He wasn't satisfied with everything, so he basically pursued nothing. He was a bona fide graduate of the School of Hard Knocks. It's sad. The wisest man who ever lived, lived like a fool. He started in the race but soon left the track altogether.

Let's face it: the prize is at the end of the race. There's only one way to get it. Stay the course—it's the single chance you have of winning!

9

ONE GOOD RUNNER WILL DRAW A CROWD

In light of the rampant immorality within, terrorism without, and widespread violence that America is experiencing, it would be easy to say there is no hope for our country today. Life, we suspect, will only get darker. Certainly nothing we could ever do as individuals could turn things around or make any kind of difference.

I want you to know that is definitely not true. If we look at the history of Israel, we see how often our history parallels it. God established the nation of Israel. He ruled over it. Despite the attempts of revisionists to rewrite our history, our founding fathers established our nation on biblical principles, and the Lord has blessed us as the years have gone by.

God intervened in the history of the nation Israel and turned it around; periodically he brought about a great revival. We can hope and pray he will do the same for us. As we look at the conditions when Elijah emerged on Israel's scene, we see that they were strikingly similar to our own. One man running well in the spiritual race did indeed make a difference.

. . . .

Elijah: The Lord Is My God

In the midst of Israel's idolatry, wickedness, and immorality, spurred on by the wicked King Ahab and Queen Jezebel, God decided to intervene. The Lord decided to raise up his man. He'd done it before. The man God sent for Israel's release was Elijah. His very name summed up his purpose; it meant "My God is Jehovah" or "The Lord is my God." In fact, Elijah's name was a rebuke to the king and queen of Israel. It essentially said, "Your god may be [the false gods] Baal or Asherah, but my God is the Lord."

As we read about the life of Elijah, he might seem a little hard to relate to. He seems almost superhuman. After all, this was the prophet who prayed down fire from heaven. This was the man God used to raise a person from the dead. This was the guy who could get rain to stop and start at his command. It's virtually impossible for us to imagine ourselves anywhere near the league of the wonder-working man of God, Elijah.

Yet, as we will discover, Elijah had his shortcomings. He had his flaws. In fact, Elijah was just as we are. Why do I bring that up? Because God is still looking for his man for this generation. He is still looking for his woman to make a difference.

Let's read about Elijah and see if we can get a handle on why he was who he was, and why the Lord used him in such a significant way. In 1 Kings 17:1 we read: "And Elijah the Tishbite...said to Ahab, 'As the LORD God of Israel lives, before whom I stand, there shall not be dew nor rain these years, except at my word.'"

What a beginning! Try to see the scene in your mind's eye: Ahab and Jezebel were legendary for their power and cruelty. People normally trembled in their presence, for, with a word they could end your life. These two had openly rebelled against and defied the true God of Israel.

Enter Elijah. What boldness he had as he stormed into their court. Elijah made no opening statement and dispensed with all formalities. He just announced that between himself and "the Lord God of Israel," the land would enjoy no rain or dew until he said so. Then, as far as we know, he turned around and walked out. Can't you see the king and queen? "Who was that guy?" "How did he get past security?" "How dare he speak to us in that way?"

. . . .

Have You Been to the Brook?

Elijah had delivered his powerful message. Ahab and Jezebel apparently let his lack of reverence pass. Then the Lord told Elijah to go into obscurity—disappear for a while—and God would provide for him there.

What a strange request! Yet we don't see Elijah arguing with God over his odd command or his rather rough provisions. Scripture says, "He went and did according to the word of the LORD, for he went and stayed by the Brook of Cherith...The ravens brought him bread and meat in the morning, and bread and meat in the evening; and he drank from the brook" (1 Kings 17:5–6).

Does Elijah's sudden turnaround sound a little familiar? Maybe things were going reasonably well in your own life, and God redirected you. It didn't necessarily make sense at the moment. Maybe you were a successful businesswoman who married and then got pregnant. You announced to all of your coworkers one day, "I am going to go home and raise this child that the Lord has given me."

They said, "Don't you know we have daycare facilities here?"

You said, "No. I want to be with this child." You turned your back and walked away, and you went to the Brook Cherith. People thought you were nuts. You knew you did the right thing.

Maybe you went to the finest university and earned a

degree. One day God spoke to you and you felt called to the mission field.

"Are you crazy?" your friends and family asked. "What about your degree?"

But you've made up your mind. You are going to the Brook Cherith. You obey when God leads you.

That is exactly what Elijah did. But the next thing we know is that the brook dried up.

Maybe that's happened to you too. Things were humming along, then one day your spouse said, "I'm leaving. I don't want to be married to you anymore." They're gone. Your brook dried up.

Maybe your ministry was flourishing. God was blessing it. Suddenly it began to shrink. It didn't make any sense. Your brook dried up.

Maybe you got a call from the place you've worked at for twenty years: "Sorry. We have to downsize." Your brook just dried up. Your world ended. Or so it seemed.

Actually, it might be a whole new beginning. When God closes one door, He opens another. Elijah was about to discover this. In fact, God was preparing him. This is very important: the Lord was getting him ready for what was ahead. We all know about Elijah and his fiery confrontation with the prophets of Baal on Mount Carmel. He wasn't ready for that yet. God first had to whip him into shape.

. . . .

The Next Assignment

Then the Lord said, "Arise, go to Zarephath . . . and dwell there. See, I have commanded a widow there to provide for you" (1 Kings 17:9). Again, Elijah obeyed.

The Lord directed the great wonder-working prophet to make himself dependent on a poor widow who had a son to raise. This was not an easy thing, being a burden to someone like that. But God was teaching Elijah humility and the widow dependence.

Though the widow didn't have enough food for herself and her son, Elijah promised God would meet her needs if she would tend to his: "You take care of me, and God will bless you and multiply what you have. In addition, you will always have enough." Sure enough, the Lord sustained her, her son, and Elijah. It was a beautiful illustration of the importance of Matthew 6:33: "Seek first the kingdom of God and His righteousness, and all these things [the needs of life] shall be added to you."

One day, the worst thing imaginable happened to this poor widow. Her beloved son unexpectedly died. But the Lord stretched her faith even more as God raised him back from the dead through Elijah the prophet.

You see, God was getting him ready, step by step, challenge by challenge. Big things were coming. The next phase was about to start. It's the same with you. If you've been told to head for the hills and be fed by birds, so to speak, if your brook has dried up, if a door has closed in your life, don't think God is done with you. You need to just trust him. He may be getting you ready for phase two. He may be whipping you into shape for something beyond your wildest dreams.

So it was for Elijah. God was going to use him in ways he never thought possible. And after his sojourn by the brook and time with the widow, he was now prepared.

Elijah was ready to rumble.

. . . .

A New Mission

In 1 Kings 18 we see his coming-out party.

> And it came to pass after many days that the word of the
> LORD came to Elijah, in the third year, saying, "Go, present

yourself to Ahab, and I will send rain on the earth." So Elijah went to present himself to Ahab; and there was a severe famine in Samaria.

And Ahab had called Obadiah, who was in charge of [Ahab's] house. (Now Obadiah feared the LORD greatly. For so it was, while Jezebel massacred the prophets of the LORD, that Obadiah had taken one hundred prophets and hidden them, fifty to a cave, and had fed them with bread and water.)

And Ahab had said to Obadiah, "Go into the land to all the springs of water and to all the brooks; perhaps we may find grass to keep the horses and mules alive, so that we will not have to kill any livestock."

So they divided the land between them to explore it; Ahab went one way by himself, and Obadiah went another way by himself.

Now as Obadiah was on his way, suddenly Elijah met him; and he recognized him, and fell on his face, and said, "Is that you, my lord Elijah?" And he answered him, "It is I. Go, tell your master, 'Elijah is here.'" (VV. 1–8)

The very next assignment was Elijah's biggest: challenging the prophets of Baal to an old-fashioned shoot-out at the OK corral.

We will look further at this story in the next chapter, but suffice it now to say that when the prophet encountered the king's servant, Obadiah, after a three-year vacation, Elijah was ready to rock.

. . . .

An Example of What Not to Do

Obadiah, however, wasn't. Let's contrast him with Elijah. He was an interesting character. Scripture tells us he feared the Lord "greatly" (1 Kings 18:3). We also read that when Jezebel was killing off the prophets, Obadiah hid one hundred of them. But even though he was a believer, he seemed to lack real backbone; otherwise he would not have served in Ahab's court. He was serving the most wicked king in the history of Israel.

Obadiah had heard and seen great atrocities against God's servants, but he had not spoken up for fear of losing his position—or his head. Obadiah's testimony was so diminished and his witness so weak that he in no way deterred Ahab from his evil. In some ways he was even an accomplice with Ahab and Jezebel in their wicked ways.

Remember, our silence can imply consent and endorsement to actions we actually oppose. If you see something wrong and you don't speak up, others may interpret your silence as approval. Think of how Elijah instantly obeyed and firmly declared God's will. That's the path you need to take.

We need more Elijahs and fewer Obadiahs. Obadiahs may believe; they fear the Lord; but they don't stand up for what is right. They are afraid of persecution. They don't want to be laughed at. They are afraid of being rejected. So they try to fly under the radar—"stealth Christians." We need more people who will stand for the Lord the way Elijah did.

I think Elijah hit the nail on the head when he said, "Obadiah, go tell your master Elijah is here." Who was Obadiah's master? Ahab. What did Jesus say? You cannot serve two masters. You will love the one and hate the other. Elijah was saying, "Obadiah, here is your problem: your master is Ahab."

We can see how fear paralyzed Obadiah when he responded, "I am not going to tell this to Ahab. I know you. You are strange. You show up and say it is not going to rain and then take off for three years. We have been looking everywhere for you! If I tell Ahab I saw Elijah, you will disappear, and I'll take the punishment." Obadiah even tried pleading: "How have I sinned, that you are delivering your servant into the hand of Ahab, to kill me?" (1 Kings 18:9).

Elijah essentially said, "Obadiah, it is time to stop being a closet believer. It is time to stand up and be counted. Stop trying to live in two worlds. Go deliver my message."

Like Obadiah, compromising Christians have too much of the Lord to be happy in the world, but too much of the world to be happy in the Lord. Like Obadiah, they know the world doesn't have the answers, yet they don't fully trust God either. It is a miserable no-man's land. As Elijah made clear then, I say now: It is time to come out. It is time to stand up for what you believe. I imagine Elijah knew Obadiah probably tried to rationalize his position by saying, "It's better that a believer is in the king's house. Perhaps I can have some influence there." Sometimes in our desire to justify ourselves, so, to gain credibility, we lose integrity. Instead of our pulling them up, the nonbelievers pull us down.

Are you compromising your personal integrity right now? Compromise prompts us to be silent for fear of offending when we ought to speak up; to give undeserved praise to keep friends; to tolerate sin because to fight it might give us enemies; to lower our standards in order to extend our reach. At what cost?

Are you an Elijah or are you an Obadiah? You are one of the two. Are you someone who is hiding away and not speaking up for your faith in Christ? Are you an Elijah who is standing up and being counted?

. . . .

How Can You and I Be Elijahs?

This passage in 1 Kings gives us some practical means by which we can be more like faithful Elijah than faithless Obadiah. Where did the prophet get his incredible courage and boldness?

1. Elijah Knew God

Elijah served a living God, not a dead one such as Baal. Like Job, Elijah could say, "I know that my Redeemer lives." Let's look at the ways Elijah stuck by God.

He was safe in the shadow. Elijah realized he stood in the presence of the most powerful King of all, and it was God himself. This was true also when Elijah stood in the presence of Ahab, because he understood what Psalm 91 meant when it said, "He who dwells in the secret place of the Most High / Shall abide under the shadow of the Almighty" (v.1). He was not afraid to stand before Ahab.

Have you ever tried to stand in someone's shadow? You have to stay very close. If he moves, you have to mirror his actions. Elijah stood in the shadow of God no matter where he was. Sometimes we forget that. We think when we leave church, we somehow leave God's presence. The truth is wherever we go, God is with us.

When you stand in the presence of God, you will not bow before any man. Proverbs 28:1 says, "The righteous are bold as a lion." Elijah was bold because he was aware that he was always standing in God's presence. He seemed to be the only one doing it at the time. Obadiah was standing in the shadow of Ahab.

He was an army of one. Have you heard the army's slogan: "An army of one"? That's what Elijah was. Do you feel as if you are an army of one? Perhaps you feel you are the only person in your class, workplace, neighborhood, or family who will speak up for Jesus Christ. You know there are other believers, but they are always fading into the woodwork. You are the single person who will stand up for the Lord.

That's not an easy thing to do. You don't want to come off like a religious nut or a prude. So maybe you compromise a bit. Maybe when someone tells a dirty joke, you laugh along with everybody else. You might wink at an indiscretion for fear of coming off too "holier than thou." You might tell a lie to get that promotion. You might make that compromise to be with the "in" crowd. I ask you today: at what cost? Elijah was no compromiser. He stood up for what was right, even when he felt he was the only one doing it.

He stood in the gap for Israel. Did you know God is still looking today for men and women who will stand in the gap for Him? What do I mean by "stand in the gap"? It's a biblical phrase, and it means interceding on someone's behalf. In Ezekiel 22:30, God said, "I sought for a man who would make a wall, and stand in the gap before Me on behalf of the land, that I should not destroy it; but I found no one." God was saying, "I am looking for someone right now to be My man, My woman. I am looking for someone to stand in the gap in that family, in that situation, in that sphere of influence. Would you be that man or woman?"

2. Elijah Was a Man of Prayer

James 5:17–18 tells us, "Elijah was a man just like us. He prayed earnestly that it would not rain, and it did not rain for three and a half years. Again he prayed, and the heavens gave rain, and the earth produced its crops" (NIV). It was Elijah's prayer in private that was the source of his power in public.

Another character in the Bible, Daniel, was similar. Every day Daniel bowed before the Lord and prayed. He boldly stood before King Nebuchadnezzar and braved lions before King Darius. Daniel seemed to have no fear. We remember also Daniel's friends, Shadrach, Meshach, and Abednego, who refused to worship the golden image the king had erected. Where did they get this power? Through prayer. Through walking in awareness of the presence of God.

Elijah was a man who knew how to pray. Up on Mount Carmel, with his life at stake and the Lord's mightiness in question, Elijah called on the Lord with passion and complete dependence. We can pray in different ways. If you are sitting down for a meal, you say quietly, "Lord, bless the food." But if you're in an extreme situation—say, one in which your life is in danger—you will cry out to Him. That is what Elijah did: he prayed with fervency, commitment, and dedication. He prayed as if lives depended on it. They did.

That is the way we all need to pray all the time. One of the reasons we see no power in our prayer is because we put so little heart in it. How can we expect God to put much heart into answering us? You might be thinking, *But come on, things aren't that serious here. Do I really need to pray so fervently?* Yes. Because lives are always at stake, even if only indirectly.

3. Elijah Faithfully Delivered the Message

God gave Elijah a simple message to deliver to King Ahab, which was, "It is not going to rain for three years." It was another way of saying, "Hard times are coming. You are going to suffer. Your subjects are going to suffer. Some of them are going to die." That was his message—not a word of hope in it! Would you have wanted to deliver such a word to the most powerful man in the nation, a man known for his wickedness? It's amazing Elijah was able to do it.

God calls us to deliver a message as well. It's called the gospel. Fortunately our message has a good-news aspect attached to it. We can tell people God loves them. We can tell people God offers hope of heaven beyond the grave. We can tell people God forgives sins.

Sometimes, though, we don't deliver the whole message. We think the listener won't want to hear everything, so we edit out parts. That's a mistake. God has called us to deliver the entire message, just as Elijah did. We have no right to speak of the glories of heaven without warning of the horrors of hell. We should not speak of the promise of forgiveness without telling people about the need for repentance.

We shouldn't tell people about the promise of wearing the crown without telling them also about the importance of taking up the cross. We can't tell them about the prize at the end of the race without telling them about all the laps involved. Sometimes we like to leave those things out for fear of offending.

Our fear should be of offending God by not delivering the whole truth, nothing but the truth. That is why Paul said, "I did not shrink from declaring to you the whole counsel of God" (Acts 20:27 ESV).

Of course, as we share this message, it's important that we do so with grace, love, and compassion. In Colossians 4:6 Paul wrote, "Let your conversation be always full of grace, seasoned with salt, that you may know how to answer everyone" (NIV). If a person rejects the message of God's grace, then you warn him of hell. But don't do it with glee; do it with sadness. The great preacher D. L. Moody said, "You should never preach on the subject of hell without tears in your eyes."

I have seen some people preaching on the topic of future judgment who seem excited about the fact that people are going to burn in hell. That's wrong. It is a serious, life-and-death message God calls us to deliver. Let's do so with compassion and tenderness.

One of the greatest communicators of this message was the apostle Paul. In the meeting on Mars Hill, he addressed a pagan crowd. He looked at the images they had erected to various gods there in the city of Athens. His opening words to the people were: "Men of Athens, I perceive that in all things you are very religious" (Acts 17:22).

That was tactful. He could have gotten up and said, "Men of Athens, you are a bunch of pagan, idolatrous heathens." Would that have been true? Technically, yes. Would that have built a bridge of communication to his audience? No. He said, "I see that you are religious. I see that you are spiritual.

I want to talk to you a little bit about your interest in spiritual things." Paul began to connect with them.

At the close of his message, he said, "Up to this point God has winked at your ignorance but now is commanding people everywhere to repent" (see Acts 17:30). He told them about Christ and what He had done. Paul built the bridge to his audience, then walked over it. He established rapport. He spoke with grace and compassion. But he also gave them the goods.

Sometimes we offend people unnecessarily by being harsh, mean, or short. Sometimes we dwell only on the negative and leave out the positive. Sometimes we give them the positive and don't tell them the ramifications of rejection of Christ. Like Elijah, like Paul, we have to faithfully share the whole message.

4. Elijah Was a Man of Faith and Obedience

Maybe Elijah felt apprehensive about his assignment. *I'm going to see the king. I have to tell him a drought is coming. This isn't going to be easy.* But he delivered the message and left with his head still on his shoulders. Amazingly, nobody said a word.

They were probably dumbfounded by it.

We don't read of anybody's trying to stop him or disagree with him. He may have walked out saying, "Lord, You are so good. That went so well. What now, Lord? Let's take on the prophets of Baal tomorrow."

As we've seen, instead, the Lord said, "I had a different plan in mind. I was thinking of your just going away for about three years and fading into obscurity." As when he delivered the message to Ahab, Elijah obeyed.

He may have wondered, *What is God doing? This is an odd path to send me on.* But God had some prep work to do in the life of the prophet.

Do you know how a mother eagle teaches her little eaglets

to fly? When the eaglets are getting to the age where they need to learn independence, the mother unceremoniously kicks them out of the nest. She lets them drop about ninety feet before swooping down and picking them up again, after which she drops them in the nest—then kicks them out again. That might seem cruel to us, but the eaglets quickly learn how to stretch those little wings and fly.

What if the mother eagles didn't do this? If they let the baby eagles stay in the nest, they would turn into teen eagles. They would just sleep and eat and never leave.

Sometimes, when we are comfortable and things have gone well, God kicks us out of the nest. He's not trying to hurt us but help us. He's teaching us how to fly. He's trying to help us grow up, realize our potential, and turn into Elijahs.

Listen to the apostle James:

> When all kinds of trials and temptations crowd into your lives, my brothers, don't treat them as intruders, but welcome them as friends! Realize that they come to test your faith and produce a quality of endurance. But let the process go on until that endurance is fully developed, and you will find you have become men of mature character, men of integrity with no weak spots. (1:2–4 PHILLIPS)

Later in the book of Kings, Elisha asked, "Where is the LORD God of Elijah?" I have another question: where are the Elijahs of the Lord God? Where are people like this today who will stand up for what is true? Would you be an Elijah to your sphere of influence?

This means you need to know God. You need to walk in a continual awareness of His presence. You need to be a person of fervent prayer. You need to obey God in faith. You need to deliver the whole truth of the Word of God and do so in love. This means you need to be willing to stand in the gap and say,

"Lord, I read you are looking for someone like this. I want to be that person."

If you will volunteer, God will take you up on it. In fact, he is looking for someone just like you—someone whose commitment to the spiritual race supersedes fear. Those who run well serve well.

Now, in the next chapter, let's take a look at how Elijah did after he'd been running a lap or two.

10
RACE TO A CAVE

I've never met a Christian who hasn't been really discouraged at some point. You know, I'm sure, how it feels to be in the depths of despair, a place from which you can see no way out. Has it ever seemed to you that you're the only person doing the hard work of standing up for faith in Jesus Christ?

If so, then you're going to commiserate with the man we've been discussing, God's miracle worker, Elijah the prophet. You might be surprised to know that Elijah, too, knew well feelings of hopelessness, loss, and isolation. Ironically, the depression he experienced came right on the heels of the greatest victory of his life and ministry. This is not necessarily all that unusual.

Have you ever followed a great celebration with enormous feelings of letdown? That's just how Elijah felt.

Remember James told us "Elijah was a man just like us" (5:17 NIV). He was subject to the same passions we are.

Here we will see that Elijah, though he had a temporary setback, was a winner in the race of life. You, too, can shake the track's dirt off, reset your pace, and get back in the race— to win. Watch how God helped Elijah do just that.

....

Who Is the Real Problem Here?

You'll remember Elijah had declared the coming of a drought, lived on raven food and a widow's mite for three years, then was sent back to face wicked King Ahab. It could not have been a meeting Elijah was eagerly anticipating.

First Kings 18 picks up the narrative.

> Then it happened, when Ahab saw Elijah, that Ahab said to him, "Is that you, O troubler of Israel?"
>
> And he answered, "I have not troubled Israel, but you and your father's house have, in that you have forsaken the commandments of the LORD and have followed the Baals. Now therefore, send and gather all Israel to me on Mount Carmel, the four hundred and fifty prophets of Baal, and the four hundred prophets of Asherah, who eat at Jezebel's table." (VV. 17–19)

Ironically, King Ahab had the gall to call Elijah a "troubler of Israel." The word Ahab used could be translated "viper" or "snake." He may have been saying, "Look who's come back to town! You snake in the grass, Elijah; you are the troubler of Israel."

Elijah quickly corrected the king, "You have that all wrong. I am not the snake in the grass. I am not the troubler of Israel. *You are,* because of your idolatry and the way you have misled the people."

No one had ever spoken to the king like that and lived to tell about it—that is, until Elijah.

Isn't it interesting how people break God's commandments—disregard what His Word says—and then, when it all comes crashing down on them, blame someone else? They blame God, or they blame the very one who could have helped them avoid the destruction they are reaping. That is exactly what Ahab was doing. He was blaming Elijah for something that was his fault.

How do you think Elijah felt about this? There he was, trying to do God's will, knowing he wasn't exactly bringing good news, and he was stuck trying to defend himself against Ahab's accusations. It was no walk in the park, to be sure. We will pay a cost for standing up for what God says. It may be mockery, it may be slander, or, as was the case with Elijah, it may be outright lies.

I want you to know, if that has happened to you, you shouldn't take it personally. Really it's a backhanded compliment. Those people in the world are seeing you as God's representative. If they share their anger at God with you, it just shows you are a chip off the old Rock. That is a good thing.

Jesus said:

When the world hates you, remember it hated me before it hated you. The world would love you if you belonged to it, but you don't. I chose you to come out of the world, and so it hates you. Do you remember what I told you? "A servant is not greater than the master." Since they persecuted me, naturally they will persecute you. And if they had listened to me, they would listen to you! (JOHN 15:18–20 NLT)

. . . .
The Battle of the Gods

Elijah didn't waste time arguing. He challenged, "Let's have a showdown! Let's meet up on Mount Carmel. You bring out the prophets of Baal and the prophets of Asherah, the goddess of sex and violence, assemble all 850 prophets, and we will have a rumble on the mountain."

Understand: this was more than a heavyweight championship between mortal men. This was the battle of the gods. The battle was to determine who was indeed the true ruler of the nation and of the universe—the Lord God of Israel or Baal and Asherah. It wasn't so much a skirmish between Ahab and Elijah as much as it was one between God and Satan.

Amazingly, Ahab agreed to this showdown. Maybe he was desperate. After all, he *really* needed to see some rain. He didn't care how he got it. Israel had been experiencing drought conditions for some three years at that point. Everything everywhere was a dingy brown. This was a crisis. Maybe, somehow, that confrontation would bring down the water. So he assembled all of the false prophets. Basically, he stepped into the trap that God's prophet had set for him.

Elijah determined that the true God would answer by fire. This seemed like a reasonable idea to Ahab, since Baal was known as the sun god. Surely the sun god could send down a stream of fire to demonstrate his mighty power.

Before the battle began, Elijah challenged the people of God: "'How long will you falter between two opinions? If the LORD is God, follow Him; but if Baal, follow him.' But the people answered him not a word" (1 Kings 18:21). Even the true believers were not willing to take a stand at that point. It sounds as though they were all stricken with "Obadia-hitis." Nobody wanted to stand up for his faith. They were faltering.

The word translated "falter" could also be translated "totter." It's a term used to describe an intoxicated person. You know how people are when they're drunk. They think they're fine, but they don't think clearly, speak coherently, or walk straight. This was the very idea Elijah was communicating: "You are like a bunch of drunks. You can't even walk a straight line. What side are you on? Are you on the Lord's side or that of the false gods? You have to make a choice."

The problem was that it was unpopular to worship the Lord in that day and age. The king and queen didn't approve. If you went along with the program, there were benefits. If you worshiped the Lord, you might be executed. Queen Jezebel had, in fact, executed a number of the Lord's prophets. For years the nation had veered back and forth between false gods and the true God, not wanting to be responsible and live fully under God's absolutes.

It sounds like America, doesn't it? We were all on our knees in the aftermath of the horrific attack on our nation on 9/11. Members of Congress sang "God Bless America" on the Capitol steps. There were prayer vigils on street corners. But that is all gone now. It seems that in America we turn to God only when we feel we need Him. But when things are going all right, or at least they seem like they are, we go back to what we were doing before.

Elijah was saying that the Israelites couldn't live that way. They had to make a choice. Each of us must do the same.

. . . .
Idols of the Heart

We may not ostensibly follow a false god, but we can have idols in our hearts. An idol is anyone or anything that takes the place of the true God in your life. It could be a relationship. It could be a possession. It could be a pursuit. It could be a career. It could be a hobby. It is anything you are more passionate about than your faith in God.

If you have an idol in your heart, if you have another god you're bowing before, know it will bring your prayer life to a screeching halt. God said in Ezekiel 14:3, "These leaders have set up idols in their hearts. They have embraced things that lead them into sin. Why should I let them ask me anything?" (NLT). If you want the ear of the Lord, your heart has to be His.

Imagine how insulting it must have been for the Lord when the Israelites turned their backs on Him. They were worshiping gods that could not save them. They had no eyes to see them, no ears to hear them, no mouth to speak to them. Yet the people bowed before them in homage.

Imagine if your spouse left you for someone else? Would that hurt you? What if your spouse left you for a mannequin they saw in a store down at the mall. You would say, "I don't get this." Your spouse would respond, "This mannequin understands me. I admit it doesn't say much, but it doesn't nag either."

Is it any more ridiculous when we leave the true God and worship some other person or thing?

. . . .
High Noon in Israel

The showdown had finally come. It was time for the duel. Elijah began by declaring that each side should place a bull on its altar, then ask its respective god(s) to send down fire to burn it up. He invited the prophets of Baal to go first.

> So they took the bull which was given them, and they prepared it, and called on the name of Baal from morning even till noon, saying, "O Baal, hear us!" But there was no voice; no one answered. Then they leaped about the altar which they had made.
>
> And so it was, at noon, that Elijah mocked them and said, "Cry aloud, for he is a god; either he is meditating, or he is busy, or he is on a journey, or perhaps he is sleeping and must be awakened."
>
> So they cried aloud, and cut themselves, as was their custom, with knives and lances, until the blood gushed out on them. And when midday was past, they prophesied until the time of the offering of the evening sacrifice. But there was no voice; no one answered, no one paid attention.
>
> (1 KINGS 18:26–29)

Elijah seemed to be having a little fun there. He mocked them. (That's one of the reasons I like this prophet.) "Yell louder," Elijah taunted. "Maybe Baal can't hear you. Maybe he's on a trip. Maybe he's sleeping." The phrase "maybe he's busy" in the original language implies that Baal had taken a trip to the celestial men's room. Or, as *The Living Bible* so bluntly puts it, Baal may have been "sitting on the toilet" (v. 27). Definitely a derogatory phrase!

The whole thing was absurd. Baal's people were screaming and twirling around, cutting themselves and bleeding. It was a grotesque circus, and everyone could see the futility. That, of course, is why Elijah did it. He was essentially saying, "These prophets have misled you. They have ripped you off. It is time for you to see that worshiping anyone but the true God is phony, empty, and idiotic." He wanted the Israelites to look at the show and think, *Why did we ever follow these people?*

Elijah finally called off the party. Before the people, he rebuilt the altar of the Lord, which the maniacs had destroyed in their raving, and dug a trench around it. He placed twelve stones on it to represent the twelve tribes of Israel. Then he restacked the wood, cut up the bull, and placed it on top. Finally, he ordered that the whole thing be doused with water— three times. And he filled the trench with water. He wanted it clear that there was no trickery, no illusion. Either God was going to answer by fire, or Elijah would pay the consequences. Like David facing his giant, this was a do-or-die scenario.

The prophet was ready then to pray. He didn't scream. He didn't moan or twirl or cut himself. He spoke with serene confidence in God's power.

. . . .
Sometimes Less Is More

This reminds us that in prayer and worship, we don't have to get worked into a frenzy. Sometimes we feel as though we have to go through spiritual acrobatics to get God's attention. The fact is when we assemble together as his people, He is already there. Jesus said, "Where two or three are gathered together in My name, I am there in the midst of them" (Matt. 18:20). God said He inhabits the praises of His people (Ps. 22:3). We don't have to rant and rave to bring God down. God is here.

If you have an emotional experience during worship, great! Enjoy it. But if you don't have an emotional experience, don't feel you have not encountered God. Maybe you were sitting in the second row one week, worshiping, and the Lord's power came on you. You could sense it. So you decide, *Every week I have to sit right here, in the exact same place!* What if someone inadvertently occupies your holy seat? "Excuse me. I have to sit there. This is my blessing spot. I had my hands lifted this high when I felt the presence of the Lord. I need to replicate that moment."

Just relax. Worship God because God is worthy of your praise. Don't worship him only when you feel like it; come into his presence with that same serene confidence Elijah had.

. . . .

Serene Confidence

Look at what happened next:

> And it came to pass, at the time of the offering of the evening sacrifice, that Elijah the prophet came near and said, "LORD God of Abraham, Isaac, and Israel, let it be known this day that You are God in Israel and I am Your servant, and that I have done all these things at Your word. Hear me, O LORD, hear me, that this people may know that you are the LORD God, and that You have turned their hearts back to You again."
>
> Then the fire of the LORD fell and consumed the burnt sacrifice, and the wood and the stones and the dust, and it licked up the water that was in the trench. Now when all the people saw it, they fell on their faces; and they said, "The LORD, He is God! The LORD, He is God!" (1 KINGS 18:36–39)

The people of Israel sure changed their tune. But the show wasn't over. Then Elijah commanded them to kill all of the prophets of Baal and Asherah. The people executed all 850 of them. That wasn't a pretty scene. God meant business.

Finally, Elijah turned to Ahab and said, "There is the sound of abundance of rain" (1 Kings 18:41). He ascended Mount Carmel, bowed before the Lord, and said, "Lord, You have sent the fire. Now it is time for the rain, so people will know I have done these things according to Your word."

Elijah sent his servant to see if the rain was coming. The servant reported there was not a cloud in the sky. Elijah kept praying. Six times he prayed and sent his servant. Finally, the seventh trip, the servant returned and said, "There is a cloud, as small as a man's hand, rising out of the sea!" (1 Kings 18:44).

That was all Elijah needed to hear.

. . . .

Not a Cloud in the Sky

Elijah's example shows the importance of persistence in prayer. Sometimes you pray, and the fire comes immediately. Other times you pray, and nothing happens. Not a cloud in the sky. Not a drop of rain. Not an answer in sight. Elijah didn't give up.

It may be that the Lord is trying to teach you some lessons of dependence upon Him. He is answering, but He is answering in His way, in His timing, and perhaps in increments.

Remember the blind man Jesus touched?

He took the blind man by the hand and led him out of the town. And when He had spit on his eyes and put His hands on him, He asked him if he saw anything. And he looked up and said, "I see men like trees, walking." Then He put His

hands on his eyes again and made him look up. And he was
restored and saw everyone clearly. (MARK 8:23–25)

Notice that Jesus didn't heal him all at once. That is often
how it starts: a little now, a little later. No thunder and light-
ning, but a cloud the size of a man's hand. Don't give up. Just
keep praying.

. . . .
Elijah the Sprinter

After the rain came, Ahab got in his chariot and left for Jezreel, where his palace was. Oddly, Elijah decided he wanted to
run for it. This is an interesting verse: "The LORD gave special
strength to Elijah. He tucked his cloak into his belt and ran
ahead of Ahab's chariot all the way to the entrance of Jezreel"
(1 Kings 18:46 NLT). Elijah the Olympic sprinter! He ran so
supernaturally fast that he beat the king in his chariot. Con-
sidering what was waiting for him there, it sort of makes you
wonder why he did it!

Ahab reached the palace . . . and Jezebel. Remember the dy-
namics of their relationship: This was a henpecked husband.
She was the power behind the throne. She ran the show.

Ahab said to his wife, "There is good news and bad news.
First the good news: it's raining again! Now the bad news: all
the prophets of Baal and Asherah are dead. And one other
piece of bad news: Elijah is back." Jezebel responded by putting out a contract on the prophet's life. When word of this
reached Elijah, how do you think he reacted? You might
think he would have just brushed it off or even laughed at
such a threat. After all, he had just faced off with most of the
idol firepower of Israel. God had answered his prayer with a
stream of fire from heaven. Why would he now cower before
the threats of this woman?

But the fact of the matter is Elijah was devastated and afraid.

1 Kings 19:3–4:

> He arose and ran for his life, and went to Beersheba, which belongs to Judah, and left his servant there. But he himself went a day's journey into the wilderness, and came and sat down under a broom tree. And he prayed that he might die, and said, "It is enough! Now, LORD, take my life, for I am no better than my fathers!"

Only hours before, Elijah had been running for God. Now he was running from Him. Our mighty prophet was giving in to depression. This reminds us of the truth of James's statement—Elijah was indeed a man just like us.

Elijah is not the only biblical figure who felt depression. At one point, the great lawgiver Moses was so despondent he asked the Lord to take his life. Jonah did much the same after seeing a great revival. It's normal for everyone to have a case of the blues now and then, even if they're great men and women of God.

Have you ever been depressed? Have you ever been down in the dumps? Maybe you are right now. Why? It could be a number of reasons: Problems at work. Problems with your family. Problems in your spiritual life. Maybe someone has threatened you in some way. It has you down.

That was how Elijah felt. Listen to his prayer: "I have been very zealous for the LORD God of hosts; for the children of Israel have forsaken Your covenant, torn down your altars, and killed Your prophets with the sword. *I alone am left*; and they seek to take my life" (1 Kings 19:10, emphasis added).

How did Elijah get into this state? We can learn much from his mistakes.

1. Elijah Lost Perspective

His emotions had gotten the best of him. Who can rationally explain fear and depression? Sometimes they just hit you and make no sense at all.

Time magazine ran a cover story on the topic of fears and phobias. Some fifty million people in the United States struggle with these, the article said. It listed fears I have never heard of. Some, frankly, seemed kooky to me. Consider ablutaphobia, which is a fear of bathing. Or cathisphobia, the fear of sitting. Then there's aloxtiphobia, the fear of opinions, and cyclephobia, the fear of bicycles. What about these: electephobia, the fear of chickens; anuptaphobia, the fear of being single; araptachulaphobia, the fear of peanut butter sticking to the roof of one's mouth; and arithmaphobia, the fear of numbers. Finally, we have automatonphobia, the fear of ventriloquist dummies.[1] It sounds as though Elijah had a bad case of Jezebelphobia.

Whatever the source, fear is a dangerous thing. It can overtake us. It can cause us to worry ourselves into a tizzy.

Elijah was doing just that. He allowed his difficulty to magnify in his mind, and he stopped thinking clearly.

2. Elijah Isolated Himself

When you are down, you need to be with God's people. Just a few statements, a fresh perspective, from a good friend can get you back on course. Elijah needed the encouragement of Godly people. But for all practical purposes, he was alone.

That is why the Bible says,

> Two are better than one,
> ...For if they fall, one will pick up his companion.
> But woe to him who is alone when he falls,
> For he has no one to help him up.
> Again, if two lie down together, they will keep warm.

But how can one keep warm alone?

Though one may be overpowered by another, two can withstand him. (ECCLESIASTES 4:9–12)

Don't avoid people when you are depressed; embrace them. They can help you get things back in perspective.

3. Elijah Let His Guard Down

Have you ever noticed that low lows often come after high highs? By that I mean, sometimes after a great victory comes a great attack. For Elijah, the battle of the gods had taken place. The Lord had won. The rainstorm had come, confirming God's word through the prophet. Sounds as though old Elijah had been running on adrenaline.

What happened was that he let his guard down. He questioned his confidence in the Lord.

I know that often after wonderful victories, I find myself feeling down. You would think that after one of my crusades, I'd be on cloud nine. But I have found that once it's over, I am depleted, drained, and tired. I don't feel that great physically or emotionally. After all, preaching to the lost is like doing battle. I once asked Billy Graham what he felt when he was giving the invitation for people to come to Christ. He responded by saying he felt as though "power was going out" of him.

Do you know what I have learned to do about those blues? Ignore them. They don't mean anything. Lows often follow highs—that's all.

We need to realize that the human bodies God gave us need maintenance, rest, and nourishment. Sometimes we over spiritualize. If you are in a depressed state, all that may really be wrong is low blood sugar. When did you sleep last? Have you had a proper, balanced meal lately? Sometimes there is a rational medical explanation.

Look at Elijah, in the depths of despair. The Lord ministered to his need: "As he lay and slept under a broom tree, suddenly an angel touched him, and said to him, 'Arise and eat.' Then he looked, and there by his head was a cake baked on coals, and a jar of water. So he ate and drank, and lay down again" (1 Kings 19:6). All Elijah needed was food and a nap! Might that be your need as well?

4. Elijah Forgot God

Look at what the Lord said to him in 1 Kings 19:11–13:

> Then He said, "Go out, and stand on the mountain before the LORD." And behold, the LORD passed by, and a great and strong wind tore into the mountains and broke the rocks in pieces before the LORD, but the LORD was not in the wind; and after the wind an earthquake, but the LORD was not in the earthquake; and after the earthquake a fire, but the LORD was not in the fire; and after the fire a still small voice.
>
> So it was, when Elijah heard it, that he wrapped his face in his mantle and went out and stood in the entrance of the cave. Suddenly a voice came to him, and said, "What are you doing here, Elijah?"

"What are you doing here? How did you get yourself into this state? Why have you lost perspective? Have you forgotten that I have brought you this far, and I am going to finish what I have begun? What are you doing here?"

Maybe God would say that to us when we worry ourselves into a frenzy. "What are you doing here? Why have you allowed yourself to end up like this, isolated from your Christian friends, ignoring the perspective of the Word of God, allowing your problems to be magnified beyond comprehension, and forgetting your God?"

. . . .
On the Road Again

What happened on that windy mountain? The Lord spoke: "I have reserved seven thousand in Israel, all whose knees have not bowed to Baal, and every mouth that has not kissed him" (1 Kings 19:18).

Elijah realized he was not alone in worshiping the Lord his God in Israel, and that he had more to do for the Lord. Elijah came to his senses, left the cave, and got back to serving the Lord.

If you are feeling a little depressed, get things back into perspective. Expect a low after a high. Take care of your body. Spend time with Godly friends. Remember that God is still on the throne.

Remember, races aren't run—or won—in caves. Let the Lord comfort you there, but then lace up those running shoes and jump back on the track. You might even beat a chariot. I'll bet you run better than ever.

11

THE ART OF SUCCESSION

This will be our last look at the life of Elijah, the great prophet of the Lord. You'll remember how the wicked monarchs Ahab and Jezebel did not heed the prophet's miracles. They continued in their unbelief despite the warnings the Lord sent through Elijah. It's like the old truth: "The same sun that softens the wax hardens the clay." The same miracle that can bring one person to belief can actually drive another deeper into his unbelief. Such was the case with Ahab and Jezebel.

Let's pick up where we left off. After his great victory up on Mount Carmel, facing off with the prophets of Baal and seeing the answer of God come through fire, Elijah got word that Jezebel threatened his life, and he descended into the lowest of the lows. He asked God to take his life. As he hid in the wilderness, the Lord came to him to encourage and restore him.

Elijah's ministry, the Lord said, was coming to a close. But he had one last mission.

The Finishing Touch

The Lord directed Elijah to go and find his successor: "Elisha the son of Shaphat of Abel Meholah you shall anoint as prophet in your place" (1 Kings 19:16). He was saying, "You are to pass your mantle on to a man named Elisha."

Because the names Elijah and Elisha are so similar, sometimes we confuse these two men. They were two very distinct individuals who spent some time together but had separate ministries. Elijah was passing the torch. It was like a relay race. Elijah was handing the baton back to Elisha to pick up and carry forward and finish the race.

Scripture says Elijah obeyed: "So he departed from there, and found Elisha the son of Shaphat, who was plowing with twelve yoke of oxen before him, and he was with the twelfth. Then Elijah passed by him and threw his mantle on him" (1 Kings 19:19).

The next step was to prepare Elisha for the work at hand. How important is this for us, even those of us who are not prophets, to do? To take all that the Lord has done in our lives and invest it in the lives of others is sometimes called *mentoring*. The biblical terminology for it is *discipling*.

We find this command in the Great Commission, when Jesus said, "Go into all the world and preach the gospel to every living creature" (Mark 16:15). In Matthew, the wording is different: "Go therefore and *make disciples* of all the nations . . . teaching them to observe all things that I have commanded you; and lo, I am with you always, even until the end of the world" (Matt. 28:19–20).

We have all heard the part about going into the world and preaching the gospel. Sometimes we miss the part that says we are to make disciples. Just in case you don't understand what that means, Jesus defined it in His challenge and call to us: "teaching them to observe all things that I have commanded you." It means we are to reproduce ourselves spiritually.

. . . .

A Whole Church—of You

What if the whole church were just like you? What if every Christian behaved exactly as you do? What kind of worship services would we have?

When it's time to worship the Lord, are you one of those people who just sits there and doesn't sing? Then a whole church of people like you would have a silent worship service.

What kind of prayer meetings would we have? Would we have to cancel them for lack of attendance? If all of the church were just like you, how many people in this world would be being reached with the gospel of Jesus Christ? Would people be hearing about him? If all of the church were just like you, would there be any resources for us to use to get the gospel out? If all of the church were just like you, how knowledgeable would we be of the Bible? Would we be a biblically illiterate church, or would we be a grounded, well-taught body of believers?

We all should be making disciples of Jesus, and people are going to learn by following our example (this is discipling). Paul said in Colossians 1:28, "We warn everyone we meet, and we teach everyone we can, all that we know about [Jesus], so that we may bring every man up to his full maturity in Christ" (PHILLIPS). In other words, our objective as Christians is to try to win people to the Lord and help them reach their full maturity and potential.

Writing to Timothy, Paul said, "You have heard me teach many things that have been confirmed by many reliable witnesses. Teach these things to trustworthy people who are able to pass them on to others" (2 Tim. 2:2 NLT). The idea is to take what God has taught us and teach it to other people. Hopefully, they will repeat the process. This is what we are all called to do: to make disciples for Jesus.

· ·

What Does Your Life Teach Others?

Are you doing that today? Have you taken someone young in the faith under your wing, and are you helping him or her to grow spiritually?

Paul discipled Timothy: "You know what I teach, Timothy, and how I live, and what my purpose in life is. You know my faith and how long I have suffered. You know my love and my patient endurance" (2 Tim. 3:10 NLT). A person should see in you an example he can follow.

This is one of the reasons a lot of us don't want to disciple anyone. We don't want people following our examples. Why? Because we are still working a few kinks out ourselves. We think that maybe when we are more mature in the faith, we will be better prepared to do it. We wouldn't want young believers to stumble over the way we live.

What is the solution? Is it that we should continue in our compromise? Well, maybe the presence of a young believer would better enable us to do what we should have been doing all along.

Your life should be something you invest in many other lives. I know sometimes you feel as if it doesn't really matter. You try to import truth that God has given to you to others, but you don't know where it is going to go. Will it bear fruit? Will it fall on deaf ears?

None of us realize the full impact of what we have done in this life. You may reach a person today who will reach her world tomorrow, but you may not live to see it. Who knows? You could take under your wing the next Billy Graham; the next man or woman who will shake a world. Just be diligent in what God has set before you.

We've all heard of such preachers as Billy Graham, Billy Sunday, and D. L. Moody. I bet you have never heard of Edward Kimball. The reason you've probably never heard of him is because he never wrote any books or pastored a church. He never conducted evangelistic events or recorded a CD. But Edward Kimball was a faithful Christian. He was a shoe salesman who wanted God to use him, and he knew he should share the gospel.

Kimball felt burdened for a young man he knew working in a shoe store in Chicago. Kimball hemmed and hawed and put it off, but he finally mustered up the courage and told the young salesman about Jesus. Much to Kimball's delight, the boy responded and gave his life to Jesus Christ.

Not long after, that shoe salesman began a preaching ministry. His name was D. L. Moody, and he was one of the greatest evangelists in church history. If that was all that ever happened from Kimball's obedience, that would have been enough. But the story continues.

When D. L. Moody was out preaching one day, a man who was already a believer was listening. Through Moody's preaching, he heard the call to go into full-time ministry. He became a pastor and wrote many wonderful books on the Christian faith. We know him as F. B. Meyer today. Kimball reached Moody. Moody reached Meyer. That is a great story, but it doesn't stop there.

A young man heard Meyer preaching and gave his life to Christ. God called him to be an evangelist. His name was Wilbur Chapman, and one of the young men he took under his wing was a former pro ball player. The ball player decided instead to preach the gospel, which he did with great success. His name was Billy Sunday.

Then Billy Sunday went to Charlotte, North Carolina, and held a crusade. Many people came to faith. The people were so thrilled they wanted to have another crusade. Sunday wasn't available. The businesspeople in Charlotte knew of another evangelist named Mordecai Hamm, so they invited him out. They erected a tent in a dairy field. It wasn't all that successful a campaign, but on one of the final nights a young, lanky farm boy walked the sawdust aisle. His friends called him Billy Frank. We know him as Billy Graham.

Kimball reached Moody, who touched Meyer, who reached Chapman, who helped Sunday, who reached the businessmen in Charlotte, who invited Hamm, who then reached Billy Graham. Talk about a legacy. You may not be Billy Graham, but you might be Edward Kimball.

Think about Andrew. He once was a disciple of John the Baptist, but one day the great baptizer knew his work was done and told his disciples to follow Jesus Christ: "Behold! The Lamb of God who takes away the sin of the world!" (John 1:29). Upon discovering Jesus as his Messiah, Andrew wanted his brother, Peter, to come to faith. Now, Peter was one of those larger-than-life figures. Andrew probably lived in his shadow most of his life, having people ask him things like "Aren't you Simon's brother? Your brother is so wonderful!" How easily Andrew could have decided to keep his newfound knowledge of Jesus as the Messiah to himself. But that thought never seemed to cross his mind.

He went out immediately, found Peter, and brought him to Jesus. Peter, along with James and John, went on to become part of Jesus' inner circle. Andrew could have resented that, but Scripture gives us no hint of anything like that.

Andrew is the model for all Christians who labor quietly where God has called them. We may not know their names as well as others', but they are known by and greatly loved by the Lord.

If we did not have Andrews, we would not have Simon Peters. If we did not have Kimballs, we would not have Moodys.

You may not be a Simon Peter, but you may be an Andrew.

There is a part for each of us to play in serving the Lord. We need an outlet for what God is doing in our lives. This is what discipling is: as you take truths in, you share them with others and bless them.

Guess what? In the process, you receive a blessing yourself. Do you know what younger believers help us do, besides live the way we ought? They help us rediscover things we have forgotten. They ask hard questions. We have to go find the answers. We get back in the Word. We start studying again. Those we are discipling challenge us, forcing us to grow and explore and remember. We are becoming a part of the process of passing it on.

. . . .

Lessons for Us

That is what Elijah did with Elisha. Here are some things he wanted Elisha to learn and understand.

1. Untie Those Apron Strings

When Elijah threw his mantle, his outer garment, on that young man, Elisha immediately understood what it meant: "I am asking you to become my successor." Look at Elisha's response: "And he left the oxen and ran after Elijah, and said, 'Please let me kiss my father and my mother, and then I will follow you.' And [Elijah] said to him, 'Go back again, for what have I done to you?'" (1 Kings 19:20).

Allow me to loosely paraphrase that: "Go home to Mommy if you want to. No one is twisting your arm. You are an adult. You know it is time to do this—will you?" This was the decisive moment in Elisha's life. Elijah knew that if Elisha were to go back home and say good-bye to his parents, he would never follow. He would get sidetracked.

This is much like the story Jesus told about the man he called to follow him. The man said, "Lord, I will follow You, but let me first go and bid them farewell who are at my house." Jesus answered, "No one, having put his hand to the plow, and looking back, is fit for the kingdom of God" (Luke 9:61–62). Why did Jesus say that? For the same reason Elijah did: he knew that if the guy went back to his family, he would never follow.

Have you ever tried to say good-bye at a family reunion? Do you know how long that takes? You haven't seen some members of your family for years. Uncle Harry has come in from Ohio, and Aunt Gertrude flew in from Florida. After a few hours you say, "We have to go."

"No," they plead, "don't go yet. Have another cup of coffee and a piece of pie." A couple more hours pass, and you say you're leaving. You start making the rounds and hugging and kissing everyone. The next thing you know, another two hours have passed. That is what Elijah was warning Elisha about: "This is the time. Let's get on with it. Ministry opportunity has just knocked on your door."

2. When Opportunity Knocks, Answer the Door

Maybe it has happened to you. Someone is in need of what you know about the Christian life. You say, "I can't do it right now. My business is taking up my time. Instead, I will put a little more in the offering. My busy schedule has no room for discipling someone. I have too much going on."

Opportunity came and you missed it. That is too bad.

Sometimes we feel the only "real" ministry is the mission field. Why do you think some supernatural thing is going to happen to you the moment you set foot on foreign soil? You want to cross the sea for Christ; why don't you start by crossing the street and talking to your neighbor?

I have an idea. I will tell you about a foreign land you can evangelize. The people speak a different language, but you'll catch on. These are people of small stature, indigenous to a certain region. They can be a bit on the wild side. It is called Sunday school. The people are called kids. They need your help and ministry. Try volunteering at your Sunday school ministry at church.

Ministry is everywhere.

God called Elisha when Elijah threw his mantle on him. Elisha was initially reluctant, but he realized he had to make his move. He accepted and began to follow the great prophet of the Lord.

When opportunity knocked, he answered.

....
A Last Conflict with Ahab's Family

At that point, Elijah could have said, "My job is done. I have found my successor. I am going to kick back on my front porch and watch the grass grow!" After all, the famine was over. But he still had a few things to do.

The next movement in the life of Elijah the prophet was quite dramatic. By then Ahab and Jezebel had died brutal deaths, as Elijah had prophesied. Their son, Ahaziah, also rebelled against God. He had failed to learn anything from the lives of his parents.

One day, the Bible tells us in 2 Kings 1, he fell through the latticework of an upper room at his palace and was seriously injured. Instead of asking the Lord for help or calling on the prophet of the Lord for assistance, King Ahaziah sent messengers to inquire in the temple of Baal whether he would live. Can you believe this?

After Baal's pathetic showing on Mount Carmel, still there was the son of Ahab and Jezebel calling on this false god.

Meanwhile the Lord spoke to Elijah the prophet and told him to intercept the messengers the king sent to the temple of Baal. Elijah confronted the men, saying, "Is there no God in Israel? You have to go to the temple of Baal to find out if the king is going to live? Since you sought Baal's counsel, the answer is no. Tell the king he won't survive."

The messengers returned to the king and reported their meeting with Elijah and the message he sent. Not surprisingly, the king was angry. He said, "I want Elijah brought here immediately."

Ahaziah sent a captain with fifty soldiers to arrest Elijah and bring him back to the palace. When the captain and his men approached Elijah, who was perched atop a hill, they said, "Man of God, the king wants to see you. Come down from that mountain."

Elijah responded, "If I am a man of God, let fire come down from heaven and consume you and your fifty men!" (2 Kings 1:10 NLT). He was a man of God. Fire came down and destroyed them.

The king heard about it and sent another captain with fifty soldiers. Ditto—Elijah called and fire came down.

A third brigade arrived, but this time the captain pleaded, "Mr. Elijah, I am just following orders. Give me a break here. I am a family man. Please come." The Lord said to Elijah, "You go with this man." Elijah delivered his message to the king's face: "Now, since you have [consulted Baal rather than God], you will never leave the bed on which you are lying, but you will surely die." The text continues, "So Ahaziah died" (2 Kings 1:16–17 NLT).

This reminds me so much of our own nation. I've mentioned that in the aftermath of 9/11, our churches were packed. People were turning to God. We were having prayer meetings in stadiums around the nation. Now that things have returned to relative calm, the people are gone.

I think that when the next crisis hits, we will see people in church again. Then, if life becomes quiet again, they will go away. Sadly, this is just what Israel did. The people called on God when things were tough, but when things went back to normal they forgot the Lord.

I pray we will see a real turning to God and that we will

really call upon the Lord. There is no military solution for the problem of terrorism. There is no single enemy we can take out. When the Japanese attacked us at Pearl Harbor, we knew where to find them. Today our enemies hide and plan disaster from afar. We have never faced anything like this before.

We need God's help.

Pray for our president. Pray for our congressmen and senators. Pray for our country.

We have seen from the life of Ahaziah that failing to call upon him shows a disrespect God cannot ignore.

. . . .

Parting Words

After Ahaziah's death, Elijah realized his time was coming to an end. He put a few challenges in Elisha's path before he went. Three times Elijah asked Elisha to stay put while he took a journey, first to Bethel, then to Jericho, then to the Jordan river. Each time, Elisha responded, "As the LORD lives, and as your soul lives, I will not leave you!" (2 Kings 2:2).

Each of these requests was a test to see if Elisha really was committed. Each time he passed.

Did you know God will test us as well to see if our faith is genuine? Many people are excited about following Jesus—at first. Then the tests come. They are persecuted for the gospel. They go through a time of difficulty. They find it is not the most popular thing to be a Christian. They don't feel that emotional high they might have felt right after conversion. They say, "That's it. I am not going to be a Christian anymore."

Elijah might have said to you, "Go home to Mommy."

Real believers stand the test and continue on. Jesus doesn't want fair-weather followers. He wants dedicated men and women—these are the kinds of people He will use to shake the world.

One day He was speaking to a huge group of people (see

John 6). The crowds had grown because He had performed his most popular miracle of all: He fed masses of people. They loved that.

Jesus looked at the multitude. They cared nothing for who He was. They cared nothing for His message. He made some radical statements to intentionally thin out the ranks. Hundreds of people left that day. Jesus turned to His own disciples and asked, "Will you also go?" Peter answered for them, "Lord, to whom shall we go? You have the words of eternal life" (John 6:68). They passed the test.

Elijah was testing Elisha: Are you sure about this? Are you ready to count the cost? Are you ready to do what God is calling you to do? Apparently he was. Are you?

. . . .

A Last Request

Now we come to the final movement in the story.

> And so it was, when they had crossed over, that Elijah said to Elisha, "Ask! What may I do for you, before I am taken away from you?" Elisha said, "Please let a double portion of your spirit be upon me."
>
> So he said, "You have asked a hard thing. Nevertheless, if you see me when I am taken from you, it shall be so for you; but if not, it shall not be so."
>
> Then it happened, as they continued on and talked, that suddenly a chariot of fire appeared with horses of fire, and separated the two of them; and Elijah went up by a whirlwind into heaven.
>
> And Elisha saw it, and he cried out, "My father, my father, the chariot of Israel and its horsemen!" So he saw him no more. (2 KINGS 2:9-12)

Elijah said, "Elisha, you have passed the test. What do you want as a reward?" Elisha answered, "I want to follow in your footsteps. I want to do what God has called me to do. I would like twice as much power as you have." I love this. Elijah said, "That is a tall order. If you see me when I am taken away, you will get what you have requested."

You can be sure Elisha kept his eyes on Elijah. Suddenly that moment came, and Elijah was caught up into the presence of the Lord. Elisha watched the whole thing. Sure enough, God's anointing came upon him in double strength. You can see that because he did twice as many miracles as Elijah had.

What kind of legacy are you leaving today? Are you discipling anyone? Do you have a life that is worth emulating? Are you just a fair-weather follower? That is the challenge before each of us.

Elijah was one of the two people in the Bible who never died. The other was Enoch, who walked with God and then "was not." This reminds us that there is a generation of people who will not see death. They will be caught up immediately into the presence of the Lord in what the Bible calls the "rapture of the church." The Bible says that in a moment, "in the twinkling of an eye," we will meet the Lord in the air (1 Cor. 15:52). From my understanding of Bible prophecy, this great event could happen at any time.

What are we supposed to be doing in the meantime? The same thing Elijah was doing: proclaiming and discipling. He made sure that before he left this world he had taught someone to continue God's work.

What else are we supposed to be doing? The same thing Elisha did with Elijah. *He watched him.* "If you see me when I am taken," his master said, "you will get what you ask."

What does the Bible say to us as believers living in the last days? Are you mentoring others? Are you looking for Jesus? With all of this uncertainty in the air, all of this tension, these threats, with Bible prophecies fulfilled before our very eyes, we need to make every moment count. This is not a time for fooling around. This is not a time for squandering our lives and resources. This is a time to follow the Lord as a true disciple and try to impact others.

We all have a part to play. You might be a Billy Graham. You might be an Edward Kimball. You may be a Simon Peter, or you may be an Andrew. Count on this: you are someone God wants to use. We need to accept the baton, our assignment, as Elijah did, and as Elisha did.

Running well the spiritual race requires that we complete each lap, no matter how hard or easy it is. When the Lord throws you a test, endure—pass it. Every lap brings you nearer to finishing, and finishing well.

12
WHEN A RACE FEELS LIKE A MARATHON

We have studied people in this book who started well in the spiritual race only to stumble later in life, never to fully recover—men such as King Saul and Samson. We have looked at those who stumbled but learned from their mistakes; they got up, ran again, and finished well—men such as David and Elijah and Elisha. This reminds us that falling down doesn't make you a failure; staying down does. Then there are those who not only start well; they run the whole race with power and finish as winners.

The story before us now is probably the ultimate spiritual success story. This is the account of a young man, who, despite dramatic setbacks that would have immobilized most people, kept going back for more. A young man who, against all odds, in the most adverse circumstances imaginable, made it to the end.

We don't ever read of his doubting God or compromising his witness in any way. We find perhaps some minor errors, but no glaring mistakes. For all practical purposes, we cannot uncover a single serious blemish in the life of this young man. God mightily blessed him as a result. His name was Joseph.

....

A Tuxedo for Field Work

The story of Joseph is really the ultimate rags-to-riches tale, where a person rose from complete obscurity and devastating setbacks to become the second-most-powerful man in the nation of Egypt. Joseph was a young man who started the race of life and finished exceptionally well. He was so amazing that, as you read about him, you might conclude he wasn't a man at all—he was somehow supernatural. No. He was a real man, all flesh and blood just like every one of us. That he started and finished his race dramatically reminds us it *can* be done.

Initially, Joseph's life showed little promise. He was a simple shepherd boy, the twelfth of thirteen children. As a young man he was apparently given to some visions of grandeur. Like any other teenager, he liked to sleep. This particular young man had some pretty remarkable dreams he believed to be from God Himself. In the beginning, Joseph's dreams got him into trouble. Thirteen years later, interpreting other people's dreams got him out of trouble.

Let's read about him in Genesis 37.

Joseph, being seventeen years old, was feeding the flock with his brothers. And the lad was with the sons of Bilhah and the sons of Zilpah, his father's wives; and Joseph brought a bad report of them to his father.

Now Israel [Jacob] loved Joseph more than all of his children, because he was the son of his old age. Also he made him a tunic of many colors. (VV. 2–3)

Jacob was an old man when Joseph was born. Young Joseph was the very apple of his eye. As we see in this passage, Jacob had many wives, but there was only one woman he ever truly loved, and her name was Rachel. The son he and Rachel produced was Joseph. As a result he doted on the young boy. Naturally, the other brothers didn't like it one bit.

One of the ways Jacob showed his favoritism toward Joseph was by giving him this so-called coat of many colors. Really it was a multicolored tunic or robe. As one translation puts it, a "richly ornamented robe" (NIV).

There is more here than meets the eye. One Old Testament commentator said the tunic was sleeved and extended to the ankles. Obviously Joseph was not going to do manual labor in a garment like that. In Joseph's day, the working garb of the people in the fields would have been a short, sleeveless tunic— a garment that kept your arms and legs free. If you showed up in a long-sleeved, full-length robe, "richly ornamented," you weren't going to be doing much that day. It would be like showing up for work in the field wearing a tuxedo. It was just not apropos.

By giving this coat to Joseph, Jacob was saying, "Son, you don't have to work the way your other brothers do. Let them tackle all the hard labor. You can sit in the shade and check up on them."

You can imagine this didn't sit well with Joseph's brothers. Day by day, they grew more resentful of him. Verse 2 tells us that Joseph had already taken a bad report about his brothers to his father. This meant that in their eyes, he was a snitch—a tattletale.

The fact of the matter is that Joseph was a Godly young man. By just showing up on the scene and being who he was, his very presence convicted his brothers. You need to know that when you are living a Godly life, you are going to offend a lot of people. As Jesus said, "Everyone practicing evil hates the light and does not come to the light, lest his deeds should be exposed" (John 3:20).

Maybe Joseph was a bit too harsh. Maybe he came down on his brothers a little too hard. We don't know. But verse 4 says, "His brothers hated Joseph because of his father's partiality. They couldn't say a kind word to him" (NLT).

One day, Joseph reported a startling dream: "There we were, binding sheaves in the field. Then behold, my sheaf arose and also stood upright; and indeed your sheaves stood all around and bowed down to my sheaf" (Gen. 37:7).

Joseph probably should have kept this one to himself: "So they hated him even more for his dreams and for his words" (v. 8). I don't know if Joseph was flaunting his position. Some people don't handle authority well. You give them a little power, especially with a uniform and a badge of some kind, and they become little tyrants. Maybe Joseph seemed a bit sanctimonious; the Bible doesn't say. Regardless, he certainly didn't deserve the type of treatment he was about to receive.

. . . .
A Dream Come True

One day his father sent him to check up on his brothers.

When Joseph's brothers saw him coming, they recognized him in the distance and made plans to kill him. "Here comes that dreamer!" they exclaimed. "Come on, let's kill him and throw him into a deep pit. We can tell our father that a wild animal has eaten him. Then we'll see what becomes of his dreams!"

But Reuben came to Joseph's rescue. "Let's not kill him," he said. "Why should we shed his blood? Let's just throw him into this pit here. That way he will die without our having to touch him." Reuben was secretly planning to help Joseph escape, and then he would bring him back to his father.

So when Joseph arrived, they pulled off his beautiful robe and threw him into the pit. The pit was normally used to store water, but it was empty at the time. Then, just as they were sitting down to eat, they noticed a caravan of camels in the distance coming toward them. It was a group of Ishmaelite traders taking spices, balm, and myrrh from Gilead to Egypt.

Judah said to the others, "What can we gain by killing our brother? That would just give us a guilty conscience. Let's sell Joseph to those Ishmaelite traders. Let's not be responsible for his death; after all, he is our brother!" And his brothers agreed. So when the traders came by, his brothers pulled Joseph out of the pit and sold him for twenty pieces of silver, and the Ishmaelite traders took him along to Egypt. (GENESIS 37:18–28 NLT)

Reuben was the firstborn of Jacob but was not the leader he should have been. The firstborn son was the heir apparent. One day he would become the spiritual leader of his family. Reuben should have been exerting some of this authority when his brothers suggested they kill Joseph. But he didn't. Jacob later described Reuben as "unstable as water" (Gen. 48:4). What an accurate assessment. He was wishy-washy, knowing what was right but unwilling to stand up for it. Ultimately the brothers prevailed.

How afraid Joseph must have felt that first night as he was taken from everything he'd ever known. But even though Joseph had been abandoned by man, he had not been forgotten by God.

Maybe you feel this way right now—that your parents, your spouse, your children, or someone you look up to spiritually has left you behind. No matter what people do to you, God never forgets you. Even when people let you down, the Lord will lift you up.

What looked like a worst-case scenario for Joseph was about to be run through God's framework of providence. This nightmare would become a dream come true. God was going to take the most adverse circumstances imaginable and turn them around for His glory.

The traders took Joseph to Egypt, which then was a pagan country filled with religious superstition. Historians tell us the Egyptian people worshiped over two thousand gods and goddesses, including the pharaoh himself. The Egyptians were also great builders. The rulers conscripted slaves to help them in their vast building projects.

Joseph was about to go on sale again.

Now when Joseph arrived in Egypt with the Ishmaelite traders, he was purchased by Potiphar, a member of the personal staff of Pharaoh, the king of Egypt. Potiphar was the captain of the palace guard.

The LORD was with Joseph and blessed him greatly as he served in the home of his Egyptian master. Potiphar noticed this and realized that the LORD was with Joseph, giving him success in everything he did. So Joseph naturally became quite a favorite with him. Potiphar soon put Joseph in charge of his entire household and entrusted him with all his business dealings. From the day Joseph was put in charge, the LORD began to bless Potiphar for Joseph's sake. All his household affairs began to run smoothly, and his crops and livestock flourished. So Potiphar gave Joseph complete administrative responsibility over everything he owned. With Joseph there, he didn't have a worry in the world, except to decide what he wanted to eat!

(GENESIS 39:1–6 NLT)

Specifically, who was Potiphar? We know he was a high-ranking Egyptian official. He was basically the head of the military police assigned to be the royal bodyguard. You might say Potiphar was the head of the Secret Service of his day. He was also responsible for the execution of criminals. Clearly Potiphar was not a man with whom you wanted to trifle. He was one bad dude, and you didn't want to mess with him.

. . . .

A Productive Pit Boy

Yet it seems that this man who could have him executed with the snap of a finger did not intimidate Joseph. Verse 2 tells us, "The LORD was with Joseph." Joseph loved and served the Lord with all of his heart. So the Lord just started blessing him, as well as Potiphar's household, because of Joseph's presence. Proverbs 22:29 says, "Do you see a man who excels in his work? / He will stand before kings; / He will not stand before unknown men." Though Joseph had been stripped of his coat, he was not stripped of his character.

Here is something we need to remember: when we work hard at what we do, it is a powerful testimony. We need more people like Joseph today who openly express their faith but also demonstrate it through hard work.

Many Christians in the workplace talk about Jesus Christ to their coworkers. They are not embarrassed to say grace over a meal. They are not ashamed to read their Bibles during their breaks. They are not standoffish about telling others about what Christ has done for them. But the problem is sometimes they don't work hard enough. They arrive late. They leave early. They make excuses about why they can't do jobs they are asked to do. That is a bad testimony.

Then we have other Christians who work very hard; they do great work. The problem is, they don't ever talk about their faith. What a testimony it is when your employer comes to you and says, "You are the best person working for me. I want to know why you work so hard." Then you can give the glory to God.

Had Joseph stayed home with his pampering father, he might not have developed the kind of character that comes from hard work and obeying orders. This was a time of testing in his life.

In time he would become a great leader, but first he had to learn how to be a faithful servant. Maybe you are at such a place in your life right now. You are laboring in obscurity. You feel as if no one notices what you do. Follow the example of Joseph: Work hard. Flip every burger for the glory of God. Create every PowerPoint presentation as though Jesus Christ Himself were going to inspect it. Hammer every nail as though you were building that house for God. Type every letter as if Jesus Himself were going to read it. Play every chord with skill and precision as if Jesus were listening. Because He is. Whatever it is you are doing, do it well. Be faithful—even if there are consequences.

Because sometimes there are.

. . . .

Lust Rears Its Ugly Head

As he often is, Satan was there in the background, carefully watching Joseph handle his experiences. Satan could see Joseph was a tough nut to crack, so he pulled out what is usually a foolproof strategy: sexual temptation. Don't forget that Joseph was just seventeen or eighteen. Scripture tells us, "Now Joseph was a very handsome and well-built young man" (Gen. 39:6 NLT). No doubt he was a typical teenager with raging hormones. He certainly could prove vulnerable to temptation of that kind.

Don't forget that no one less than the man after God's own heart, King David, fell for this sin. Then, of course, there was Samson. The devil probably reasoned that if he could bring down David and Samson, he could bring down Joseph, too.

I'm sure Potiphar's wife was attractive. She probably dressed in a sexually provocative way to get Joseph to notice her. But he just kept on with his work, never taking the bait. Finally, she decided to cast half-measures aside and just cut to the chase.

She approached him and said, "Sleep with me. I want you, and I want you now." Impressively, Joseph refused her advances. She did not give up. If anything, his rejection only spurred her on. She was relentless.

Joseph could have rationalized sin, thinking, *If I give in to her advances, she will speak highly of me to her husband, and I will get a promotion. I will be even more influential.* Or *If I cross her, she will turn against me. She is very powerful. She could destroy my life. Besides, if I had sex with her, who would ever know?* But deep in his heart he knew God would know. We need to remember that God is watching us as well.

Genesis 39:8 simply says, "Joseph refused" (NLT). Joseph recognized that temptation is a call to battle. He armed himself and prepared to fight. Verse 10 tells us, "She kept putting pressure on him day after day, but he refused to sleep with her, and he kept out of her way as much as possible" (NLT).

There was a smart boy. I am sure Potiphar's wife used every visual and verbal seductive technique she could. I am sure she tried every trick in the book to excite him and move him in her direction. He wisely kept as much distance from her as possible.

Isn't that an obvious action we all should take? We all have areas of vulnerability, don't we?

. . . .

A Personal Example

Let me make a little confession.

One night I spoke for a friend of mine who pastors a church. His name is Skip Heitzig. We saw 150 people make commitments to Christ that night, and we were blessed.

How do Christians celebrate? We eat. Skip said, "Do you want to go out for dinner after church?" I said, "I ate before, Skip. I better not eat late." He said, "How about dessert?" I said, "I don't want dessert either." Skip would not take no for an answer so I ended up going.

We went to this incredible bakery with unbelievable des-

serts. Skip said, "What do you want? Greg, get something."
I was vacillating between the key lime pie and the apple pie.
Skip ordered the apple, and I ordered the key lime.

We sat down. Skip went to get silverware. I took one little
bite of his apple pie, and it was so good I ate all of it before he
returned. He said, "What happened to my apple pie?" I said,
"I traded. You can have mine." He ate a couple of bites. He
didn't want it. And I ended up eating that too!

I never should have gone to that bakery. Quite honestly, if I
had returned to my hotel room, I wouldn't have been dream-
ing about key lime or apple pie. I would have gone to bed, and
that would have been the end of it. But I didn't, and I had to
accept the consequences.

The best thing to do is to stay away from temptation.

. . . .
Keys to Overcoming

In Joseph's life, we find a couple of powerful keys to overcom-
ing temptation. These will better enable us to run the spiritual
race well and win.

1. Joseph Called Sin "Sin"

Once Potiphar's wife said, "Come and sleep with me," he answered, "How then can I do this great wickedness, and sin
against God?" (Gen. 39:9). He was right. He saw sin clearly for
what it was. It would have been wrong.

Nowadays we don't call sin "sin." People don't seem to say
that word anymore.

If you lie, you don't admit it; you lie about the lie. Instead
of saying, "I lied and got caught," you say, "I misspoke." Who
came up with phrases like that? My favorite one is "Mistakes
were made." Not "I have made a mistake" or even "We have
made a mistake." "Mistakes were made" suggests that no one
knows who made them. Talk about passing the buck!

These days, if you are an alcoholic or a drug addict, you may call your problem "a disease." Adultery is "having an affair" or a "fling." This soft terminology makes us more comfortable with sin. Shakespeare said, "A rose by any other name would smell as sweet." It could also be said that sin in any other form will smell just as bad.

2. Joseph Realized That All Sin Was Against God

This is the strongest deterrent against sin—not our fear of what will happen if we get caught, though that is not a bad thing to keep in mind. The ultimate deterrent is a love for God. In fact, our response to temptation is an accurate barometer of our love for God. If we want to boast about how much we love the Lord, we have to resist sin.

Someone may counter, "I show my love for the Lord in worship." I am glad you do. Or "I show my love for the Lord through giving." That's good too. But one of the most important ways to show your love for God is simply to resist temptation and obey God.

Jesus himself said, "Whoever has my commandments and obeys them, he is the one who loves me" (John 14:21 NIV).

Psalm 97:10 instructs, "Let those who love the LORD hate evil, / for he guards the lives of his faithful ones / and delivers them from the hand of the wicked" (NIV). Romans 12:9 says, "Hate what is evil; cling to what is good" (NIV). If we really love God, we should hate evil. If we really love God, we should seek to resist temptation.

. . . .

From Potiphar's Servant to Prisoner

How does the story end? Pretty strangely. Potiphar's wife was an attractive woman probably used to men falling at her feet. When Joseph avoided or outright rejected her, she finally decided, *I'll have to force him.* When he walked by one day, she tried to literally pull him down on her bed. Joseph escaped her grasp, but he didn't escape her influence.

Potiphar's wife was so angry and humiliated that she cried "Rape!" The fact that she had his garment in her hand was serious evidence. She said as much to her husband. I suspect Potiphar had seen this before. Personally, I don't think Potiphar bought it. I also think he didn't want to mess with his wife. So he did the only "honorable" thing in the eyes of his spouse: he sent Joseph to prison.

At that point, do you think Joseph doubted God? Did he say, "Lord, I don't understand. One day I wake up, I visit my brothers, I tell them about the great dreams You are giving me. They sell me as a slave for twenty pieces of silver. I don't get it. I am taken to this land of pagan idolatry. I honor You. I work hard. Potiphar elevates me. I am beginning to see what You are doing and give You the glory. Then his wife starts hitting on me. By Your power I resist her. Now she has accused me of rape. Here I am in a prison cell. Why? I thought that by doing good, I would receive Your blessing. Instead I am being punished for it."

Yes, he could have said that. And if he had, we would have understood. Maybe in his place we would have said something like that. Maybe in other situations we already have. Joseph didn't. He just trusted God.

That's not to say Joseph enjoyed himself in prison. But do you think he ever questioned his decisions?

I know there are times when temptations are *very* tempting. After you resist them, the devil whispers in your ear, "Have you lost your mind? You could have had her [or him]. You could have had that position! You could have had that experience! You said no. What are you thinking?"

Sometimes people who are living in sin appear to be getting away with it. A guy commits adultery. He is married. His family is intact, and he is doing this thing on the side. He tells you what a great time he is having. You wonder how he is keeping this affair a secret.

A person lies on her résumé. Because of that, she gets the job you wanted. Now she's your boss.

Someone steals something, and he never gets caught. He is enjoying the thing he stole—in fact, you wish you had one yourself, but you can't afford it.

It seems sometimes that the wicked are prospering, and we are being punished for doing the right thing. Just hang on. As time passes, you will see the wisdom of God's Word. The guy who has been getting away with the fling will get busted. His little house of cards will come crashing down. It will all catch up with him.

That woman who lied on her résumé will one day prove she doesn't have the skills or experience she claimed to have. Something or someone will blow the whistle on her. She will be publicly humiliated and lose her position.

The guy who stole something will have his dishonesty fall back on him. A jealous person will steal from him. He will not get to enjoy his possession forever.

Not that that is any comfort, but it simply is a reminder that the Bible is true when it tells us, "You will reap what you sow" (see Gal. 6:7). Sin always ends up coming out.

Joseph would see. He was in a prison cell for a little while, but the next thing you know, he was Pharaoh's right-hand man. We'll read about his very satisfying payback in the next chapter.

Maybe you are in one of those in-between times right now. You are honoring the Lord, but you have made some sacrifices. Others have progressed by dishonest means. It has been hard. Here is my advice to you: *Just hang in there.* You are doing the right thing, and you will never regret it. God will give you the strength to resist the temptation you are facing today, no matter how strong it might be.

Apply yourself; like Joseph, reach down inside for some more perseverance. He kept running even when the other racers knocked him down on their way down the track. He kept getting up. You need to do the same. It's the only way to be a consistently great runner in the race of life.

And remember, there is a special blessing promised to the person who effectively resists temptation, not only in this life, but in the life to come. "Blessed is the man who endures temptation; for when he has been approved, he will receive the crown of life which the Lord has promised to those who love Him" (James 1:12).

13

DROPPING DEADWEIGHT *FOR* A FASTER RACE

The term *unforgiving Christian* is an oxymoron. An oxymoron, as you know, is one of those expressions that seem to contradict itself. We hear lots of these: "genuine imitation leather"; "found missing"; "freezer burn"; "fresh frozen"; "jumbo shrimp." Here's another one to add to the list: *unforgiving Christian.* Jesus constantly pressed the issue of forgiving others. His sermons and His parables, so many of the things He said, dealt with our need to forgive each other. As we continue our look at Joseph, we're going to see one of the most dramatic demonstrations of forgiveness to be found in the pages of the Bible.

Once Joseph was second in command to the king of Egypt, he possessed unlimited powers. He was in a position to execute the ultimate payback on anyone who annoyed him. He had the resources to utterly destroy lives, especially those very brothers of his who had heartlessly betrayed and sold him out.

In fact, Joseph faced a prime opportunity to abandon the race of life altogether. Pull out of the competition. Forfeit the prize in favor of revenge. But he made a different choice, one that made him a winner, not a loser.

. . . .

A Blameless Man

We have discovered in this book that the Bible does not flatter its heroes. Even if a man or a woman of God lived beautifully and suffered only a single lapse, the Bible records it. When we looked at the life of Elijah, for instance, we saw his glorious, powerful, and victorious life and ministry. But when he had a little lapse of faith, a little side trip into self-pity, Scripture recorded it clearly.

Amazingly, we find nothing this damaging in the record of Joseph. This leads me to believe he was truly an upstanding man, an unusually Godly individual. We find not a single critical word about him in all of the chapters devoted to him in the book of Genesis.

You'll remember Joseph endured some serious setbacks: jealous brothers, hateful plots, slavery, false accusations, unjust imprisonment. Joseph had that Midas touch, though, and everywhere he landed, he prospered. One minute a lie threw him in jail; the next thing you know, Joseph was running the prison.

Let's start by taking a look at Genesis 39:

The LORD was with Joseph and showed him mercy, and He gave him favor in the sight of the keeper of the prison. And the keeper of the prison committed to Joseph's hand all the prisoners who were in the prison; whatever they did there, it was his doing. The keeper of the prison did not look into anything that was under Joseph's authority, because the LORD was with him; and whatever he did, the LORD made it possible. (VV. 21–23)

Things were going as well as they could in prison, but Joseph's fortunes were about to take another turn. One day, who arrived in jail but the king's cupbearer and his baker? What they did we don't know. Whatever it was, they offended the king. One day, the palace, the next, a prison.

The two men had troubling dreams one night. They mentioned it to Joseph, who replied, "Do not interpretations belong to God? Tell me your dreams" (Gen. 40:8 NIV). In other words, "I have been able to interpret a dream or two, by the power of God. Let me have a go."

The cupbearer described his dream to Joseph, which Joseph said meant he was going to get out of prison, and he would be serving in the king's presence in no time at all. Joseph added,

> But remember me when all goes well with you, and please show kindness to me; make mention of me to Pharaoh, and get me out of this house. For indeed I was stolen away from the land of the Hebrews; and also I have done nothing here that they should put me into the dungeon. (GENESIS 40:14–15)

"Help me out," Joseph pleaded. "Say a kind word for me." The baker, encouraged by this, then described his dream. Joseph had the distasteful job of revealing the devastating interpretation of his dream: "You are going to be dead in a few days."

That is exactly what happened. The baker was executed. The cupbearer returned to serve the king. But, the Bible says, he forgot about Joseph.

. . . .

Our Timing versus God's

Two full years passed while Joseph remained in that prison. That would have been upsetting, right? Joseph could have prayed, "Lord, I thought Your bringing the cupbearer to me and giving me the interpretation of his dream was my deliverance. It was my ticket out. What happened here?" But he didn't complain. He just waited. God was preparing him for an amazing responsibility.

With God, timing is everything.

Who knows but that God is preparing you for something in your future as well? You might be in a transitional time right now. Maybe you want a certain thing to happen, but the Lord says, "You better wait." You want to get married. The Lord says, "You are not ready yet. You need to wait. He isn't the right man. [Or 'She isn't the right woman.'] That is why I put the brakes on it." Trust Him—the Lord has to get you into shape first.

Maybe you are retirement age now, and your busiest years seem to be finished. Who knows that they are not just beginning? All of your experiences, all that you have gone through, all that you have learned—who knows what God can do with you still?

God's timing can vary from person to person. One person is ready for his greatest task at the age of eighteen. Another isn't ready until the age of eighty. Don't assume it is over. Who knows what the Lord has in store?

Maybe you're in a not-so-good transition time right now. Maybe you're in a Joseph-like prison. See if any of these scenarios fit. Maybe...

- you have been the victim of false accusations.
- because you are a Christian, people have tried to damage your testimony.
- you, like Joseph, have been separated from a parent you love.
- you have all but lost contact with one or all of your siblings.
- you helped someone out, and he fully took advantage of you.

- you are a husband whose wife violated her marital vows (or vice versa).
- a pastor or a spiritual leader has let you down.

What are you to do? Learn from the life of Joseph: forgive and forget. That is exactly what he did, passing every test that came his way. It is true that the cupbearer forgot about Joseph, but God did not.

. . . .
From Desperation to His Destiny

One day Pharaoh had a dream. It greatly troubled him. Then he had another dream similar to it. So disturbed was he that he called in all of the astrologers and soothsayers who were supposed to be able to interpret dreams. They were clueless.

Then the cupbearer had an epiphany:

> Today I am reminded of my shortcomings. Pharaoh was once angry with his servants, and he imprisoned me and the chief baker in the house of the captain of the guard. Each of us had a dream the same night, and each dream had a meaning of its own. Now a young Hebrew was there with us, a servant of the captain of the guard. We told him our dreams, and he interpreted them for us, giving each man the interpretation of his dream. And things turned out exactly as he interpreted them to us: I was restored to my position, and the other man was hanged. (GENESIS 41:9–13 NIV)

"Oh, King," he said, "there is this Jewish fellow in prison . . ." Pharaoh was sufficiently impressed. He said, "I want to talk to him. Bring him up here right now."

Imagine Joseph. He got up that morning as he did every day. It was just another day in this stinking prison. Suddenly someone came in and said, "The Pharaoh wants to see you."

Joseph enjoyed a long-overdue shower and shave. He was given new clothes. Then he was brought before the most powerful man in the land. In a matter of minutes Joseph moved from the prison to the palace, from the worst filth imaginable to the most palatial of surroundings. He went from desperation to his destiny.

He seemed to take it all in stride, much like the apostle Paul, who wrote,

> I have learned how to get along happily whether I have much or little. I know how to live on almost nothing or with everything. I have learned the secret of living in every situation, whether it is with a full stomach or empty, with plenty or little. For I can do everything with the help of Christ who gives me the strength I need.
>
> (PHILIPPIANS 4:11–13 NLT)

Paul was saying, "I know what it's like to be on the bottom and on the top. I am pretty much content wherever I go, because my contentment doesn't come from what I have. It comes from whom I know." That is a good principle for life. He didn't seem to be affected by where he was. He was a seasoned and prepared young man who trusted in his God.

The pharaoh described his dream to Joseph. Joseph said, "I know what that dream is about: You are going to have seven years of plenty. Your crops are going to produce more than they normally would, and you will have more food than you can eat. Immediately following that, you are going to have seven years of famine."

Notice what Joseph said next: "This will happen just as I have described it, for God has shown you what he is about to do" (Gen. 41:28 NLT). Joseph remembered his Deliverer, the source of his insight. He made that clear to Pharaoh.

Then he offered a word of advice: "What you need to do

is store the extra from the first seven years to prepare for the next seven years. You had better get somebody who is wise to do this for you. Then you will be able to survive it."

Pharaoh said, "That sounds good to me. I like that. I know just the man for the job: it is *you.*"

In a matter of minutes Joseph was taken from the lowest of the low positions to become the second-most-powerful man in the kingdom. He waited on God's timing and was blessed because of it. He had unlimited financial authority. The Pharaoh gave him a special signet ring that meant he could authorize any expenditure. Joseph had social prestige because he dressed in royal garments, and had his own private chariot, which would be the equivalent of a presidential limo. He had his own Secret Service. All of this, mind you, at the age of thirty.

I wonder if Potiphar was standing by while all this happened.

As head of Pharaoh's secret service he most likely was. If so, he was shaking in his sandals, because Joseph was now far more powerful then he was. In fact, Joseph's new authority was second only to the Pharoah himself.

What is amazing is that Joseph's change of fortune did not seem to turn his head in any way. He wasn't filled with arrogance or pride. We know what happens to some men when they come into prosperity—it destroys them. Not Joseph. He handled it well.

. . . .
Mercy Reigns

Notice that Joseph did not misuse his power. How easily he could have said, "I am the second-most-powerful man in the kingdom. I want to see Potiphar and his wife right now. They are now dead people. After that, I want a search party sent out to find my wicked brothers. They are going to be executed."

He didn't do anything of the kind. Once again, he worked

hard at his job, and he was a roaring success. We have evidence he had not only forgiven but also forgotten the pain others caused him. The Bible tells us he had two sons with his wife, Asenath. One he named Manasseh, and the other Ephraim. The meaning of the names is significant. *Manasseh* means "forgetting." Joseph had forgotten about all of the pain and hardship he had endured. *Ephraim* means "doubly fruitful." God had blessed Joseph as he had waited upon the Lord.

Then the story took another turn. If Hollywood scripted this, Joseph's brothers would show up, and he would kill them. The scriptwriters would have stretched this out and shown him hunting down each brother and dealing each a dramatic death. The scriptwriters would have saved the most wicked brother of all for the worst possible death. That's how the movies work: Good guy is hurt. Good guy destroys everyone in the end. We cheer good guy. That's entertainment!

This is the Bible. It's a little different. Joseph was in a position to do anything he wanted, but he refused the temptation to abuse his authority.

The massive famine he predicted had reached even the family of Jacob, who thought he was dead. Jacob took charge and sent his sons to find provision: "I have heard there is grain in Egypt. Go down and buy some for us before we all starve to death" (Gen. 42:2 NLT).

Off they went to Egypt, where one day someone alerted Joseph, "Some Jewish men want to see you about some food."

"Could it possibly be my family?" Joseph wondered.

It was.

Picture the scene: there was Joseph, sitting regally on his throne, and before him were his brothers. They didn't recognize him. I think maybe he had aged a bit more than normal because of all of the hardship he had endured. Suffering can certainly take its toll, and, truth be told, young Joseph had suffered a lot.

Also, because of where and who he was, he would have had a shaved head, the style the Egyptians wore. I mentioned that he would have been dressed in royal robes. He would have spoken in the Egyptian dialect. Jacob's sons really had no way of knowing Joseph was before them. They probably thought he was long dead, or toiling as a slave somewhere, far from the throne room of Egypt.

But he knew who they were—and at first he didn't tell them. He pretended not to understand their language. He carefully listened to their conversations in Hebrew, but they did not realize he understood every word of what they were saying. He even put them up to a few tasks and tests, to make them sweat a little. But finally:

> Joseph could stand it no longer. "Out, all of you!" he cried out to his attendants. He wanted to be alone with his brothers when he told them who he was. Then he broke down and wept aloud. His sobs could be heard throughout the palace, and the news was quickly carried to Pharaoh's palace.
>
> "I am Joseph!" he said to his brothers. "Is my father still alive?" But his brothers were speechless! They were stunned to realize that Joseph was standing there in front of them. "Come over here," he said. So they came closer. And he said again, "I am Joseph, your brother whom you sold into Egypt. But don't be angry with yourselves that you did this to me, for God did it. He sent me here ahead of you to preserve your lives." (GENESIS 45:1–5 NLT)

This was high drama. When the brothers heard this powerful man of Egypt weeping, they had to be thinking, *This cannot possibly be good. What did we say? We have to get out of here!* When the royal then ordered, "Everyone leave. I want to be alone with these men," things certainly looked bad. Then he dropped the bombshell: "I am Joseph!"

Their jaws must have dropped to the ground. Now there was no question they were dead.

But look at the improbable words that fall from Joseph's lips. "God did it!"

Incredible. Joseph didn't even say, "God *allowed* it." He simply said, "God did it." He knew God was in control of everything that had happened to him. His brothers couldn't believe their ears.

The rest of the account continues the drama. Jacob found out his sons were a bunch of habitual liars who had covered up their wicked and selfish deception for years, but anger turned to anticipation when he also found out his beloved Joseph was alive. They were reunited. What a joy it was for dear Jacob to reunite with his beloved Joseph after thinking him dead those many years.

The brothers felt none too secure. They thought amongst themselves, *Wait until the old man is dead. Joseph's going to kill us all.* It's just a matter of time.

Jacob did die. The brothers saw their mortality hanging in the balance and sent Joseph an urgent message:

"Before your father died, he instructed us to say to you: 'Forgive your brothers for the great evil they did to you.' So we, the servants of the God of your father, beg you to forgive us." When Joseph received the message, he broke down and wept. Then his brothers came and bowed low before him. "We are your slaves," they said.

But Joseph told them, "Don't be afraid of me. Am I God, to judge and punish you? As far as I am concerned, God turned into good what you meant for evil. He brought me to the high position I have today so I could save the lives of many people. No, don't be afraid. Indeed, I myself will take care of you and your families." And he spoke very kindly to them, reassuring them. (GENESIS 50:16–21 NLT)

In spite of everything, Joseph was still willing to extend mercy. He was making a variation on his first statement. First he said, "God did it." Then he said, "God meant it for good." He was saying, "I know you meant it for evil. But God meant it for good to save many people."

....

Ingredients for a Forgiving Heart

How could Joseph make such a statement? Two reasons we need to remember in our own lives:

1. Joseph Knew God Is Sovereign

In other words, he knew nothing happens in the life of a child of God that He has not first approved. Did you know that? We forget sometimes.

Remember when Satan wanted to attack God's servant Job? He first had to get permission. Though the Lord did allow hardship and pain in Job's life, the Lord knew what Job could handle.

God knows what you can handle as well. He will never give you more than you can bear. Whenever God allows his children to go through fiery trials, He always keeps an eye on them and a finger on the thermostat.

Remember, the word *oops* is not in God's vocabulary.

2. Joseph Knew God Is Good

We need to balance the truth of God's sovereignty with this truth: God is good. Therefore the things that come into our lives by God's sovereignty are for our benefit and others'.

Sometimes we believe God is sovereign but that He is mean. "He is powerful," you acknowledge, "and He won't let anything happen He doesn't want to happen. But you don't know what He's going to do next. He's not exactly...trustworthy."

This is wrong. Yes, He is sovereign. Yes, He is all-powerful.

Yes, He is all-knowing. But don't forget that God is *all good,* and He loves you and has a good plan for your life. We've seen this verse earlier in the book, but it's worth repeating: God says, "For I know the thoughts that I think toward you, says the LORD, thoughts of peace and not of evil, to give you a future and a hope" (Jer. 29:11).

. . . .

"Good" According to God

One verse you cannot help but quote when you read the story of Joseph. It's one every believer should know: "All things work together for good to those who love God, to those who are the called according to His purpose" (Rom. 8:28). It certainly is a promise we need to know. It's certainly a promise we need to quote. It's also a promise we need to understand. I think sometimes we fail to do that.

Many think the verse says everything that happens will always turn into a good thing. Not exactly. Certainly there are times in our lives when something adverse or unexpected happens, and God turns it around so that something great comes of it. But then there are some events that, quite frankly, we don't fully understand. Maybe all things work for good, but it depends on how you define "good." If "good" is what makes us happy now, what makes us experience a certain sense of well-being, well, when we experience something difficult or draining, how can we call that "good"?

We need to remember that after Romans 8:28 comes Romans 8:29. Think about what these verses say in context with one another: "All things work together for good to those who love God, and are the called according to His purpose. For whom He foreknew, He also predestined to be conformed to the image of His Son."

This gives us the big picture. Whatever happens in your life is something God has allowed. It will always *ultimately* work for your good in that it will make you more like Jesus. In other words, although we are interested in what is temporarily good, God is interested in what is eternally good. He is looking at the long term to make us more like the Lord Jesus Himself.

How?

Let's say a loved one dies what we deem prematurely. This we cannot understand. There seems to be no good in it. But maybe at his memorial service, ten people come to Christ. Then, as the years pass, those ten people reach ten more, and so on. Maybe when it is all said and done, a thousand people are in heaven as a result. In the end, even things we cannot understand do work for good.

Thinking about this reminds me of when I was a boy. For a number of years I lived with my grandparents, Charles and Stella McDaniel. We all called them Mama Stella and Daddy Charles. They were from Arkansas, so we had a regular diet of good old-fashioned southern cooking: black-eyed peas, collard greens, and fresh mashed potatoes. My grandmother believed in making every meal from scratch. We never had leftovers. When she wanted to cook a chicken, my grandfather often went out in the backyard and killed one. That's how fresh it was. She made incredible food.

Mama Stella's crowning achievement was her biscuits. I have never had a better biscuit made by anyone anywhere. I used to watch her make them. She used vegetable oil, self-rising flour, and of course buttermilk. No ingredient she used was appealing to me on its own. But when she mixed them all together with expert hands and put them in a very hot oven, they made some very good biscuits.

In the same way, when God takes the events of our lives—the good things and the so-called bad things—and puts them in the oven of adversity, when it is all done, we say, "That is good." It may take time. It may take a lifetime.

. . . .

What We *Can* Control

You and I cannot control our circumstances. But there is something we can control: how we react. When people have wronged us (and they will), when people disappoint us (and they will), when people betray us (and they will), and when they turn against us, we can forgive. We can forget.

You may say, "Greg, they don't deserve it." That's probably true. Do you? Forgive as you have been forgiven. Ephesians 4:32 says, "Be kind and compassionate to one another, forgiving each other, just as in Christ God forgave you" (NIV). Romans 12:18 says, "Do your part to live in peace with everyone, as much as possible" (NLT). When you carry bitterness and anger toward someone, it eats you up inside. You need to commit it to God and obey His Word. Joseph had done this before his brothers even showed up—that is so clear from his actions. Forgiven people should be forgiving people.

You may say, "Greg, it is easy for you to tell your biscuit stories and say these things to us, but forgiveness *isn't* easy." I know that. I have been through some hard stuff in my life, too. I have been wronged, many times, and not just before my conversion, but afterward. But I know firsthand that all things work together for good to those who love God. I can see how God has turned my life's setbacks around. He is going to do the same for you. Again, we can't control our circumstances, but we can control the way we react to them. Choose to forgive. Choose to forget. You will be glad you did.

No doubt Joseph was. By doing so, he threw off "everything that hinders and the sin that so easily entangles" (Heb. 12:1 NIV). That was one of the reasons he ran his whole race well and finished a winner: by dropping all the deadweight, he gained wings.

14
THE LEAST LIKELY RUNNER EVER

Let me ask you a question. Have you known anyone you just could not imagine becoming a Christian? But maybe you took him to church, and he went forward and gave his life to the Lord. It surpassed all of your expectations of what God could do.

Maybe you know someone who is especially vocal about her opposition to your faith in Jesus Christ. This person seems to go out of her way to harass you because you follow the Lord. It's as if she lives for it. You might be surprised to learn that the very person who gives you such a hard time about your faith may be closer to coming to the Lord than anyone else you know. It's been said, "When you throw a rock into a pack of dogs, the one that barks the loudest is the one that got hit!"

In the same way, those who protest (or "bark") the most, those who always have an argument waiting for us about our faith, are probably the ones getting hit. They are under the conviction of the Holy Spirit.

In Acts 8 is the story of a man who was both the most unlikely candidate for conversion and one who specialized in mocking and harassing Christians. His story is one of the most radical and unexpected turnarounds in the history of the Christian life.

Of course I am speaking of the conversion of the feared Saul of Tarsus. Against all odds, a man whose very name probably sent a shiver down the backbones of most believers became a leader of the earthly church. Saul of Tarsus was transformed into the beloved apostle Paul.

. . . .
Paul the Front-Runner

Remember, it was Paul himself who compared the Christian life to running a race. Speaking to the elders in Acts 20, as he realized his life was coming to an end, he said, "I want to finish my race with joy, and the ministry which I received from the Lord" (v. 24). Paul knew that the point was not to start well but to finish well; to learn how to pace himself and make it across the finish line.

It was Paul who wrote, "Do you not know that those who run in a race all run, but only one receives the prize?" (1 Cor. 9:24). It was Paul who wrote in Philippians, "Forgetting those things which are behind and reaching forward to those things which are ahead, I press toward the goal for the prize of the upward call of God in Christ Jesus" (3:13–14).

When you get down to it, if ever there was a winner in the spiritual race…a man who had a less-than-promising beginning…a man you never expected to see following Jesus…a man who turned his world upside down…it was the apostle Paul. To appreciate how dramatic and unexpected his conversion was, we need to understand the background of the man known as Saul of Tarsus.

Saul was named after the first king of Israel. He was a young man who did everything wholeheartedly. Young Saul grew up in a strict Jewish home where he learned the Scripture from his youth. He also came from the best Jewish soil: the tribe of

Benjamin, from which rose Israel's first king. But like Israel's first king, Saul of Tarsus also "played the fool and erred exceedingly" for many years of his life.

Saul opted to become a Pharisee, a part of a very select group of people never numbering more than six thousand. Each Pharisee took a solemn vow before three witnesses that he would devote every moment of his life to obeying the Ten Commandments. Saul was a careful student who studied under the famous Gamaliel. So profound was the influence of this Jewish rabbi that at his death it was said, "Since Gamaliel has died, the glory of the Law has ceased." He was the ultimate teacher, and under his tutelage, this zealous young Jewish man grew by the day, as did his knowledge of Scripture and his grasp of the Law.

You wonder, *How could someone so religious be so wicked?* It was Saul, later to become Paul, who eventually confessed, "I was formerly a blasphemer" (1 Tim. 1:13). He described himself as the "chief of all sinners" (see 1 Tim. 1:15). How could this happen? Quite simply, it was religion. There is a big difference between religion and a relationship with Jesus Christ. It was religion that drove Saul to his wicked state.

. . . .
Religion That Harms

Some people assert that religion can solve the problems of the world. I would have to disagree with that. If we are quite honest about it, religion is the cause of a lot of the world's problems today. Those wicked suicide bombers who take their lives and the lives of many others do so in the name of their religion. It's clear what a destructive power that is.

In Ireland today, a bloody conflict continues between the Protestants and the Catholics, all in the name of religion. Many people lost their lives in the Dark Ages, all in the name of religion. We must keep in mind that it was religious people, the Pharisees, who ultimately put Christ on the cross.

Let me clarify the fact that none of this religious activity has anything to do with Jesus Christ. When we are proclaiming the gospel, we are not promoting religion. We are promoting a relationship with God. When a man substitutes religion for a relationship with God, trouble will inevitably result. And clearly God would never have us engage in evangelism with threats, but rather with love. Not coercion but conversion. Not with the threat of death but with the promise of life.

Saul was blinded by his own twisted religion. He believed these followers of Jesus were heretics and were to be hunted down, tortured, and executed!

. . . .
Escalating Conflict

It's quite possible Saul worked his way up through the religious ranks by becoming a member of the Jewish Sanhedrin, which was the elite ruling group over Israel at that time. Then, Israel's civil and religious lives were closely intertwined. Therefore the Sanhedrin not only made civil decisions as the Supreme Court does in our country, but it also passed down religious decisions. Needless to say, being a member of the Sanhedrin meant that you were very influential and powerful and, yes, feared.

As Jesus' followers grew in number, they created maddening times for the Sanhedrin. The Sanhedrin's attempt to silence the followers of Christ actually backfired. The members thought that once Jesus was dead, that would be the end of it. But, of course, that was only the beginning. It was the very death of Jesus and His resurrection from the dead that transformed a disorganized bunch of fishermen, tax collectors, and other common folk into powerful preachers of the gospel. Unwittingly the Sanhedrin and religious leaders helped to bring about the purpose and plan of God by executing Jesus.

There it is again: what was meant for evil ultimately produced good.

That was hard for Jesus' devoted followers to understand as they saw His beaten and bloodied frame hanging on a Roman cross. But the Resurrection would change all of that—and their lives—forever.

The Sanhedrin leaders decided they would start imprisoning the believers. That only made the Christians bolder. It was as though the religious leaders were trying to put a fire out with gasoline—it just grew and grew. The Sanhedrin thought it was time to take it to the next level; threat of imprisonment was not enough. They decided to execute those who followed Jesus. Saul of Tarsus was one of those who took that task to heart.

. . . .

The First Martyr

The first one to die was a courageous young man whose name was Stephen. It's worth noting that Stephen was not an apostle. He was not even a leader in the church. If anything, he was something of an understudy. When the apostles selected men to handle the more mundane conflicts in the early church, one of the men was Stephen. Stephen faithfully took care of those problems, and he also preached the gospel. God was using him. Miracles were occurring. So he was called before the Sanhedrin and told to cease and desist from all such activity.

If Stephen had played his cards right, he could have gone home to dinner that night with his family. Instead, being a young man with vision, he thought, *Here I am before the Jewish Sanhedrin. God could reach them! I can imagine their influence if they used their office to help people come to faith!*

Stephen began to rehearse systematically the history of the

nation Israel, showing its pattern of rebellion against the various prophets God had raised up, all of which culminated in the crucifixion of Jesus Christ. Then he looked them right in the eyes and boldly said, "You are stubborn, and you don't listen to what God is saying." That did not go over well: "When they heard these things they were cut to the heart, and they gnashed at him with their teeth" (Acts 7:54).

Stephen was undeterred. Suddenly he cried out, "Look! I see the heavens opened and the Son of Man standing at the right hand of God!" That was it. They couldn't take any more: "Then they cried out with a loud voice, stopped their ears, and ran at him with one accord; and they cast him out of the city and stoned him." As life drained from his young body, Stephen's final words were, "Lord Jesus, do not charge them with this sin" (Acts 7:56, 57, 59). A tragic story, but Stephen shined brightly in that dark moment of his life. He forgave.

Why do I tell this story? To remind you what a powerful testimony it is when a Christian forgives someone who has horribly wronged him. Stephen reflected what our Lord did on the cross. As the Roman soldiers crucified him, he said, "Father, forgive them, for they do not know what they do" (Luke 23:34). The young man of faith might have even reflected back on Joseph's story of forgiving his brothers when he offered that prayer for forgiveness to the Lord he would soon join. I believe Stephen's very prayer, which was but a reflection of Jesus' prayer, ultimately resulted in the conversion of the feared Saul of Tarsus. Stephen did not live a long life, but he lived a productive one.

By the way, let me remind you that it is the greatest honor imaginable if God allows you to suffer for His name's sake. If a man like Saul is persecuting you, even if it is as subtle as harassment or mockery or ostracism, the Bible says this is an indication that you are living a Godly life. Scripture tells us,

"All who desire to live Godly in Christ Jesus will suffer persecution" (1 Tim. 3:12).

Know that you are in good company. Jesus said, "Blessed are you when they revile and persecute you, and say all kinds of evil against you falsely for My sake. Rejoice and be exceedingly glad, for great is your reward in heaven, for so they persecuted the prophets who were before you" (Matt. 5:11–12).

....
Blinded by the Light

Let's pick up the story after Stephen's death.

> Now Saul was consenting to his death. At that time a great persecution arose against the church which was at Jerusalem; and they were all scattered throughout the regions of Judea and Samaria, except the apostles.
>
> And devout men carried Stephen to his burial, and made great lamentation over him.
>
> As for Saul, he made havoc of the church, entering every house, and dragging off men and women, committing them to prison.
>
> Therefore those who were scattered went everywhere preaching the word. (ACTS 8:1–4)

At that point, the persecution of the church was intense. In other parts of the book of Acts, Paul gave a few details about his actions as an enemy of Christ. In Acts 26 he mentioned that he not only arrested Christians but he "punished them often in every synagogue and compelled them to blaspheme...I persecuted them even to foreign cities" (v. 11). This implies that he tortured them. He also mentioned that whenever the chief priests were deciding the fate of a Christian to death, Paul always voted for execution (v. 10). He was a coldhearted murderer who blindly thought he was doing the will of God.

What drove Saul to have such a hatred for Christians? He was under the intense conviction of the Holy Spirit and did not know it. He was actually quite close to conversion, and no one was aware of it except God Himself.

Saul and Stephen had a few things in common but many differences. Stephen was a truly spiritual man; Saul was religious. Stephen was humble, saved by the grace of God; Saul was self-righteous, arrogant, and proud. Stephen defended the gospel; Saul persecuted it. In God's plan, ironically, Saul ultimately carried on Stephen's task.

How did that happen?

Then Saul, still breathing threats and murder against the disciples of the Lord, went to the high priest and asked letters from him to the synagogues of Damascus, so that if he found any who were of the Way, whether men or women, he might bring them bound to Jerusalem.

As he journeyed he came near Damascus, and suddenly a light shone around him from heaven. Then he fell to the ground, and heard a voice saying to him, "Saul, Saul, why are you persecuting Me?" And he said, "Who are You, Lord?" Then the Lord said, "I am Jesus, whom you are persecuting. It is hard for you to kick against the goads."

So he, trembling and astonished, said, "Lord, what do you want me to do?" Then the Lord said to him, "Arise and go into the city, and you will be told what you must do." And the men who journeyed with him stood speechless, hearing a voice but seeing no one.

Then Saul arose from the ground, and when his eyes were opened he saw no one. But they led him by the hand and brought him into Damascus. (ACTS 9:1–8)

On his way to hunt down Christians, Saul was "breathing threats." This is an interesting phrase in the Greek. It could be translated "to breathe in and out." Just as a wild animal stalks its prey, breathing hard as it is in pursuit, Saul lived on hate. He breathed it like oxygen. His mind was blinded by prejudice, and fury fueled his every act.

I love verse 3. *"Suddenly"* Saul encountered Jesus. Isn't that just like the Lord? No announcement ahead of time. Without warning, the course of Saul's life changed dramatically and unexpectedly. This is a reminder to us that God will always have the last word.

On the day you became a Christian, did you know that was going to happen? It's quite possible you did. I have heard the stories of many who have come to our evangelistic events intending to make commitments to Christ. They know they are going to respond to the invitation to come forward and make a public profession to follow Christ, which I always give at the end of each service. Then there are others who had no plan to convert. They reluctantly attended with a friend or a family member. I was one of those people. On the day I gave my life to the Lord, I can assure you the last thing on my mind was conversion to Christianity.

Multiply that a hundred or a thousand times, and you have an idea of how Saul felt. This reminds us that someone can be so set in his ways, so wicked, yet instantaneously God's Holy Spirit can intervene in his life and turn him around. Conversion is the work of the Spirit. It can occur in the most unexpected circumstances and times and ways.

. . . .
Saul's Encounter with Jesus

Notice what Jesus said first: "Saul, Saul, why are you persecuting Me?" Whenever you see a person's name repeated twice in the Bible, it's because it is a term of endearment. It shows affection. The very Jesus Saul had been maligning tenderly reached out to him and asked, "Saul...*Saul*...Why are you persecuting Me?" Can you imagine how the word "Me" reverberated through Saul as he realized in a moment what he had actually been doing? "Why are you persecuting *Me*?"

This shows that Jesus closely identifies with us in our afflictions. Nothing escapes His attention. When a persecutor raises a hand against a follower of Jesus, he is indeed raising his hand against the very Lord Himself.

In verse 5 Jesus said, "It is hard for you to kick against the goads." "Kick against the goads" was a common expression in Greek and Latin literature. It described a farmer poking his oxen with a sharpened stick. When his oxen weren't moving, he gave them a poke. Sometimes the oxen resisted and kicked against the goad the farmer was using. That caused them even more pain.

Jesus used the rural expression to describe what Saul had been going through for the previous few months. The Lord had been goading him, poking him, pricking his conscience, and saying, "Saul, you need to believe in Me." Despite the goading, Saul said, "No way." His religion had kept him blind to truth.

....

The Enemies of a Twisted Mind

What goads was Saul kicking against?

1. The Very Life of Jesus

Saul was alive when Jesus had His ministry. It's quite possible Saul personally heard and saw Jesus speak. Being a leading Pharisee, and possibly a member of the Sanhedrin, Saul was probably in the thick of the conflicts between Jesus and the religious leaders and knew all about the plans to execute Jesus.

Saul would also have been aware of the famed religious leader Nicodemus going to see Jesus by night. That was a goad. It got his attention. Saul probably thought Nicodemus had fallen under Jesus' hypnotic spells, but he knew better.

Perhaps when Jesus appeared to Saul on the Damascus road, Saul recognized the Lord. "Saul, remember Me? I am alive still."

2. The Spread of the Christian Faith and the Commitment of Its Followers

The Christians Saul tortured probably died calling on God. The more he attacked Jesus' followers, the more their numbers grew. He had never seen anything like that in his own legalistic religion. The Christians reflected changed lives and persistence even in the face of death.

3. The Peaceful Death of Stephen and His Forgiveness of His Persecutors

The Bible says Stephen's face looked like that of an angel when he preached to the Sanhedrin. Then, when he gave his life for the faith and prayed, "Lord, don't lay this sin against their charge," it pierced Saul's hardened heart. But not all the way, until his encounter on the Damascus road.

Here is something to remember regarding the three points I just noted: a goad is not comfortable. It is not pleasant to be poked with a stick. Conversion begins with discomfort and results in eternal comfort.

Sometimes we don't want to create conflict with nonbelievers by sharing our faith with them. We don't want to offend. We don't want to get into an argument. So we try to blend into the woodwork.

When we do that, we make a big mistake. The very friction and discomfort a real follower of Jesus provides ultimately produces conversion. I'm not suggesting we be obnoxious or overly pushy. I'm simply saying we need to be what we are: a bright light in a dark place, and sometimes a pinch of salt in a wound.

Maybe your family, a bunch of nonbelievers, gets together. The whole mood changes the moment you enter the room. Of course, whenever a family gathers, they want to have their token prayer, especially if it's Thanksgiving or Christmas. It usually falls on you as the Christian.

You don't like the tension. You wish they would call on someone else.

I'm telling you this tension, this uncomfortable feeling, can be a very good thing. And remember this: when you are asked to pray, you have the floor! So take full advantage of it for the gospel.

In 2004 I was asked to offer a two-minute opening prayer at the Republican National Convention, to be televised internationally. This was a great honor, and I wanted to use it for the gospel. I wanted to point people to Jesus Christ. I wanted to take it beyond merely saying "In Jesus' name" at the end. As I was preparing it I sought the counsel of Godly people like Billy Graham and Chuck Smith.

I was given two minutes to pray and was asked to first submit my prayer to the RNC for approval. Much to my delight, the RNC approved it, even though it was a strong prayer.

Here is some of what I prayed:

Heavenly Father,

We come tonight to pray for our nation, the United States of America. You have blessed us in so many ways, but sometimes we have taken that for granted. We remember the wise words of President Abraham Lincoln when he said "We have forgotten You, and have vainly imagined in the deceitfulness of our hearts that all these blessings that we see in our country were produced by some superior wisdom and virtue of our own." It is true, Lord; we have forgotten You in many ways in our culture. We have forgotten the sanctity You place on human life. We have forgotten the value You have placed on the family unit.

But we are grateful that You have not forgotten us. And You have reminded us that "righteousness exalts a nation, but sin brings a reproach to it." Lord, we want to see righteousness exalting America again. We want to do what is right. But we have sinned against You. Yet You loved us so much that You sent Your Son, Jesus Christ, to live the perfect life, then voluntarily go to a Cross to receive the penalty for our sin by dying for us, so that if we will turn from our sin and turn to You, in faith, we can be forgiven.

Thank you God for second chances. You have told us in Scripture that if we "would humble ourselves and pray and seek Your face and turn from our wicked ways that You would forgive our sin and heal our land." We humble ourselves tonight.

We ask you to "heal our land."

Billy Graham told me that I should be prepared for noise in the hall as I prayed, as he had experienced that when he prayed at conventions in the past. But amazingly, the room went silent.

And when I was done the people applauded. I think there were a lot of Christians out there agreeing with me.

So take advantage of those opportunities to pray.

. . . .
Spiritual Encounter with a Bodybuilder

Once I was getting my cell phone repaired, and, while I was waiting, I went next door to one of those bodybuilding stores. I quickly scoped it out and could not find a thing I needed. As I was walking toward the door, a very muscular guy looked me in the eyes and said, "You're Greg Laurie, aren't you?" Another equally pumped-up guy was behind the counter watching with great interest.

I replied, "Yes, I am."

He said, "I have a question for you. I'm living with my girl-friend. Why is that a sin?"

I thought for a moment. *I don't know if this guy is going to appreciate the answer I have for him here. Yet, I don't really have a choice in the matter.*

So I responded, "Because the Bible says it is."

He said, "Let me ask you this: if I died, would I go to hell?"

I said, "You probably would." I thought, *This is crazy. These two guys could put the hurt on me.* There was quite a bit of friction in that room. I tried to be very loving. I didn't scream the truth in his face. I spoke calmly but firmly.

As we talked more, he softened. He admitted he had made a commitment to Christ but had fallen away. He knew he shouldn't have been living with his girlfriend.

I told him he needed to recommit his life to the Lord. I said, "Would you like to do that right now?"

"No way."

I said, "I am going to pray for you."

He took a step back and responded, "Oh no. Don't do that."

I said, "You know what? I have never been in here before. Obviously I don't frequent this store. This was a divine appointment. The Lord led me in here to tell you these things because He loves you and wants you to get right with Him."

Believe me, there was tension. I tried to diffuse any unnecessary friction without compromising my message. I believe God used this as a goad in this man's life. I am sure he had been using other things and encounters to get his attention as well.

God got Saul's attention through different goads. You might be a goad in someone else's life. You just hang in there and "goad" for it!

. . . .
Two Questions We All Should Ask

Saul asked two very important questions on the day of his conversion: "Who are You, Lord, and what do You want me to do?" Every follower of Jesus should ask the same things. We need to dedicate our lives to discovering who Jesus is. Certainly Paul did that. He said it best himself in Philippians: "My determined purpose is that I may become intimately and more personally acquainted with Him. I want to know Him and the power of His resurrection" (3:10; see The Amplified Bible). That is a good way to live your life: getting to know the Lord.

"What do You want Me to do?" This is a question I think many believers have never asked the Lord. Have you? "Lord, what is Your plan for my life? What do You want me to do with my future? How do You want me to invest my time, my money, my energy?" If you ask, I believe the Lord will give you an answer. He gave one to Saul; He will give one to you too.

Saul's story did not stop at his conversion. That was just the beginning. The man who had dedicated his life to the destruction of the Christian church then dedicated his life to its spread. He who had been controlled by hate was now to be controlled by love.

After his encounter with Christ, Saul blazed a trail, creating countless churches and converts. He fearlessly preached to philosophers, Pharisees, rulers, soldiers, sorcerers, slaves, sailors, and quite possibly Caesar himself.

Saul's conversion was such an unlikely event that a British agnostic of the last century thought it would not be too difficult to disprove. In doing that, he thought he could also show that the rest of the New Testament was not credible and thus undermine the entire foundation of the Christian faith. George Lloyd Littleton went to work on his book, *Observations on the Conversion and Apostleship of Saint Paul.*

But a funny thing happened to Littleton as he researched Paul's story. He came to a far different conclusion than he had anticipated. At the end of his book, he made this statement: "Paul's conversion and apostleship alone duly considered are a demonstration sufficient to prove Christianity to be a divine revelation." As it turned out, Littleton was actually converted in the study of the transformation that took place in Saul's life.

Saul may have done damage to God's people prior to starting the race, but he spent the rest of his life trying to make up for it. He set the pace for all who would follow.

15
THE LAST LAP

Just after Saul's conversion, we read in Acts 9 that God directed a man named Ananias to seek out the new convert. The Lord told him to go to a certain place where he would recognize Saul because he would be praying.

Ananias was understandably reluctant. He reminded God that Saul had been the persecutor of the church: "Lord, I have heard much from many about this man, how much harm he has done to Your saints in Jerusalem. And here he has authority from the chief priests to bind all who call on Your name." God responded, "Go, for he is a chosen vessel of Mine to bear My name before Gentiles, kings, and the children of Israel. For I will show him how many things he must suffer for My name's sake" (Acts 9:13–16).

It is interesting that when God wanted to raise up someone to minister to Saul, he did not choose an apostle such as Peter or John, but an ordinary and unknown man. Did Ananias write any book of the New Testament? Did he ever perform a miracle? Did he raise a dead person? Did he give a notable sermon that we know about? No. But he did come at a critical time into the life of a man who would change his world, and, indeed, world history.

I thank God for the Ananiases of the kingdom. By that I mean those who faithfully work behind the scenes. We rarely hear their names, yet they faithfully deliver their messages, minister to the sick and the hurting, pray, give, labor away in obscurity on the mission field. We don't know about them. They are unknown to man, but they are beloved of God.

Who knows but that God could not use you in such a way? He could raise you up to be like the apostle Paul or like the humble Ananias.

. . . .
My Story

A young man did this for me. His name was Mark. Shortly after my unexpected conversion, Mark sought me out and helped me acclimate to this new world of Christianity I knew nothing about.

First, let me tell you a little about my background. I was not raised in the church. For the most part, I didn't read the Bible or pray. I always believed, however, there was a God somewhere, but I never knew He could be known personally.

I grew up in a very dysfunctional home. My mother was married and divorced some seven times and was also a full-blown alcoholic. I spent far too much time in smoky bars waiting for my mom to tire and be ready to return home. Many times I feared for my life as she drunkenly tried to find her way back to our house in the car. Countless nights I was awakened very late to hear my mother screaming obscenities and throwing things. The next morning she remembered nothing and never made mention of it. Then the pattern repeated the next evening. This went on for years.

As a result of this bizarre upbringing, I quickly developed survival skills and a pretty tough skin. I was known for my quick, biting, sarcastic wit, which got me into quite a bit of trouble in the various schools I attended over the years. The funny thing is, on the inside I was almost a romantic, believing that somewhere in the world was a good, wholesome, and loving life. But on the outside I was hard and bitter.

Despite the horrific example of my mother, I myself turned to a partying lifestyle. Tiring of that, I got caught up in the drug culture for a few years. This only exacerbated my problems.

I was very unhappy with the course my life was taking and desperately wanted to have some meaning and purpose in my life. I was to find that in an unexpected place.

It all started with a girl on my high-school campus who caught my eye. She was attractive, but there was more to her than that. I could not quite put my finger on it. I really wanted to meet her and try and discover what made her different from so many of the other girls on campus. One day she was talking to one of my friends, so I thought that would be as good a time as any to make my move.

I walked up to them as they talked and waited for a break in the conversation. I looked down and saw her notebook, a textbook for a class, and something unexpected: a Bible! I thought, *Oh no! She's one of those Jesus freaks!*

At a lull in our conversation, I introduced myself. She did not jump down my throat with the gospel. She just radiated Jesus Christ. I wondered, *Is there something to all of this?*

That lunchtime I went into "enemy territory" and decided to eavesdrop on the Christians as they had their Bible study on the front lawn of Newport Harbor High School in Orange County, California.

I carefully surveyed the group of Christians in attendance that day. I was sitting at a distance but close enough to hear what was being said. A young man from a local church called Calvary Chapel got up and spoke about who Jesus Christ was and how one could know Him personally. Though, as a very young man, I had prayed at a Christian camp and asked Jesus Christ into my life, I really had no idea then what I was really doing. But suddenly it was crystal clear.

God loved me. He sent His Son to die on the cross in my place. I needed to believe in and follow Him.

My heart pounded so hard it seemed as though people sitting around me could hear it. I hung my head and thought, *It all sounds so great. It really does. But this would never work for me personally.* I just did not see myself as the religious type. I was far too cynical, skeptical, and reluctant to follow the Christian crowd.

But God was working on me that day. The conviction of the Holy Spirit did not let up, and, much to my own amazement, I found myself praying with some others to make a commitment to Jesus Christ. Even as I prayed, I was thinking God was going to somehow turn me down cold.

But He did not. He came into my life and forgave me of my sins that day.

When others I knew on campus found out, they could not believe it: "Laurie is a Jesus freak now?" Yes, I was. But I could have fallen through the cracks were it not for a young man named Mark

. . . .
A Crucial Role

So, there I was, a brand-new Christian. Frankly, I did not know what to do next.

No one came to me with a Bible or told me to go to church. No one even explained what had happened to me, and I was perplexed. Despite the fact that I was now a newly minted Christian, I still felt a bit awkward around the other believers. I did not understand their lingo or lifestyles in many ways. So,

I went back to hang out with my old nonbelieving friends for a few days.

But the things I used to enjoy suddenly had no appeal to me. The jokes weren't funny anymore. The absolute waste of life was evident, so I disconnected from them.

I was in danger of quickly falling through the cracks. That is, until Mark came along.

He came up to me out of the blue one day at school and told me he had seen me pray and receive Christ. I was a bit cold and standoffish, thinking, *What does this guy want?*

Mark was patient with me and asked if I had a Bible yet. He then proceeded to get me one and even explained how best to start reading it. I opened this wonderful book for the first time and was absolutely amazed at what I read. It was so relevant to my life.

Mark started having personal Bible studies with me, explaining the basics of the Christian faith. He also took me to church and introduced me to other Christians.

He was my Ananias.

Could you be that for someone else?

. . . .

Secrets of Paul's Success

Returning to Paul's story: Ananias was understandably hesitant, but in obedience he did what God told him to do. He found Saul, who had been blinded after his dazzling meeting with Jesus, and prayed that the Lord would restore his sight.

This encounter brings us to a few secrets of Saul-turned-Paul's life that I want to bring to your attention. These principles will help us to understand why God so powerfully used him.

1. Paul Was a Praying Man

God told Ananias to look for Saul, a guy who would be praying. Sure enough, that's exactly what Saul was doing when

Ananias came upon him. What was he praying about? I am sure he was seeking forgiveness of his sins.

Can you imagine how hard it would be to accept God's forgiveness if you were a murderer? And Saul was not just someone who took the lives of others, but someone who specifically hunted down the followers of Jesus Christ and brought about their premature deaths. When Paul later wrote that he was "forgetting the things which are behind and reaching forward to those things which are ahead," you have to understand that he had a lot to forget. He had a lot of sin to put behind him. So he prayed.

Prayer actually characterized his life of faith. You can't help but notice that. So many of his epistles begin or end with beautiful prayers he offered on behalf of the people to whom he was writing. It was Paul who told us that men ought to pray (1 Tim. 2:8). He told us we should remember to be people of prayer and to "pray without ceasing" (1 Thess. 5:17).

Paul practiced what he preached. We read in Acts 16 that Paul and Silas were thrown into a dungeon for preaching the gospel. Their backs had been ripped open by a whip. Their feet were fastened in stocks. There, in that dark, stinking hole, the Bible says that at midnight Paul and Silas prayed and sang praises to God. Who would want to pray at a time like that? It would make more sense if at midnight Paul and Silas wept or cried out to God or sat in stunned silence. No. The Bible says they prayed and worshiped God. Instead of cursing men, they were blessing God. No wonder the other prisoners were listening to them.

Paul discovered through prayer that he could enjoy an intimate relationship with the God he had known of previously only in a cold, distant way through dead legalism and orthodoxy. He later wrote, "For you did not receive the spirit of bondage again to fear, but you received the Spirit adoption by whom we cry out, 'Abba, Father'" (Rom. 8:15). "Abba" was the affectionate cry of a beloved child. Our modern equivalent would be "Daddy" or "Papa." Paul developed an intimacy with God.

This was the transformation that took part in the life of Paul. He was a man of prayer. Are you a man of prayer? Are you a woman of prayer? Does prayer characterize your life? It ought to. If you want to finish well in the spiritual race, you need to learn how to pray.

2. Paul Was a Humble Man

Now, he wasn't always humble. At one time he was probably the proudest guy around—filled with himself and his accomplishments, knowledge, and skills. Later God transformed him into a man of deep and genuine humility.

Right after his conversion Paul started preaching the gospel in Damascus (Acts 9). He was so powerful and persuasive that the religious leaders wanted him dead right then and there. He was a threat. The believers found out about it and hatched a scheme by which they could get Paul out of the city. They put him into a basket and lowered it over the city walls at nighttime.

Think of the irony of that situation. Just a short time earlier, he had been Saul of Tarsus with his entourage that arrested and executed Christians. Next thing you know, Christians were taking extraordinary precautions to save his life by lowering him over the city wall in a basket.

Even his name gives us an insight into what he was all about at that point. He changed his name from Saul to Paul. Saul was the name of the first king of Israel; it was a respected and powerful name. Then he took the name of Paul, which means "little." I don't know if he took that name because he was small in stature; I think Saul took the name Paul to describe the change that had happened in his life. One name, Saul, denoted power, greatness, influence. The other, Paul, spoke of smallness, insignificance, humility.

This was like having the name *Spike* and changing it to *Squirt.* God had transformed him. The hunter had become the hunted. The man who persecuted others was getting a taste of his own medicine.

Yet instead of striking out, he practiced humility. Let's explore the ways in which he did so.

A humble man endures obscurity. The Lord took Paul away and put him into obscurity in the desert of Arabia for a period of time (Gal.1:17). What happened there we are not told. We can only presume that it was then that he drew close to the Lord in fellowship and communion. Most likely it was there that he refined the theology we see in the great epistles that God inspired him to write.

It was typical of how God dealt with many people He prepared for service: he placed them on "pause" for a time. You remember after Elijah made his bold pronouncement to Ahab and Jezebel, God sent him to the Brook Cherith for a couple of years. Moses had forty years of training to get him into shape to deliver the children of Israel. Even after the young teenager David was anointed to be king, it wasn't until he reached the age of thirty that he actually ascended to the throne. Even after Joseph flourished in the house of Potiphar, he lived in prison for two very long years.

God isolated these men only because he was preparing them for his work. God did the same for Paul.

It has been said that it takes a steady hand to hold a full cup. God was going to give a full cup to Paul. He was going to use him powerfully. He had to be prepared and properly equipped to withstand the challenges. The Lord humbled him and made him ready for the tasks that were ahead. Only then did He take Paul back into society.

The Lord may be preparing you today for a greater work He wants to do with you tomorrow.

A humble man prefers worshiping God to being worshiped

himself. An interesting series of events unfolded. According to Acts 14, when Paul was in Lystra, he saw a crippled man. God revealed to Paul that he wanted to heal the man, so Paul, under the inspiration of the Holy Spirit, said, "Get up and walk." The man got up and walked. The people in that city, who were largely pagan, were so moved by this demonstration of faith and power that they thought Paul and his companion, Barnabas, were Greek gods come to life. They called them Zeus and Hermes, and they began to offer animal sacrifices to them.

Paul was a humble man, as was Barnabas. Scripture says, "When the apostles Barnabas and Paul heard this, they tore their clothes and ran in among the multitude, crying out and saying, 'Men, why are you doing these things? We also are men with the same nature as you'" (Acts 14:14–15).

Paul proceeded to preach the gospel to them. The leaders were so outraged at Paul's audacity to confront them with the truth that they decided to put him to death. They turned the same multitude that had been ready to sacrifice to him against him.

We read in Acts 14: "Now some Jews arrived from Antioch and Iconium and turned the crowds into a murderous mob. They stoned Paul and dragged him out of the city, apparently dead" (v. 19 NLT). It was probably at this point Paul had his "third heaven" experience. In 2 Corinthians 12, Paul described it this way:

It is doubtless not profitable for me to boast. I will come to visions and revelations of the Lord: I know a man in Christ who fourteen years ago—whether in the body I do not know, or whether out of the body I do not know, God knows—such a one was caught up to the third heaven. And I know such a man—whether in the body or out of the body I do not know, God knows—how he was caught up into

Paradise and heard inexpressible words, which is not lawful for a man to utter. Of such a one I will boast; yet of myself I will not boast, except in my infirmities. For though I might desire to boast, I will not be a fool; for I will speak the truth. But I refrain, lest anyone should think of me above what he sees me to be or hears from me. (VV. 1–6)

Paul was saying he died, went to heaven, and heard things that he could not repeat. He was saying he didn't even want to boast about hearing these words from God.

It is my opinion that the event we read about in Acts is when this transpired. Paul was preaching. The crowd turned against him. They stoned him, and he died. He was immediately ushered into the presence of God Almighty.

This passage reminds us that we should never feel sorrow for people who have died in the Lord. Sure, we miss them desperately. Yes, we wish we could still hear their voices and look into their eyes.

But don't feel sorry for them. Where they are is far better than where you are right now. They would want you to know that.

That's why Paul said, "How can I describe it? It was Paradise! I am telling you that it is not something I can put into human words."

This shows us the humility of the apostle. If I personally had died, gone to heaven, and come back, I would talk about it every day. I would bring it up in every conversation. In fact, the title of this book would have been something along the lines of *How I Went to Heaven and Came Back to Earth*.

Paul mentioned it once, but we never read of it again.

A humble man knows where his strength lies. The Lord knew that this supernatural experience could potentially boost Paul's pride. We read:

Lest I should be exalted above measure by the abundance of the revelations, a thorn in the flesh was given to me, a messenger of Satan to buffet me, lest I be exalted above measure.

Concerning this thing I pleaded with the Lord three times that it might depart from me. And He said to me, "My grace is sufficient for you, for My strength is made perfect in weakness." (2 CORINTHIANS 12:7-9)

What this thorn was we don't know. I will tell you this: in the original language it could be better translated "a stake in the flesh." It was a brutal thing. Some commentators think it was a disability; perhaps he was born with it. Others believe it might have been something that didn't heal after he was stoned. I think that is probably the case. Whatever it was, three times he asked the Lord to take it away.

Understand God had used Paul to pray for other people to be well, but God didn't heal the apostle himself. Rather He just extended His grace. Why? Paul said, "I don't know, but I will tell you this much: I rejoice in these things." I love his words in verse 9–10,

Now I am glad to boast about my weaknesses, so that the power of Christ may work through me. Since I know it is all for Christ's good, I am quite content with my weaknesses and with insults, hardships, persecutions, and calamities. For when I am weak, then I am strong. (NLT)

Sometimes we want God to take a certain thing away. We pray over and over for Him to remove it. Did you ever stop to think God is using it in your life?

Something else to consider: when you have gone through hardship, you can more effectively minister to others who are going through the same thing. Paul wrote in 2 Corinthians 1:

He comforts us in all our troubles so that we can comfort
others. When others are troubled, we will be able to give
them the same comfort God has given us...For when God
comforts us, it is so that we, in turn, can be an encouragement to you. Then you can patiently endure the same things
we suffer. (VV. 4, 6 NLT)

You have endured tragedies in life that others will endure
as well. You can comfort someone else with the comfort you
have received from the Lord. Nothing happens by accident in
the life of the Christian.

3. Paul Was a Loving Man

Paul had once been so filled with hate. Remember, the Bible
says that he was "breathing threats and murder against the
disciples of the Lord" (Acts 9:1). It is a vivid picture of a wild
animal seething in hostility and anger as it hunts its prey. Paul
once lived on hate; then God transformed him into the apostle
of love. He wrote the greatest chapter on love in human history in 1 Corinthians 13: "Though I speak with the tongues of
men and of angels, but have not love, I have become sound-
ing brass or crashing cymbal...Love suffers long and is kind"
(vv. 1, 4). These were not the hollow words of a man who merely
liked the sentiment of love. This was a man who lived it.

Paul probably did more to remove barriers between Jews and
Gentiles than anybody else in the first-century Christian church.
What kept him going through the persecutions and hardships:
he loved God, and he loved people. It was Paul who wrote, "The
love of Christ constrains and motivates me" (see 2 Cor. 5:14).

. . . .
Paul's Obituary

Paul's turbulent life was coming to an end. He had touched
thousands of lives. He had fearlessly preached the gospel to

great leaders and common people. God had wrought miracles through him. He had written the wonderful epistles we so value today as much of the New Testament.

We read his final words in 2 Timothy 4. When Paul wrote this, he was in the Mamertine prison in Rome. He had appealed to Caesar. We have good reason to believe he eventually stood before the Roman emperor Nero himself. God had somehow revealed to Paul that this was it—his time had come to an end.

> I am already being poured out as a drink offering, and the time of my departure is at hand. I have fought the good fight, I have finished the race, I have kept the faith. Finally, there is laid up for me the crown of righteousness, which the Lord, the righteous Judge, will give to me on that Day, and not to me only but also to all who have loved His appearing. (VV. 6–8)

If I am going someplace I don't like, I dread the trip. But if I am going somewhere I like, I look forward to the trip. The trip is relatively painless, even sitting in coach with a person reclined in front of me. It is okay. The destination makes it worth it.

Paul had been in pain. Paul had suffered. He had endured hardship. How do you imagine he looked in those moments, as he stood before Caesar? Don't think of a depressed old man—think of a person whose face was radiating with joy. "My departure is at hand. I have fought the good fight. I have kept the faith. I finished the course."

If you died today, would you be able to say that? I am not suggesting you should be able to say, "I am a perfect person. I never made a mistake." No one could. But could you say, in general, that you have kept the faith and finished the race? We should all be able to say it.

Paul compared himself as a Christian to three different types of people:

1. A Wrestler

"I have fought the good fight." The word translated "fight" points to the Greek wrestling matches in which men struggled against each other with all of their might, sometimes fighting even to the death. It was like a street brawl. Paul was saying, "I have fought this fight to the death."

Make no mistake about it: the Christian life is a fight. The moment you give your life to Jesus, the battle begins. Conversion has made our hearts a battleground. The Spirit wars against the flesh, and the flesh wars against the Spirit. You have the devil, the flesh, and the world as your enemies. The raging fight will not end until the day you are safely in the arms of Jesus. There will always be that dynamic of struggle and conflict because you are in a spiritual war.

It was Paul who wrote, "We do not wrestle against flesh and blood, but against principalities, against powers, against the rulers of the darkness of this age, against spiritual hosts of this wickedness in the heavenly places" (Eph. 6:12).

2. A Runner

Paul said, "I have finished the race." Notice that he used the word "finished." He didn't say that he merely ran the race. As we have seen, it is possible to run the race poorly, to give up halfway through it. Paul was able to say, "I finished the race." That is the goal: to finish what we have begun.

In Philippians 3:14, you'll remember that Paul wrote, "I press toward the goal for the prize of the upward call of God in Christ Jesus." The word he used for "press" comes from the Greek word *agonizo*. We get the English word *agonize* from it. It gives us a picture of a runner in the last lap of a race. Pain is wracking his body. He can see the ribbon. He is almost there.

Are you finishing the race?

3. A Soldier

Paul said, "I have kept the faith." The word "kept" means having guarded the faith as an armed soldier would guard his post against enemy attack. In other words, Paul was saying that he had not strayed from the truth in his words or in his life.

If your life were to end today, would you be able to say that you had fought the good fight, you had kept the faith and finished the course? Have you been winning in this fight and struggle against Satan and personal sin? Have you kept up the pace in the race of life? Have you guarded and kept the faith in the way you live? If so, then the reward that Paul was looking forward to will be yours as well.

Paul concluded in 2 Timothy 4:8: "Finally, there is laid up for me the crown of righteousness, which the Lord, the righteous Judge, will give to me on that Day, and not to me only but also to all who have loved His appearing."

If you are looking forward to the appearing of Christ, then Christ has a crown of righteousness for you. If you are truly anticipating the Lord's return, it should affect the way you live.

Life will come to an end. We don't know when. It might be many years from now; it might not. We all need to give thought to our legacy—to what we are living for and what our lives are all about. What do you think your last words will be? What will your obituary say? Can you sum up your life the way Paul did?

Don't waste your life. Fight the good fight. Finish that race. Keep the faith. Run this way, and you will win a crown for a prize.

16

NECK AND NECK . . . WITH HIMSELF

A dramatic moment took place in the Olympic competitions a number of years ago in Mexico City. It was seven in the evening on October 20, 1968. It was almost dark. The last of the marathon runners were stumbling across the finish line. Finally the very last, a lone runner wearing the colors of Tanzania, staggered into the stadium. His name was John Steven Okiwari. His leg had been injured in a fall. It was crudely bandaged. As the crowd looked on, he hobbled the final lap around the track.

When he finally finished, the crowd stood in unison and gave him an ovation. He actually received greater applause than the winner of the race had. Why? Because he had, against all odds, finished this incredible race. Afterward someone asked why he had not quit. This was the response he gave: "My country did not send me seven thousand miles to start the race. They sent me seven thousand miles to finish the race."

When I read that, I couldn't help but think of the person in the Bible who, like Okiwari, finished his race, but not without some serious injuries. He, too, made a dramatic comeback and crossed the finishing line with flying colors. This man's faux pas were legendary, his statements priceless, his mistakes public. Of course I am speaking of Simon Peter.

. . . .

A Man Like Any Other

You have to love Peter. He was such a classically human character. We can admire a man like the apostle Paul for his great courage, dedication, and commitment. We can stand in awe of a man like the apostle John for the deep love and devotion he had for the Lord. But when we look at Simon Peter, we just step back and say, "That is me." He is a guy we can so easily relate to.

The key to understanding this man is in his name. He was given the name Simon by his parents. He was given the new name of Peter by Jesus.

That tells us who he was and who he was to become. All of his life, he remained both Simon and Peter. Sometimes Simon prevailed; other times Peter did. If that doesn't make any sense to you, look at John 1:40–42.

> One of the two who heard John speak, and followed Him, was Andrew, Simon Peter's brother. He first found his own brother Simon, and said to him, "We have found the Messiah" (which is translated, the Christ). And he brought him to Jesus. Now when Jesus looked at him, He said, "You are Simon the son of Jonah. You shall be called Cephas" (which is translated, A Stone).

His given name, Simon, means "a listener" or "a hearer." Upon seeing him for the first time, Jesus essentially gave him a nickname—a new title to describe the person he was going to become. He said, "Your name is going to be Peter or 'Rock' (the literal meaning)."

I think the others might have done a little snickering at

that point. If there was anything Simon was not, it was a rock. A rock is stable and solid. Peter was given to the emotion of a moment. He could be hotheaded. But God saw him for what he would become.

. . . .

A Name to Reflect One's Potential

Maybe your parents gave you a name you don't particularly like. I heard about a mom and dad who decided to give their child the very curious name of Odd. Poor kid! Obviously that invited ridicule and mockery all through grade school, high school, and college. But the jibes made him want to achieve, and he became a very successful lawyer.

Because people ribbed him his entire life, he decided that upon his death, he wanted an unmarked tombstone placed at his grave so his name would never be uttered again. His wishes were honored. The problem was when people saw this tombstone without an inscription, they almost always said, "That's odd."

Jesus gave to Simon this new name of Rock. Why? He knew Peter would eventually grow into the name. The phrase that is translated "Jesus looked at Peter" means that He looked right through him.

Have you ever had anyone look right through you? Let me restate the question. Do you have a mother? Then you know what it is like to have someone look right through you. You find yourself confessing wrongs you never even committed.

We know Jesus knew what He was getting. He knew Peter would fail. He knew that Peter would fall short. He knew even that Peter would ultimately deny Him. But Jesus also knew Peter would make a comeback. He knew that after his early failure, "the rock" would courageously serve the Lord all the days of his life. He looked right through him, and He saw potential.

In the same way Jesus looks at you and doesn't see you just for what you are. He sees you for what you can become. We see a lump of clay; God sees a beautiful vase. We see a blank canvas; God sees a finished painting. We see a lump of coal; God sees a refined diamond. We see problems; God sees solutions. We see failures; God sees potential success. We see a Jacob; God sees an Israel. We see a Simon; God sees an apostle Peter.

....
Failure Turned to Success

God can take the failures of our lives and use them for His glory. That doesn't mean we should go out and intentionally fail. It means that when we do, we can learn from those mistakes. It has been said that the doorway to success is entered through the hallway of failure. It has also been said that if at first you don't succeed, relax—you are just like the rest of us!

Have you ever tried to do something for God that was a complete failure? Perhaps it was your feeble attempt to share the gospel with some friends. They not only failed to respond in the affirmative, they became angry with you.

It may have been a prayer for someone to get better physically, who actually got worse. I remember once a friend was feeling nauseated and asked if I would pray. I did just that, and his nausea increased! He said he would never ask me to pray for him again!

Perhaps you started a home Bible study, and no one showed up.

Let me say to you: thank you for your failures! I would far rather try and fail than never do anything at all. Besides, failure is not always such a bad thing. We learn from our mistakes. Failure can indeed teach success.

Successful people know how to handle failure. Many failed initially only to succeed later. Albert Einstein failed at math before he discovered the theory of relativity. Isaac Newton had to have an apple fall on his head before discovering the theory of gravity. Michael Jordan failed to make his high-school basketball team before making the NBA.

You might say, "But I have failed horribly." You can't change your past, but you can choose your response to it. God can take your endings and turn them into beginnings.

. . . .
Peter's Failures Help Us

We certainly see that in the life of Simon Peter. The gospels are full of his adventures and statements. No disciple spoke as often as he did, and out of necessity, no disciple was corrected as many times as Peter was. Sometimes he opened his mouth merely to change feet. Other times what he said was absolutely profound. Jesus commended him like no other and at the same time sometimes harshly criticized him. Sometimes both at once.

You might say Peter was the patron saint of ordinary people. In short, Peter was a man just like us. This is important, because sometimes we see the apostles in stained glass. We think that they were incapable of shortcomings or mistakes. That is simply not true. Again, the Bible is a thoroughly honest book. We will see Peter's victories, but we will also see his vulnerabilities.

The point: God can take an ordinary person and do something extraordinary. Jesus did not choose the apostles because they were great. Rather, their greatness came as a result of Jesus' choosing them. In the same way, God did not choose you because you were great. You aren't. Nor am I. Yet in His grace and mercy, He can do something wonderful with both of our lives.

For example, you can take a golf club that you bought at a garage sale, give it to me, and ask me to impress you. You are going to be very disappointed. I have no golfing skills whatsoever. You wouldn't even want me for a partner in miniature golf.

Yet you could take that same club, as flawed and worn as it is, put it in the hands of a master golfer like Tiger Woods, and see a contest won. It all depends on who has the club.

In the same way, you are an instrument in the hands of God. God can make you into someone you were not before to touch this world.

. . . .
Dual Personalities

It is interesting to note how Jesus said to Simon, "You shall be called Peter [Rock]" in John 1. He didn't say, "You are Peter." He was only Simon at that point. It was only after Simon's encounter with Jesus at Caesarea Philippi that anyone referred to him as Peter.

In Matthew 16, we read:

He asked His disciples, saying, "Who do men say that I, the Son of Man, am?"

So they said, "Some say John the Baptist, some Elijah, and others Jeremiah or one of the prophets."

He said to them, "But who do you say that I am?"

Simon Peter answered, "You are the Christ, the Son of the living God."

Jesus answered and said to him, "Blessed are you, Simon Bar-Jonah, for flesh and blood has not revealed this to you, but My Father who is in heaven. And I also say to you that you are Peter." (VV. 13–18)

The Lord had said previously, "You will be called Peter." Then, after Simon had confessed that Jesus was the Christ, he says, "You are Peter." He was a new man with a new name.

In the same way, when we put our trust in Jesus Christ, we, too, receive a new name: *Christian.* With that new name God gives us a new nature. We have the power to live this life in a way we never could before. The Holy Spirit of God resides within us, leading us to obey God.

Unfortunately, just as Simon Peter had two natures that constantly battled one another, we, too, have the battle between the old and the new natures. As in Galatians 5:17,

The old sinful nature loves to do evil, which is just opposite from what the Holy Spirit wants. And the Spirit gives us desires that are opposite from what the sinful nature desires. These two forces are constantly fighting each other, and your choices are never free from this conflict. (NLT)

You know what this is like. It's not a day-by-day issue; it's a moment-by-moment issue. Every morning when we get up, we face thousands of opportunities to decide: *Am I going to yield to the flesh, or will I yield to the Spirit?* We can go back to our old ways and disobey God, or we can surrender to the leading of the Spirit and do what is right.

Just to show you how quickly this can happen, right after Peter had said, "You are the Christ, the Son of the living God," the Lord went on to describe His future: He was going to be arrested, crucified, and rise again on the third day. Simon, probably feeling that he was on some kind of a roll, protested and said, "Lord, far be it from you" (Matt. 16:22). He began to rebuke Jesus.

Can you imagine rebuking Jesus? "Lord, now this is the Rock talking!" Peter blurted out. "You gave me a new name.

I have to give You a little career advice. This is a bad move. You don't want to have Yourself crucified. This would be a good time for You to establish Your kingdom. There is no way death could be God's plan for You."

Jesus said to him, "Get behind Me, Satan! You are an offense to Me" (Matt. 16:23). One moment the Father in heaven inspired Peter. The next moment the devil from hell told him what to say.

In the same way, you can do so well spiritually, and then you mess up. You can't believe you did it. You can be driving down the freeway listening to a worship CD, singing, "Lord, I love You so much." Suddenly, some guy cuts you off and you explode with anger, screaming and shaking your fist at him.

It shocks you. *How could I be praising God, then do something like that?* Answer: it is human nature. I am not excusing or justifying it. I am just trying to explain that that nature is always there just beneath the surface, ready to come in for the kill. You need to remember that.

How do you deal with it? Jesus gave us a great example when He said to the spirit that inspired Simon Peter, "Get behind Me, Satan." When the devil comes knocking on your door with the temptation, don't give him the time of day.

The Lord had called Simon. He had given him a new name. But right off the bat, just seconds after the name was official, he did something to contradict it. Instead of acting like the apostle Peter, he behaved far more like Simon.

. . . .
Peter: Humanity 101

That wasn't the only time, either. We learn in Luke 5 that Peter had turned away from following Jesus after a while. The other gospels record that he had already been called by Jesus; he had left his nets and become a disciple. Yet in Luke we see that he, along with his two buddies James and John, had at least temporarily returned to fishing.

Nothing wrong with that. That is what they did for a living; they were hardworking men. Peter still believed in Jesus. He still trusted. The point, however, was that Jesus had called them to be fishers of men; in other words, they had the privilege of being called to serve God and they had basically gone AWOL. They were men who knew better. They were men whom God had marked for His service, and they were not following through.

Jesus did something unique to enter into their little universe and bring them to a point of deeper commitment.

So it was, as the multitude pressed about Him to hear the word of God, that He stood by the Lake of Gennesaret, and saw two boats standing by the lake; but the fishermen had gone from them and were washing their nets.

Then He got into one of the boats, which was Simon's, and asked him to put out a little from the land. And He sat down and taught the multitudes from the boat.

When He had stopped speaking, He said to Simon, "Launch out into the deep and let down your nets for a catch." But Simon answered and said to Him, "Master, we have toiled all night and caught nothing; nevertheless at Your word I will let down the net."

And when they had done this, they caught a great number of fish, and their net was breaking. So they signaled to their partners in the other boat to come and help them. And they came and filled both the boats, so that they began to sink.

When Simon Peter saw it, he fell down at Jesus' knees, saying, "Depart from me, for I am a sinful man, O Lord!" For he and all who were with him were astonished at the catch of fish which they had taken; and so also were James and John, the sons of Zebedee, who were partners with Simon.

And Jesus said to Simon, "Do not be afraid. From now on you will catch men." So when they had brought their boats to land, they forsook all and followed Him. (vv. 1–11)

When Jesus stepped into Simon's boat and asked him to row out a bit, it may have seemed a little forward on Jesus' part. But He had a work He wanted to do in Simon Peter's life. Note that when the Scripture describes Peter in this passage, it starts by using the name "Simon." It is not until verse 8, when Simon fell down at the feet of Jesus, that Scripture refers to him as Simon Peter. There is that conflict of natures. He wasn't acting like the Rock. He was acting like Simon again.

He and his friends had gone back to fishing and had caught nothing. They were not realizing the potential that Jesus had for them. They had no idea what their future would be. Jesus desired to mold them into powerful spiritual leaders who would write the very Scripture we hold in our hands today. They were to be the leaders of His church and evangelists to the world. They quite literally would change their world, and that impact would continue for generations and generations.

But they did not understand or fully appreciate that. He had to whip them into shape first.

When Jesus climbed into the boat and told Peter to row out, Peter was probably waiting for the Lord to wheel around and rebuke him. Jesus didn't. Jesus recognized Peter was a half-hearted follower who needed a personal touch.

I wonder if some of us right now are in the same boat as Peter. By that I mean that you believe in Jesus; you have asked Him to be your Savior and friend. You trust Him for salvation. But are you glorifying Him? Are you really offering your life to God and giving Him control? Are you serving Him as Master and Lord?

. . . .
Whose Honor and Glory Are You After?

Have you ever thought about dedicating your career to God, saying, "Lord, here is what I do for a living. I want to do it to Your glory. I want to find ways in which I can honor You through the skills and abilities You have given me. Lord, here are the talents I have. They may not be a lot, but I am willing to dedicate them to You. Do with them what You will." If you were to do that, it could make all the difference in the world.

Maybe you are like Peter. You have been fishing all night and have caught nothing. You are working hard, yet barely getting by. You have no opportunities, foresee no successes. I am not saying that if you commit your career to Jesus, suddenly you are going to make more money than you can spend. The Lord may prosper you in that way, or you may actually make less for a while. I will say this, though: if you give your work to the Lord, you will be living your life the way God meant you to—to His honor and glory. And when you have done that, you will be your happiest.

There was a film made some years ago called *Chariots of Fire*. It was based in part on the life of Eric Liddell. He was an Olympic runner and one of the fastest men of his time. Eric was also a very committed Christian. It was his desire to go on the mission field and serve the Lord, which he eventually did.

In an early scene in the film, Eric's sister Jenny is concerned that he is still involved in his running when she thought he should already be on the mission field. Eric turned to her and said, "Jenny, I believe God made me for a purpose... But He also made me fast. And when I run, I feel His pleasure."

I loved that line. Not all of us are called to the mission field per se, but all of us are called with a sense of mission. You may be in business, or a stay-at-home mom. You may be a construction worker or a musician. A teacher or a computer programmer. Whatever you do, you can do for the glory of

God. And when you do so, you, like Eric Liddell, will also "feel His pleasure." That is all that matters in the long run. Leave the results in His hands.

. . . .

Only a Personal Encounter Will Do

That's what was happening with Peter. He was in an area of noncommitment. He believed, but he wasn't really giving his all to Jesus. Jesus intervened in a personal way for Peter. Jesus produced a miracle that dazzled the seasoned fisherman.

Understand that Simon Peter had seen miracles already. He had seen his own mother-in-law, who was very ill, restored to health. But none of these miracles necessarily appeared to move him much. Jesus' personalized miracle would convince Peter.

Everybody has to have his own personal encounter with Jesus Christ. No one can live off of somebody else's faith. You can talk until you are blue in the face to someone about his need for Christ. But you need to pray that God will make Himself known to him. It's not your clever arguments that will convince him. Something needs to happen to get his attention, and God will do it.

He did it for Peter. After speaking to the multitudes, Jesus told him, "Launch out into the deep and let down your nets for a catch." Peter said, "Lord, we will let down our net for a catch."

Notice Jesus said "nets," and Peter said "net." Peter had fished those waters since childhood. He knew the most favorable climatic conditions for fishing and when they were most likely to be caught. In Peter's mind, Jesus was basically a landlubber giving him fishing advice. Peter was saying, "Lord, with all due respect, when You open the Word of God we hang on Your every word, but when it comes to fishing, we are men who know what we're doing. We are experienced. This is not something You necessarily know about."

You say, "Greg, how can you read that into the text?" By judging by what Peter did. Jesus said to let down the "nets," and Peter let down a "net." That was not obedience. Partial obedience is disobedience. Of course, then there were so many fish that they were overwhelmed.

We know that because of archeological studies that have found these first-century fishing boats from the time of Christ. They would have been about seven feet wide and about twenty-seven feet long. When Peter and his crew began to pull in the net, two of these boats began to sink. This means they were pulling in tons of fish. It was supernatural, and they knew it.

A boatload of fish may not impress us, but it impressed them because they were fishermen. They knew well this sort of thing did not just happen. God came to them in a way that they could understand.

Peter was overwhelmed with gratitude and guilt when he saw this. He said in Luke 5:8, "Depart from me, for I am a sinful man, O Lord!" In other words, "Lord, You saw me before. You looked right through me and gave me this new name. I hate to disappoint You, but I haven't been the Rock. I have fallen short. I appreciate Your call in my life, but I am only going to disappoint You. Get someone else. Don't waste Your time on me. I am just not worth it."

Have you ever felt that way? Have you felt you were totally inadequate for the task of serving God? Good. You are just the man or woman for whom God is looking. He isn't looking for people who are arrogant or self-sufficient, but people who see themselves for what they really are: deficient and in great need of God's help to get anything done.

This reminds me of Job when he came into God's presence and said, "I have heard of You by the hearing of the ear, / but now my eye sees You. / Therefore I abhor myself, / And repent in dust and ashes" (42:5–6).

Isaiah said something similar: "I saw the Lord sitting on a throne, high and lifted up, and the train of His robe filled the temple. / ... I said, 'Woe is me, for I am undone! / Because I am a man of unclean lips'" (6:1, 5). In the presence of God, Isaiah became immediately aware of his shortcomings. As he saw God for who He was, he saw himself for who he was.

In the same way, Peter saw himself as a sinner, which he was. But this was good because he had come to the end of himself; thus he was coming to the beginning of God.

. . . .
Have You Left All for Him?

How did Jesus respond to Rock's statement? In Luke 5:10 He said, "Do not be afraid. From now on you will catch men." This is an interesting concept. It appears just two times in the Bible, here and in 2 Timothy 2:26, where the apostle Paul talked about those whom Satan had "taken captive to do his will." That phrase "taken captive" could be translated "they are caught alive."

It comes down to this; either the devil is going to catch people alive, or we are going to catch people alive. Either they are under the control of Satan, or under the control of Jesus Christ. That is why the Lord has called us to go fishing for men.

Luke 5:11 says, "They forsook all and followed Him." Have you done that? Perhaps you are still stuck in one spot. You made an initial commitment to Christ, but your old nature has been prevailing. You need to say, "Lord, I turn it over to You. I ask You to do what You want with my life, my marriage, my career. I ask You to be Lord over everything that I have. Be the Master of my life."

If you have said that, like Peter you can enjoy a fruitful life.

You may stumble out of the blocks. You may limp along at times as if you've got two left feet. But Jesus sees potential in you, and He knows you can do it.

In the next chapter we'll see how Simon Peter redeemed a rocky start in his own race.

17

A RACE CRASH

Everyone has taken an unanticipated spill. A number of years ago, I was riding my bicycle to meet my wife at a restaurant for breakfast. Unbeknownst to me, somebody had loosened the little levers that hold the front tire on the bike. When I popped off a curb, crossed a street, and came up to another curb, I pulled up on the handlebars...but the wheel kept going straight. I hit the ground with the forks, flew over the front of the bike, and slammed onto the ground face-first.

I blacked out for a few seconds. When I came to, some man was standing over me, asking, "Are you okay?" I was bloody and bruised. I had lost consciousness.

I thought I was fine, but after a few hours passed I realized I wasn't. I ached everywhere.

In the same way I didn't see that accident coming, we can fail to see a spiritual fall coming. But when people fall away from the Lord, when they crash and burn, they have already taken steps leading up to that event. Maybe they were not fully aware of the steps, but that doesn't change the fact they were taking them. Nobody falls away from the Lord overnight or immediately. There is always a process that unfolds over a period of time.

That is certainly what happened to Simon Peter. We need to remember the fact that his spiritual crash came as no surprise to Jesus—in fact, He warned him specifically of the sin he was about to commit. Yet no one was more shocked when it happened than Peter.

....
A Rock in Progress

We've seen that Simon needed some time to grow into his new name of Peter (the Rock). You will recall that at Caesarea Philippi, Peter had great insight into who Jesus was, declaring, "You are the Christ, the Son of the living God." Jesus commended him and said, "Flesh and blood has not revealed this to you, but My Father who is in heaven" (Matt. 16:16–17).

Not all that long after that, Peter denied the Lord.

That was the story of Peter's life: the man of dual natures. We certainly see into his character at the transfiguration of Jesus. What a glorious moment that must have been as Jesus took Peter, James, and John with Him up a mountain. Suddenly they saw Jesus shining like the sun. On one side of Him was the great law-giver himself, Moses. On the other side the miracle-working prophet Elijah.

Some people say it was a great miracle that Jesus shone like the sun. The miracle was not that Jesus shone on that day, but that He did not shine that way the rest of the time! Remember, He was God in human form. The Transfiguration showed what He really was: God shrouded in human flesh. As the old Christmas hymn so beautifully states:

> Veiled in flesh the Godhead see,
> Hail the incarnate Deity!

Pleased with man with men to dwell,
Jesus our Immanuel.

In that blazing moment, Jesus had an in-depth conversation with Moses and Elijah. Were they discussing His impending death, that He was going to the cross to suffer and die?

Most people would be spellbound at such an event. They would stand in awe, speechless. Peter, however, thought it was a great opportunity to say a few words. He blurted out, "It is good for us to be here; if You wish, let us make here three tabernacles: one for You, one for Moses, and one for Elijah" (Matt. 17:4). Mark's gospel tells us that Peter didn't know what to say, so that's what came out.

You can relate to that. Have you ever said the wrong thing at the wrong time? The moment you said it, you wished you could have taken your words back.

Peter was excited, and he wanted to throw in his two cents' worth. I think the operative word that Peter used is "here": "It is good for us to be *here*." In other words, "Lord, it is time for You to forget about this idea of being crucified. It is time for You to stop talking about going to a cross. This is where You belong. It is on the mount with Moses and Elijah shining like the sun. This is where we need to stay. Let's just stay here on the mountain and bask in Your glory!"

In the same way, sometimes we as Christians want to remove ourselves from the secular culture we are living in and just stay in a place of continual bliss. If it was possible, we would never leave church. Yet we must understand that the purpose of the church is to provide a place for believers to grow and learn. It is a place for us to refocus. It is also a place that helps us to go back out into the world, refreshed and equipped to do battle. It is sort of like a gas station—a place to get refilled and recharged.

I don't know about you, but I don't like to go to gas stations.

My wife likes it even less than I do. I wait until the tank is just above empty and then reluctantly pull over. Some of us treat church that way: *I'll go only when I have to.* If we are wise, we will go for constant refills. Top it off. Get a little bit more. The danger is that we can isolate ourselves from the world to which God has called us. But God has not called us to isolate. He has called us to infiltrate. Jesus did not say that the whole world should go to church. Rather He said that the church should go to the whole world.

Peter was saying, "It is good for us to be here. We want to stay away from that world. We don't want You to go down there, and we don't want to watch You die." But they had to descend from the mountaintop. They had to go back into the real world.

Almost joining the Lord Jesus in correcting the wayward apostle, God the Father chimed in: "A bright cloud overshadowed them; and suddenly a voice came out of the cloud, saying, 'This is My beloved Son, in whom I am well pleased. *Hear Him!*'" (Matt. 17:5). The Father was saying to Peter, "If My Son tells you He must go to Jerusalem to suffer and die, then believe Him. If He tells you to take up your cross and follow Him, that is what you need to do."

. . . .
Just Like Us

I don't know about you, but I'm sure I would've been a bit sheepish if God himself had to reprimand me for speaking out of turn. But that's the way Peter was. He just couldn't seem to keep a low profile. You certainly always knew where you stood with him.

Remember his classic moment when Jesus was walking on the water? I can just picture it. The disciples had endured a rough night on the Sea of Galilee. They were frightened; they despaired of life. Who came strolling up to them on the top of the water but our Lord? Of course the disciples were terrified, and they thought He was a ghost. Jesus said to them, "Take courage! It is I. Don't be afraid" (Matt. 14:27 NIV).

It was another holy moment. It was something to take in. There was the Lord, walking on water. Peter should have savored it.

Instead, again he spoke. "Lord, if it's you, tell me to come to you on the water" (v. 28 NIV).

Now, in Peter's defense, he did ask the Lord's permission first. Jesus then gave it, and Peter did the impossible. When the Lord said, "Come," Peter threw one leg over the side of the boat and set it down on the water. It supported him. He put the other leg over the side and stood up. He took his first step and his second. Then, probably seeing how crazy it was, and taking his eyes off of the Lord and putting them on his circumstances, he began to sink. He cried out, "Lord, save me!" (vv. 29–30 NIV).

That was Peter—always saying what he thought. He was either knocking it out of the park or he was striking out. There was rarely anything in between. Everything he did, he threw himself into wholeheartedly.

. . . .
"Satan Is Asking for You"

Unfortunately, this also included his fall. Peter fell big. All of the disciples were in hiding the night Jesus was taken to be crucified. On one hand, Peter wanted to be close to Jesus, but on the other, he overtly distanced himself from the Lord.

In John 13, we read that the Lord had gathered His disciples in the upper room to discuss some very important matters. It would be their final Passover meal together.

Not surprisingly, the atmosphere wasn't joyful or festive, as other Passovers had been. The tension was so thick you could cut it with a knife.

A storm was brewing, but the disciples did not know exactly what was happening. They could see the burden Jesus was carrying, the pressure closing in on Him. Then the Lord Himself did something completely unexpected. He took off His outer garment, wrapped Himself in a towel, got down on His hands and knees, and with a basin of water, began to wash the disciples' feet.

Can you imagine this? The Creator of the universe, in human form, washing the dirt of the feet of His disciples. That is nothing short of amazing. But what's even more amazing is the fact that He also included the betrayer himself in that foot-washing.

Jesus poured water on and removed the dirt from the feet of Judas Iscariot. The very man, who, in just moments, would coldheartedly leave to complete his act of betrayal.

Jesus, being God, had complete foreknowledge of this, yet in that act of sacrificial love and compassion, He humbled Himself.

As Jesus made His way to each of His boys, the men He had chosen, no doubt a hush filled the room. This was a holy moment. A time to just "be still and know that He is God." But Peter, true to form, had to offer a bit of commentary. Peter protested and told Jesus He would never wash his feet.

In fairness, Peter felt he was too undeserving of such an act of humility from Jesus. Jesus then looked at the protesting Peter and firmly said, "If I do not wash you, you have no part with Me" (John 13:8).

Then the Lord dropped a bombshell on the disciples.

And the Lord said, "Simon, Simon! Indeed, Satan has asked for you, that he may sift you as wheat. But I have prayed for you, that your faith should not fail; and when you have returned to Me, strengthen your brethren."

But he said to Him, "Lord, I am ready to go with You, both to prison and to death."

Then He said, "I tell you, Peter, the rooster shall not crow this day before you will deny three times that you know me." (LUKE 22:31–34)

Can you imagine hearing Jesus say this to you? Put yourself in Peter's sandals for just a moment. Jesus said, "Satan has been asking for you." A literal translation of that phrase would be "Satan has been asking for you specifically by name." Jesus was saying, "Simon, Lucifer, the devil himself, has been personally asking for *you*."

If this would not make your blood cold, I don't know what would.

Fortunately for Peter, Jesus answered the door. "Peter, don't panic. I have prayed for you!" (see Luke 22:32).

In other words, Jesus was saying to His terrified follower that, despite the fact that the very devil of hell was asking for him, he need not be afraid, because Jesus Himself would be there to answer him.(I want you to notice that Satan did have to ask God first. He can do nothing in the life of the child without our Father's permission. God was watching over Peter.)

You might read this and think, *I wish Jesus was standing for me that way too.* He is! Jesus is interceding for you as well. Romans 8:34 says, "Who is he that condemns? Christ Jesus who died—more than that, who was raised to life—is at the right hand of God and is also interceding for us" (NIV). Paul continued, "Who shall separate us from the love of Christ? Shall trouble or hardship or persecution or famine or nakedness or danger or sword?" (v. 35 NIV).

Were it not for the prayers of Jesus, Peter would not have stood a chance. Were it not for the intercession of Jesus, we wouldn't stand a chance either.

What did Jesus pray for Peter? Did He pray that he would not be tempted? Did He pray he wouldn't go through a time of trial? No. He prayed that Peter's faith would not fail. Peter was about to take a graduate-level course in the School of Hard Knocks. He would be a better man for it.

Why did the devil set his sights on the salty fisherman? Simply because he was a mighty instrument in the hand of God. The devil targets leaders today as well—that is why we must pray for them. It is easy to play armchair quarterback and second-guess every decision a leader makes: "If I were the pastor, I would never have done that. If I were the person in charge, I would not have made this decision." Everyone is entitled to his opinion, but you may not be privy to all of the information that went into the decision-making process. Not that every decision every leader makes is right; that is why you ought to pray for each one and understand that they come under attack.

For that matter, any man or woman who is making a difference for the kingdom of God is going to be a candidate for the onslaught of Satan. If God is using you to bring people into the kingdom, to touch people for Jesus Christ, to bring His Word to people, the devil is going to try to bring you down. But remember that Jesus, God's Son, intercedes for you as He did for Peter.

. . . .
Steps to a Fall

Yes, Peter did deny the Lord, just as Jesus said he would. But the steps that led to that denial were subtle and very significant—steps that we can easily follow if we are not careful.

Let's look at the steps that led to Peter's fall, that we may try to avoid them in our own spiritual race.

1. Peter Was Overconfident

According to Matthew's gospel, Peter made this statement: "Even if all are made to stumble because of You, I will never be made to stumble" (26:33). Why did Peter say that? Because Jesus pointed out that one of them was going to be a traitor. Peter thought it was a great opportunity to boast of his love for the Lord. "Judas may betray you, but I will never do anything like that. I will never let You down." Jesus was basically saying, "Well, Peter, since you brought it up: you are going to deny Me *three times*."

You should never boast of your love for the Lord. Rather boast of His love for you. Sometimes I hear people say, "I just love the Lord so much." That is good. But I would rather boast of how much the Lord loves me. My love can be so fickle, so hot or cold, depending upon my mood. In contrast, God's love is consistent.

I love the way the apostle John described himself in his gospel: "the disciple whom Jesus loved"(see John 13:23).Some might critique John for saying that because it implies Jesus loved him more than the others. I disagree. Would you rather he said that he was the apostle that *loved Jesus*? Instead of boasting of his love for the Lord, he boasted of the Lord's love for him. That is a smart thing to do.

You know what? You, too, are a disciple Jesus loves.

Peter was boasting of his dedication, of his commitment, of his tenacity. His first step down was overconfidence. In speaking those words, Peter was not only revealing an unfounded faith in himself, but he also was directly contradicting the Lord's prediction that he would deny him. What he should have said was, "Lord, I have a hard time believing I am capable of such a thing, but You said it, therefore it is true."

Instead he said, "Jesus, You are wrong. No way. Even though You are the Creator and Truth incarnate and know all things, You are wrong on this thing. I know me. I know that

I will not deny You." No, Peter did not know himself as well as he thought.

Nor do you or I. Nobody knows you better than Jesus.

Mark's gospel records that Peter repeatedly insisted on his loyalty. At first blush, this could almost seem commendable, but in fact it was sinful. He was full of himself. When you see somebody fall into a sin like lust or greed, at the foundation of that sin was overconfidence. By that I mean the one who fell was probably a person who said, "I would never do such a thing. No matter what, I would never cave in to such a temptation. I am above that."

Be careful. Know that you have this vulnerability, even a propensity toward doing the wrong thing.

In Scripture many men who were known for one trait were also known for its opposite. For instance, when you think of Elijah the prophet, what comes to mind? Courage. Bravery. We remember his facing off with the prophets of Baal on Mount Carmel. We also recall that Elijah fled in panic and sank into depression when he heard a threat from Queen Jezebel. This man who was known for courage also was filled with fear.

What comes to mind when you think of the great patriarch Abraham? Faith. But we know that Abraham had lapses. On one occasion he asked his wife, Sarah, to say she was his sister because he was afraid the strangers whose land they were visiting would kill him to get her. Then he had sexual relations with Sarah's handmaid, Hagar, instead of waiting on the Lord for the fulfillment of his promise to give a child to Abraham and Sarah.

We need to realize that any great strength we have can also be an area of weakness. We all need a good dose of reality when it comes to our vulnerability for doing the wrong thing— regardless of how many years we have known the Lord.

2. Peter Was Prayerless

Look at Luke 22:39–46.

> Coming out, He went to the Mount of Olives, as He was accustomed, and His disciples also followed Him. When He came to the place, He said to them, "Pray that you may not enter into temptation." And He was withdrawn from them about a stone's throw, and He knelt down and prayed, saying, "Father, if it is Your will, take this cup away from Me; nevertheless not My will, but Yours, be done." Then an angel appeared to Him from heaven, strengthening Him.
>
> And being in agony, He prayed more earnestly. Then His sweat became like great drops of blood falling down to the ground. When He rose up from prayer, and had come to His disciples, He found them sleeping from sorrow. Then He said to them, "Why do you sleep? Rise and pray, lest you enter into temptation."

This was a direct result of the first sin of overconfidence. Even after Jesus had specifically instructed Peter, James, and John to pray, they decided to sleep instead. Granted, they were emotionally and spiritually drained from the events of the day. They were sleeping "from sorrow," the Bible tells us. This probably means they cried themselves to sleep. But our Lord had specifically told them to pray not to enter into temptation, and that the flesh was weak. Peter, James, and John should have been on high alert. Clearly the Lord was warning that something significant was coming.

In the same way, we often pray when we think we need to, but we don't when things seem to be stable and secure. That is human nature for you. We need to pray in the good times as well as the bad. Paul said we should pray at all times (1 Thess. 5:17).

While the three disciples were sawing logs and counting

sheep, Judas, the temple guard, and Roman soldiers appre-
hended the Lord. Judas Iscariot betrayed him with a kiss.
When Peter awoke, he was outraged. How dare Judas do this to
Jesus! "Don't worry, Lord, I will defend you! Rock is here!"

He started swinging his sword and cut off a bystander's ear
in the process. Soldiers led the Lord away, and Peter's world
came crashing down.

Because of prayerlessness, Peter was unprepared for the
very temptation of which Jesus spoke.

3. Peter Followed at a Distance

Luke 22:54: "Having arrested Him, they led Him, and brought
Him into the high priest's house. But Peter followed at a distance."

This distance from the Lord in closeness and fellowship is
always at the foundation of all spiritual regression. Granted,
Peter was following, but not closely.

Here is Simon Peter's dual nature once again. On one hand,
he was terrified of what others would say about him. On the
other hand, he wanted to be close to Jesus—just not as close
as he had been before. At best, at that moment, Peter's was a
halfhearted commitment.

Many people like Peter go to church. Granted, they are
there, but they are following at a distance. This kind of person
often sits at the very back of the church and is the last one in
and first one out. During the time of worship, he doesn't sing.
When the offering plate is passed, he keeps his hands in his
pockets. He doesn't want to engage. He wouldn't even think of
going to a midweek Bible study. He gives only his bare mini-
mum to the Lord. His is a halfhearted commitment.

It is so sad when people do that. They miss out on what God
wants to do in their lives. They miss out on all that church
could be to them, and all they could be to the church. Yes, they
are following, but they do so from a distance.

Have you ever noticed in nature-type programs on TV that the animal that ends up being picked off is usually the animal that has strayed from the rest of the pack? He is vulnerable. He is weak. He is an easy target. He is lunch.

Whom do you think the devil is going to pounce on? It is easiest to bring down someone who is following at a distance—someone who is separated from fellow believers.

4. Peter Warmed Himself by the Enemy's Fire

At the courtyard of Caiaphas, the Lord was being falsely charged in a kangaroo court of gross injustice. People were gathered around, warming themselves by a fire in the courtyard.

The chill of sin is strong, and the warmth of trust Peter had known before was shattered by his denial. Peter was hoping to go unnoticed in the large crowd. He stepped near the fire.

At that point, he was worn down, weak, and vulnerable. He was a train wreck waiting to happen. To Peter's eternal credit, at least he was there, but only at a distance, and, frankly, he had run out of ideas. He was just waiting for the end of this nightmare to finally come.

Matthew's gospel says that Peter sat down with the servants at Caiaphas's house to watch the proceedings. Peter was at the wrong place with the wrong people, about to do the wrong thing. It wasn't the fire itself that was bad. It was the people around the fire. He was in a place where he shouldn't have been.

5. Peter Tried to Escape Reality

Luke 22:56–57: "And a certain servant girl, seeing him as he sat by the fire, looked intently at him, and said, 'This man was also with Him.' But he denied Him, saying, 'Woman, I do not know Him.'"

Peter was already busted. He could not escape recognition, but he tried to take refuge in a lie.

6. Peter Remained Among the Enemy

Luke 22:58: "And after a little while another saw him and said, 'You also are of them.' But Peter said, 'Man, I am not!'"

Note that a little time had passed. Peter had had some minutes or perhaps even an hour or two to think about his first denial and the spiritual danger he was in. Yet he stayed put among the enemy. Not only had he denied knowing Jesus; then he denied being one of His disciples.

7. Peter Lost All Awareness of God

Luke 22:59–60: "Then after about an hour had passed, another confidently affirmed, saying, 'Surely this fellow also was with Him, for he is a Galilean.' But Peter said, 'Man, I do not know what you are saying!'"

Galileans didn't normally hang around near Jerusalem, especially in the courtyard of Caiaphas. To those in the sophisticated city, a Galilean was akin to what we might refer to as a "country bumpkin." That is what the person said to Peter: "You are a *Galilean.*" If we were to put it in our modern vernacular, it would be like calling someone "trailer trash" or worse. There was disdain in the person's voice.

According to Matthew's gospel, at that point Peter "began to curse and swear" (Matt. 26:74). This does not mean that he swore like a sailor (though he was one); Peter was taking an oath. It is an interesting phrase that means "to pronounce death on one's self by the hand of God if he is lying." Peter essentially said, "May God kill me if I am not speaking the truth." That is taking the Lord's name in vain.

Peter had lost all sense of reality and awareness of God. Luke 22:60–62:

Immediately, while he was still speaking, the rooster crowed. And the Lord turned and looked at Peter. Then Peter remembered the word of the Lord, how He had said to him, "Before the rooster crows, you will deny Me three times." And Peter went out and wept bitterly.

Jesus looked at him. Can you imagine this scene? Put yourself there if you can. Peter has denied the Lord three times. Now he has called down God's judgment on himself if he has been lying. The rooster crows. He spins around, and there stands Jesus, looking right into his eyes. Can you feel the intensity of that gaze—the feelings it ignited in Peter?

Did the denial come as a shock or a surprise to Jesus? Absolutely not. Did this denial come as a shock and surprise to Simon Peter? Absolutely. But the Lord knew he would fail. He predicted it.

Did Peter let the Lord down? Yes. Did Peter deny the Lord? Yes. Was he still a believer? Was he still loved by Jesus? Yes. Peter needed to remember what else the Lord said to him: "And when you have returned to Me, go and strengthen your brethren" (Luke 22:32). In other words, "The setback is going to be temporary, and you will be back."

Remember, God gives second chances. He gives third, fourth, and fifth ones. Remember, nobody is above falling into sin.

. . . .
Peter Is All Too Familiar

Maybe some of us can identify with the failings of this great follower of Jesus. Maybe right now you are where he was: in some way, you have denied the Lord. Maybe you have fallen into some gross sin, and you need God's forgiveness today.

Then again, maybe you are somewhere along the road Peter traveled. You are not quite at the bottom, but you are headed there. Overconfident, prayerless, following Jesus only at a distance, drawing near and camping out by the enemy's fire: you are flirting with disaster. You are walking along a precipice.

The race no longer seems as enticing as the sin that is calling your name.

Don't mistake Peter's restoration to Jesus as an excuse to sin. Remember the agony he felt in catching Jesus' gaze at the courtyard. His was an intensely painful fall, and it took a miracle to restore him to his Savior. Don't let that happen to you.

Run the race. Stay on the right track. If you crash, recover. Jump up and get back in the race. Go for the prize.

Let's see how Peter pursued his own prize.

18

A COMPASSIONATE COACH

Have you ever failed miserably in life? You wanted your marriage to thrive, and it has ended in divorce. You had hoped that one day you would get a degree from a leading university, but you had to drop out for some reason. You were hoping you would be very successful in business at this point in life, but you are fighting for survival.

Maybe you set goals in your spiritual life as well. You hoped to be at a certain place right now spiritually—stable, invested in others' lives, full of purpose—that you have not reached. You have faced failure after failure, so many that you have even begun to wonder if you are a child of God. You have questioned whether you really love the Lord or not.

If this is the case, you're in good company. As we've seen, one of Jesus' closest followers felt this way after he denied the Lord. Yet we know Peter went on to preach the gospel to thousands, to author two books of the Bible, to become a powerful apostle of the Lord. Something had to happen between those disastrous denials and his eventual glory.

What happened for Peter can happen also for you.

· ·

It's Raining Regrets

The last sight Simon Peter had of his Lord was of Him hanging on a cross, beaten and bloodied beyond recognition. Poor Peter. All that he held dear was placed in a tomb. He had so many regrets. He wanted to say that he was sorry.

You know what this is like if you have experienced the sudden death of a loved one. You think about your last conversation and encounter with him; maybe you had a disagreement, or you just didn't leave on the best terms. You deeply regret that. You wish you could tell that person how much you loved him. Imagine how Simon felt—not only that he had blown it big with Jesus, but he couldn't even sustain the thought of forgiveness. It seemed impossible.

Of course, three days later our Lord rose from the dead. An angel outside His tomb told Mary Magdalene, "Go, tell His disciples—and Peter—that He is going before you into Galilee; there you will see Him" (Mark 16:7). One could interpret that statement two ways—as a promise of coming revenge or one of hope and encouragement. Clearly it was the latter.

Peter did indeed encounter the Lord, and they spent time together we don't know much about because the Scripture doesn't address it. We can be confident that it was there that the Lord forgave Peter and pardoned him for all of his sin.

As the story begins, we read: "Simon Peter said to them, 'I am going fishing.' They said to him, 'We are going with you also.' They went out and immediately got into the boat, and that night they caught nothing" (John 21:3).The disciples had fished all night. They didn't know what else to do at that point. The Lord had risen. He had been making appearances to various disciples. But he had delivered no clear marching orders, so they went back to what they knew how to do: fish. But once again, they were pulling up nothing but empty nets.

It was a picture the Lord was going to draw on: the futility and uselessness of living without His direction and blessing. Sometimes God will not let you get what you want. You will try to achieve something, and the Lord will simply say no. Other times, God will allow you to accomplish your goals to teach you a lesson. As the Scripture says of the nation Israel, "He gave them their request / But sent leanness into their soul" (Ps. 106:15). As has been said, "There are two sources of unhappiness in life. One is not getting what you want, and the other is getting it."

Sometimes success can be a form of failure. What cost did you pay to achieve it? Deception? Betrayal? Abandoning your principles? Sacrificing your integrity? Neglecting your family and friends? Forgetting or perhaps even denying Christ? If so, your so-called success is a glaring failure.

This is what was happening with the disciples and especially with Peter. They had failed, in a sense, by abandoning Jesus at the cross. But remember, failure can often be the doorway that leads to real success.

What is success, anyway? How would you classify successful people? We would probably say they are wealthy, powerful, popular, and they have others' respect. If we applied those standards to Jesus Christ, would we say He was a success? Was Jesus popular? For a time, He was. But the fickle multitudes soon turned against Him.

Was Jesus a person who had a lot of friends? For a time, He did. When trouble came, most of them ran for cover. Did Jesus have money and possessions? We know He didn't have a home or a place to hang His hat (so to speak). We know He had a single garment that people gambled over after his crucifixion.

Did Jesus' peers respect Him? If you classify His peers as the religious leaders of the day, the answer would have to be no.

Despite these apparent failures, Jesus Christ has changed

millions of lives over the centuries. In the world's eyes, maybe He was a failure, but in God's eyes He was the ultimate success. He accomplished the Father's goals.

Now He was saying to His own disciples, to Peter, "You have had some failures. Let Me teach you through them."

....

The Other Side of Failure

An interesting scenario unfolded that early morning. John 21:4: "But when the morning had now come, Jesus stood on the shore; yet the disciples did not know that it was Jesus." A figure stood on the beach, which was not uncommon. Often those who sold the fish in the market waited there for the fishermen to bring in the catch.

"Then Jesus said to them, 'Children, have you any food?' They answered him, 'No'" (John 21:5). A better translation would be, "*Boys,* did you catch anything?" I like the word *boys.* It is a word you would use only with someone you knew well. It implies a parental role. You can imagine the disciples bristling. "Who's He calling 'boys'? We are adult men." I wonder what Peter was thinking—perhaps that he deserved to be called a child?

Why did Jesus ask this question? He wanted the disciples to answer it. He wanted them to admit their failure. But why?

So He could bring them to the other side of failure.

God often asks probing questions. After Adam's sin, what did the Lord ask? "Adam, have you eaten of the tree that I commanded you not to eat of?" Was God ignorant of what Adam had done? No. Why did God ask the question? He wanted confession.

Remember, after Elijah had his great encounter with the prophets of Baal up on Mount Carmel, Queen Jezebel threatened him. He hid in a cave. The Lord came to Elijah and asked,

"What are you doing here?" Why did God ask him that question? He wanted Elijah to acknowledge his real condition.

In the same way Jesus asked Peter and the disciples, "Did you catch anything? Have you been successful? Have things gone the way you had hoped? Are you satisfied?"

They needed to say, "No, Lord. We are not satisfied. We have not been successful." Then he could say, "Then do it My way": "And He said to them, 'Cast the net on the right side of the boat, and you will find some.' So they cast, and now they were not able to draw it in because of the multitude of fish" (John 21:6).

John, the spiritually perceptive one, exclaimed, "It is the Lord!" (v. 7). Peter was so excited that he jumped out of the boat and swam to shore. He couldn't wait to get close to Jesus.

"Then, as soon as they had come to land, they saw a fire of coals there, and fish laid on it, and bread. Jesus said to them, 'Bring some of the fish which you have just caught'" (John 21:9–10). This amazes me. The Lord who had been crucified and risen again was making breakfast for His boys. You would think He had better things to do. Certainly He didn't need their fish. He could have spoken that breakfast into existence.

But instead He said, "Bring Me the fish you have caught." What do we learn from this? God doesn't need us, but He wants our participation in the work He is doing. Jesus had fish already, but he said, "Bring yours too. Let Me prepare it. Let Me serve you."

That must have been an interesting moment. No one knew quite what to say. There was probably an awkward silence as they slowly chewed their food. There in the fire's flicker, Peter may have been flashing back to his earlier denial and the moment when he and Jesus met each other's glance.

Peter most likely felt a searing shame. His heart was broken for what he had done, but it was so good to be near Jesus again.

....

Steps Leading Back to Success

Finally the Lord broke the silence with this probing question: "Simon, son of Jonah, do you love Me?" Notice that He didn't say, "Simon Peter." Remember, Jesus used the names Simon and Peter interchangeably, depending on how the fisherman was behaving. Simon had not been behaving like a rock lately. So Jesus asked, "Simon, do you love Me?"

This is interesting. If we were going to try to determine a person's spirituality, we would probably want to know about his theology. What are his views on this or that topic? We would want to know if he had been obedient to God. These are valid issues, and we should look for them in another believer's life.

But Jesus did not say, "Simon, are you theologically correct?" Nor did He ask Peter, "Are you full of faith?" or "Have you been obedient?" Rather, the Lord said, "Do you love Me?"

Why is that significant? If you really love the Lord, you will want to be doctrinally correct. You will want to study His Word. If you really love the Lord, you really will grow in your faith. If you love the Lord, it will be your delight to obey Him. Love for God is at the basis of everything else. If you don't love God, nothing else much matters.

That is why the Lord said:

"You must love the Lord your God with all your heart, all your soul, and all your mind." This is the first and greatest commandment. A second is equally important: "Love your neighbor as yourself." All the other commandments and all

the demands of the prophets are based on these two commandments. (MATT 22:37–40 NLT)

. . . .
Three Questions, Three Tests

There are three tests in the questions Jesus asked Peter.

Test 1: Have You Learned Anything?

The first question, "Do you love Me more than these?" meant
"Are you still the same boastful Simon of a few days ago?"
I think the old Peter would have said, "Do I love You more
than these? Are You kidding? Do fish swim? Of course I do. I
am Your most devoted disciple on the face of the earth."

But the new, improved, repentant Simon Peter, who had
gotten a glimpse of how weak he was, simply said, "Lord, I
love You."

Jesus accepted that answer. He said in response, "Feed My
sheep." Allow me to loosely paraphrase: "Very good. You got
that right. Feed My sheep."

What does it mean to feed sheep? Jesus was saying, "I am
commissioning you to service. I am calling you to tend the
flock. Up to this point you have been a fisher of men, but now
I am calling you to be a tender of sheep." This was an investment in Peter's life. It was an acknowledgment that Jesus was
recommissioning Peter to service.

Test 2: Do You Love Me with a Sacrificial Love?

Again, Jesus asked Peter, "Do you love me?" (v.16). In the
original language, different words for *love* were used. Jesus
was using the Greek word *agape*. Peter was using the Greek
word *phileo*.

Agape is a very important word in the New Testament.
Paul's definition of the word *love* in 1 Corinthians 13 is the
Greek word *agape*. When you read, "Greater love has no one

than this, than to lay down one's life for his friends," that is *agape* (John 15:13). "For God so *agaped* [or loved] the world that He gave His only begotten Son" (John 3:16). Agape love speaks of an all-consuming, sacrificial, 100 percent love. It is the highest of all loves because it is utterly unselfish.

Jesus asked, "Peter do you *agape* Me? Do you have a sacrificial, all-consuming, dedicated love?" Peter answered, "Lord, I *phileo* You."

Phileo refers to brotherly love. It is the kind you have for a close friend or companion. It is not unconditional. You basically *phileo*-love people with whom you like to spend time. It is a give-and-take love. Jesus asked, "Do you have this *agape* all-consuming love?" Peter answered, "Lord, I love You like a brother."

In our English vernacular, the conversation would be this: "Do you love Me?" "Lord, I like You."

In high school, if a girl you loved said to you, "I love you like a friend," she was really saying, "Forget about it." That was her nice way of trying to let you down easily.

You must be thinking, "Peter should have said he *agape*-loved the Lord." But I think Peter's answer was just right. He was saying, "Lord, all I can commit to is this. I can't trust myself with more right now." If Jesus were dissatisfied with the answer, He would have said so. Rather He accepted Peter's answer; we know this because He responded by saying, "Tend my sheep. That is good enough, Peter."

Test 3: Is Your Love for Me Real, or Just Words?

Jesus questioned Peter a third time. This time Jesus used the same word Peter used: "Peter, do you *phileo* Me? Do you love Me like a friend? Are you sure about this? Have you thought this through?"

This irritated Peter. In John 21:17, he answered, "Lord, You know all things; You know that I love You." In other words,

"Lord, You know. You know what is in my heart. To the best of my ability, I love You."

Are you disappointed in Peter's response? I would rather see this than someone boast about a nonexistent love for God. The proof is in the pudding. We can talk all day long about how much we love God, but the Lord is looking for action. He is looking for reality, not boastful words.

Peter had learned a lesson. He said, "I am not going to boast about my love for You anymore. I am going to just say I like You a lot." The bottom line? Peter did love the Lord. Peter did indeed *agape* the Lord Jesus. His courageous preaching on the Day of Pentecost in the book of Acts proves this. The suffering he endured for preaching the gospel proves this. Peter was martyred for his faith—this proves he loved the Lord.

But that day, face-to-face with Jesus, he was communicating, "Lord, I want to try to demonstrate it to You from this point on. I am tired of talking about it. Let me show it to You."

. . . .
How to Know If Your Love Is Real

Let's bring it to our world. Let's say Jesus Christ was sitting next to you right now. He turns to you and asks, "Do you love Me?" What would you say? "Yes, Lord, I love You." That is a good answer if you mean it.

How can you tell if you really love the Lord? Let me give to you five litmus tests to determine whether or not you love God.

1. You Long for Personal Communion with God
King David wrote:

> My soul thirsts for you;
> my whole body longs for you

in this parched and weary land
    where there is no water.
I have seen you in your sanctuary
    and gazed upon your power and glory.
Your unfailing love is better to me than life itself;
    how I praise you!
I will honor you as long as I live,
    lifting up my hands to you in prayer.
(PSALM 63:1–4 NLT)

This is a man who was in love with God. A person who loves the Lord will delight in communion with God.

How do we commune with God? If you really love the Lord, you will have an active prayer life. If you really love the Lord, you will open up His Word and see what it has to say to you. It is not a duty. It is a delight. It should not be a drudgery. It should be your heartfelt desire. In church, it will be your joy, not your burden, to worship God.

This is so important. The last time you went to church, were you looking forward to a time of worship? Were you anticipating hearing a message from the Word of God? Were you looking forward to having fellowship with your Christian friends? Were you anticipating the offering as your opportunity to contribute to God's work?

All of these are acts of worship, of personal communion with God.

2. You Love the Things the Lord Loves

The psalmist wrote, "Oh, how I love Your law! / It is my meditation all the day" (119:97). If you love God, you will love the Word of God. You will love the church.

I have heard people say, "I love the Lord, but I can't stand Christians." I know the church has its flaws. We are just sinners saved by grace. Don't expect perfection from everyone.

You need to love the church; the church is God's people. If you really love the Lord, you will love His people as He does.

If you really love the Lord, you will also love lost people. The Lord's heart aches for them as well.

3. You Hate the Things He Hates

Did you know there is a place for hatred in the Christian life? What are we to hate? Psalm 97:10 says, "You that love the LORD, hate evil! / He protects the lives of his Godly people / and rescues them from the power of the wicked" (NLT). Paul wrote in Romans 12:9, "Abhor what is evil. Cling to what is good." God hates sin, and we should do the same.

We are often fascinated by evil. It is not that we want to participate in it, but we kind of like to look at it. When you are stopped in backed-up traffic on the freeway because there has been an accident, do you take a long look at it as you drive by?

Sometimes we do that with sin. We think, *I would never do such a thing. That is horrible. But, just look at it.* Watch out now. Romans 1:32 says that it is not only wrong to do these things, but to take pleasure in those who do them.

4. You Long for the Return of Jesus Christ

Paul said in 2 Timothy 4:8, "There is laid up for me a crown of righteousness, which the Lord, the righteous Judge, will give to me on that Day, and not to me only but to all who have loved His appearing."

If you are a true Christian, you will love His appearing. You should look forward to the day when Christ comes back. When you are reminded that Jesus is coming soon, it should send joy to your heart. If you find instead that you have a sense of dread, remorse, or fear, something is not right with you spiritually. A man or woman who is walking with the Lord will look forward to the Lord's return.

5. *You Keep His Commandments*

Jesus said in John 14:21, "He who has My commandments and keeps them, it is he who loves Me. And he who loves Me will be loved by My Father, and I will love him and manifest Myself to Him." Those who love the Lord do what God tells them to do.

. . . .

How About You?

Peter, I believe, passed all five tests with flying colors. As a result, Jesus recommissioned him for service.

Do you need to be recommissioned today? Do you need to be restored? Maybe you have failed the Lord recently. You have done things of which you are ashamed. You know what Peter must have felt: you've been reluctant to look at Jesus. You are hesitant to go to church because of the shame in your life.

You need to get right with God. Jesus is asking you and me, "Do you love Me?" If you do, then you need to get on with the business of walking with and obeying Him. These things cannot take the place of love, but if you love Him, you should certainly do them. God will restore and forgive you if you will come to Him.

What did Peter have to do first? He had to admit his condition. You need to admit your failure. Then you need to say, "Lord, I want to do it Your way. I am not going to pledge some great love that I am not sure I have. I am going to come with all I do have to You. Here I am."

If you will go to God like that, He will forgive you. Perhaps you once received a distinct call of God on your life—a specific goal to race toward. Maybe the path has been much rougher than you expected, and you are off course. God's Holy Spirit is bringing it to the forefront of your mind as you read this.

God would like to recommission you today—put you back on the track with fresh energy and renewed hope. Come back.

Give what love you have to Him, and watch Him multiply it. Yes, Simon grew into that name Peter in time. He stumbled in the race of life, but he got back up again and he was a winner in the race of life.

If you are down, it's time to get up. It's time to grow into your new name: Christian.

19
GOD'S STOPWATCH

Have you ever misused your time? Maybe you bought a car or house on impulse. Maybe you signed a contract you did not carefully read. Maybe you entered a business deal with someone you didn't know well enough. Maybe you got married without seeking the Lord about it first. Whatever the case, you are sorry you did it now.

Ecclesiastes 3:1 says, "There is a time for everything, / a season for every activity under heaven " (NLT). Timing is important in the race of life as well. The fastest runner wins—the one who finishes as well as he started gets the prize. I have come to discover that just as important as the will of God is the timing of God.

This is something a certain biblical character had to learn. This guy had really bad timing. If he were in a race, he would have come out of nowhere to take the lead—then suddenly fallen hard. So hard, in fact, you would never have expected him to get up again. But he did. His name was Moses.

. . . .

More Than a Movie

If you were to draw up a short list of men God has used in a powerful way, Moses would be at the top: Moses the great law-giver. Moses, the man who through his personal godliness and integrity kept three million people from turning to idolatry. Perhaps the best description of all: Moses the man of God.

It is hard for us to take Moses off of his pedestal. We see him engraved in stone by a great artist like Michelangelo with light emanating from him. We see him in *The Prince of Egypt* as a powerful youth. We see him portrayed by Charlton Heston in *The Ten Commandments* parting the Red Sea. It is difficult to separate fact from fiction.

Yes, Moses was one of the greatest men of God—one who ran to win the prize—but he also was a man who endured serious setbacks and committed a serious sin or two. It is worth noting that, along with Saul of Tarsus, Moses is one of the men God used who was guilty of the very sin of murder.

Moses was born during hard times for the Jewish people. As you recall, they were living as slaves in Egypt. They were about three million strong, so naturally the pharaoh thought of them as a potential threat. He did his best to quell the people's growing power: he told the midwives that when a Jewish woman gave birth to a son, they were to kill the baby and declare it stillborn. The midwives feared the Lord and would not do it. In frustration, the pharaoh decreed that all Jewish baby boys were to be drowned in the Nile River. That's how bad things had gotten.

God once made a promise that still stands today. Years before he had said to Abraham, speaking of the Jews:

I will make you a great nation;
  I will bless you
And make your name great.

I will bless those who bless you,
And I will curse him who curses you. (GEN. 12:2-3)

Satan has been busy over the years attacking and seeking to exterminate the Jewish race, because they are God's chosen people. There is another reason that Satan hates the Jews: he knew that through them the Messiah would come. The battle lines were drawn clear back in the book of Genesis. After the serpent beguiled Adam and Eve, the Lord told Satan one was coming who "will crush your head, and you will strike his heel" (Gen. 3:15 NLT). The devil knew a Deliverer was coming for Israel. The pharaoh's killing the Jewish baby boys was Satan's attempt to stop the Messiah, who eventually arose from the Jews.

The Jewish people were suffering. They were crying out day and night to God for deliverance. Enter Moses the man of God.

. . . .
Beautiful Boy

As soon as Moses was born, his parents knew he was special. The Bible says he was "beautiful" and that his mother, Jochebed, hid him successfully for three months. She knew she couldn't hide him forever, so she came up with a plan: waterproof a basket, place Moses in it, and put it in the river. She trusted in the providence of God to protect him.

Sometimes in the retelling of the story, the facts get changed. Some say Jochebed sent Moses downstream in his basket. The Bible says, however, that she placed that little basket in the reeds by the edge of the Nile. She knew that would be a good place for him because she knew what happened in that particular spot on a regular basis.

Timing was everything—even a matter of life or death.

Then the daughter of Pharaoh came down to bathe at the river. And her maidens walked along the riverside; and when she saw the ark among the reeds, she sent her maid to get it.

And when she opened it, she saw the child, and behold, the baby wept. So she had compassion on him, and said, "This is one of the Hebrews' children."

Then his sister said to Pharaoh's daughter, "Shall I go and call a nurse for you from the Hebrew women, that she may nurse the child for you?" And Pharaoh's daughter said to her, "Go."

So the maiden went and called the child's mother. Then Pharaoh's daughter said to her, "Take this child away and nurse him for me, and I will give you your wages." So the woman took the child and nursed him.

And the child grew, and she brought him to Pharaoh's daughter, and he became her son. So she called his name Moses, saying, "Because I drew him out of the water."

(EXODUS 2:5–10)

You have to love Jochebed, the mother of Moses. She was apparently aware of the fact that the pharaoh's daughter bathed every day at that particular bank of the Nile. I think she intentionally positioned that little basket there, hoping this royal woman would rescue her son. She could not be certain of what would happen, but she certainly took practical steps to save her child.

Sometimes we say, "Lord, I need You to provide for me. I need money to pay the rent. I need food. I am praying You will provide it." We say this as we are kicked back in the reclined position in our La-Z-Boys, watching television. What we ought to be doing is looking through the want ads for employment. And as we are handing out our résumés to prospective employers, we should pray. Sometimes we pray, but we don't take practical steps.

I think Jochebed knew that her son's fate was ultimately in the hands of God, but she wanted to do her best to save him as well. Her plan went smoothly. She even got paid for nursing her own son! Everything worked out beautifully.

. . . .

An Inauspicious Beginning

In Acts 7 we learn that "Moses was taught all the wisdom of the Egyptians, and he became mighty in both speech and action" (v. 22 NLT).

The Jewish historian Josephus tells us the pharaoh had no son or heir; therefore Moses was groomed to become the next king of Egypt. He was raised as a royal person. He was schooled in all Egypt had to offer.

At that time in history, Egypt was a marvel. It was highly developed. The people had extensive knowledge in engineering, mathematics, and astronomy. That very knowledge of astronomy helped them develop an amazingly accurate calendar. Their engineers planned and supervised the construction of edifices that still stand today, such as the pyramids and the Sphinx. As we look at Egyptian antiquities, we marvel at the skill and craftsmanship. They were also experts in embalming. Their sophistication was impressive.

Moses learned the way of Egyptian military tactics, art, music, painting, philosophy, law, and even their religion. He learned about the thousands of gods that the Egyptians worshiped. They believed that the Nile River was a god. They believed animals were a god. They even believed Pharaoh was a god. Pretty much, you name it, they worshiped it.

In the midst of all of this, Moses knew who he was. He was a true believer in the Lord God. Underneath those Egyptian robes of royalty beat the heart of a Jew. And he wanted to get out.

You might say Moses should have played it cool; if he had

laid low—if he'd hung back until the final turn and then snuck up from the outside—he could have become the pharaoh of Egypt and released the Jews. But for him that would have been a compromise. Deep inside, he knew living compromised in the very lap of Egyptian luxury and comfort was bringing him down spiritually. He saw the mistreatment of his fellow Jews while he was living in wealth and extravagance. He had to do something.

Hebrews 11 tells us:

> It was by faith that Moses, when he grew up, refused to be treated as the son of Pharaoh's daughter. He chose to share the oppression of God's people instead of enjoying the fleeting pleasures of sin. He thought it was better to suffer for the sake of the Messiah than to own the treasures of Egypt, for he was looking ahead to the reward that God would give him. (VV. 24–26 NLT)

Moses' heart was in the right place, but his choices were foolhardy, to say the least. When he took action, it was one of the worst mistakes of his life.

> Now it came to pass in those days, when Moses was grown, that he went out to his brethren and looked at their burdens. And he saw an Egyptian beating a Hebrew, one of his brethren. So he looked this way and that way, and when he saw no one, he killed the Egyptian and hid him in the sand. (EXODUS 2:11–12)

Clearly the Lord had not told Moses to do this. Notice how the passage says, "He looked this way and that way." He should have looked *up*. If he had done that, the Lord would have said no. God wants us to do His will in His way in His time. Sometimes we want the will of God, but we will go about it in our own way, according to our own timetable.

. . . .

God's Will in God's Way

I read about a guy who decided to rob a Baptist church. He grabbed the loot and tried to escape through a bathroom window. At six feet and 235 pounds, he required four police officers' pushing and pulling to get him out. That's about how subtle Moses was when he tried to bury the guy in the sand. It was Moses who later said in Numbers 32:23, "Your sin will find you out."

Are you trying to cover up something? Is there a secret sin in your life? May I make a suggestion? Just confess it. Otherwise, sooner or later, it will be exposed. Nothing is hidden from God.

. . . .

A Leader in Training

Moses probably thought his fellow Jews would applaud his act of courage. He was hoping they would say, "That Moses is something. Here he is the son of the pharaoh, but he risks everything to help us. He is our hero." Things didn't go as he had hoped.

The next day he saw a couple of fellow Hebrews arguing. When he tried to settle the argument, they said, "Who made you a prince and a ruler over us? Are you going to kill us the way you did that Egyptian yesterday?" Moses realized that everybody knew. He thought he had hidden his sin, but it was on the front page of the Egyptian *National Inquirer*. He realized he was in trouble.

He was right. When the pharaoh heard about it, he said, "Moses is a dead man." Moses had to flee for his life, and he escaped to the desert.

Now it could have looked as if Moses' chance at leadership was over—that he'd blown it. Not true. It wasn't that Moses wasn't leader material; it was just that he needed time. Moses was a leader in training. He wasn't ready yet.

People often ask, "How can I become a leader in the church?" The best course of action is to serve wherever you can. A good leader needs to learn how to be a good servant first. You should also try leading to see if anyone follows you. If not, maybe you aren't a leader. At least not yet.

You may, however, be a leader in training.

Moses was gifted to be a leader, but he wasn't quite ready. He had to flee for his life. He had lost everything: his position, his people, his reputation. But he had not lost God. Moses made a huge mess for himself, but God had not turned against him. What looked like the end of his life was actually the beginning of his training for a new life.

. . . .
Wait Training

There are lessons we can learn from Moses' failure.

1. Bad Choice

First, Moses did the wrong thing in the wrong way at the wrong time. His heart was in the right place, but he went about it all wrong. There was no need to kill the Egyptian who was mistreating the Hebrew. I'm sure there was a lot of pent-up anger in Moses' heart after seeing the Jews so miserably mistreated, but it was a serious sin and crime that would haunt him for years.

2. Bad Timing

Second, Moses' timing was horribly off—about forty years, to be exact. Moses' life can be divided into three forty-year increments. Moses spent forty years in Pharaoh's court finding out he was a somebody. He spent forty years in the wilderness finding out he was a nobody. Then he spent forty years finding out what God can do with a *somebody* who realizes he is a *nobody*!

After he murdered the Egyptian, Moses entered the "nobody" phase where he would live in a desert. There he found a family who befriended him. He married one of the daughters and ended up a shepherd for his father-in-law. That is probably where he thought he was going to die: in obscurity, in the desert, far from his people, watching his sheep. You might say he had taken an early retirement. He was sure he was disqualified in the race of life and never expected to run again.

God had other plans.

> Now Moses was tending the flock of Jethro his father-in-law, the priest of Midian. And he led the flock to the back of the desert, and came to Horeb, the mountain of God.
>
> And the Angel of the LORD appeared to him in a flame of fire from the midst of a bush. So he looked, and behold, the bush was burning with fire, but the bush was not consumed.
>
> Then Moses said, "I will now turn aside and see this great sight, why the bush does not burn."
>
> So when the LORD saw that he turned aside to look, God called to him from the midst of the bush and said, "Moses, Moses!" And he said, "Here I am." Then He said, "Do not draw near this place. Take your sandals off your feet, for the place where you stand is holy ground." (EXODUS 3:1–5)

God told Moses he had seen the suffering of His people. God appointed Moses to go to the pharaoh and lead the Jews to freedom. Moses was stunned, to say the least. He'd thought he was done.

What Moses did not realize was that God had been preparing him all of that time he spent watching sheep. The Lord was getting him ready to lead a human flock numbering more than three million to freedom. God was seasoning him. When he woke up that day, Moses had no idea that his life would forever change. It came unexpectedly.

. . . .

Look for the Lord in the Unusual

Moses encountered God in a burning bush. Now, Moses had spent a lot of time in the desert; he'd seen plenty of tumbleweeds. He'd seen bushes catch fire and burn out. This bush was different. It continued to burn, yet it did not dissipate. It was an ordinary bush doing an extraordinary thing—something God used to get Moses' attention. Then the Lord spoke.

I have discovered that when something out of the ordinary happens in my life, it may signal that the Lord is trying to speak to me. When you have an unexpected change of plans, you may think it's a disaster. Look again. It might be the hand of God trying to direct you a certain way. What may seem like a coincidence may actually be providence. Disappointment is His appointment.

Note that this was an ordinary bush that God touched—just like Moses at that point in his life. He was an older man. His skin was weathered and tanned from the sun. He was seasoned, wiser. But, unbeknownst to himself, old Moses was ready to rumble.

God was saying, "Look at that old bush. See how it keeps burning. That is what I am going to do with you. I am going to take an old bush like you and set you on fire. You are going to keep burning until My purpose is accomplished. Are you up for that?"

Listen to what God said in Exodus 3:6: "I am the God of your father—the God of Abraham, the God of Isaac, and the God of Jacob." What was God really saying? Though we often look at these men through rose-colored glasses, Abraham and Jacob both had lapses of faith. God was telling Moses, "I am the God of men who have failed. I am the God of ordinary men who have accomplished extraordinary things. There is hope for you. I am not just the God of Abraham, Isaac, and Jacob. I am the God of Moses. I am calling you. I am giving you a second chance."

In verse 7, God further explained Moses' mission: "I have surely seen the oppression of My people who are in Egypt, and have heard their cry because of their taskmasters, for I have known their sorrows." God had seen. He had heard. He was aware. "I have come to deliver," he said. "You are My man. Moses, just as this old bush burns, you are going to burn with My message. Are you ready for this?"

. . . .
Moses Fumbles His First Play

What Moses should have said was, "Absolutely. Thank You for calling me." Instead he offered up a plethora of excuses. People offer the same ones today as to why they think God cannot possibly use them.

1. "I Don't Have All the Answers"

> Then Moses said to God, "Indeed, when I come to the children of Israel and say to them, 'The God of your fathers has sent me to you,' and they say to me, 'What is His name?' what shall I say to them?"
> And God said to Moses, "I AM WHO I AM." And He said, "Thus you shall say to the children of Israel, 'I AM has sent me to you.'" (EXODUS 3:13–14)

We say the same thing: "I can't do that. I can't share the gospel. What if that person asks a question I can't answer?" "I can't teach a Bible study. I just don't know enough."

Don't misunderstand. There is definitely a place for preparation and study. But God can use you in some capacity wherever you are in your Christian life.

I began preaching at nineteen and pastoring at twenty. I had been a Christian for three years. My knowledge of the Bible was limited, to say the least. Prior to my conversion, I had no background in the Scriptures or in the church. It was all relatively new to me.

So I taught everything I had learned to that point, and then I continued to study and prepare myself with on-the-job training from that day to the present. My point is that I took what little I had and offered it to the Lord. You can do the same.

You have much more information in your head than you may realize. You don't know that because you have never tapped it. You have surrounded yourself with people who have the same level of knowledge you do. If you were to speak to a nonbeliever, he or she might fire some questions at you. In that case, you might be surprised at what you have to say under the inspiration of the Holy Spirit.

That is why God reassured Moses, "Don't sweat it. I will be with you. Nothing will overwhelm you."

2. "I Am Not a Good Speaker"

"Moses pleaded with the LORD, 'O Lord, I'm just not a good speaker. I never have been, and I'm not now, even after you have spoken to me. I'm clumsy with words'" (Ex. 4:10 NLT).

Maybe you are afraid to speak publicly. That may be an advantage. Sometimes people who lack self-confidence are better communicators than those who have it. Some people can talk you into anything. They can sell ice to an Eskimo. Such people can sometimes be manipulative.

A person who isn't overconfident may be the very person who should be a preacher. A person who isn't even comfortable standing up in front of people, who is a little embarrassed or shy, is a person who will depend totally on God. Then when he speaks, his message and persuasion will be from heaven instead of manipulative techniques.

You may know me as a pastor and evangelist, but I have to remind you that this is not anything I aspired to. When I was in school, I didn't like to be in front of crowds. I didn't like to study. Frankly, I was a bit of a goof-off. So God called me to be a person who had to be dedicated to study and public proclamation. It is the very opposite of what I felt prepared for humanly.

In fact, after I gave my life to the Lord I had a secret fear that God would call me to preach. I recoiled from the idea. I wanted to serve the Lord in some other capacity. I was a graphic designer, so I wanted to do artwork.

One day when I was a brand-new believer, I went to Big Corona Beach in Newport Beach, Orange County, to attend a baptism. I arrived late, though, and the baptism was over. I saw a group of Christians gathered, singing songs. I sat down with them and joined in the singing.

I was waiting for somebody to say something. I realized there was no leader. My heart started to burn as if the Lord wanted me to say something. I finally said (with a very shaky voice), "I would like to share what the Lord showed me in the Bible this week." As I spoke, I saw people nodding in agreement. When I was done, I offered up a silent prayer of thanks to God for allowing me that opportunity. I was so glad it was done.

God wasn't finished. I was feeling good about having the courage to speak when two girls said, "We missed the baptism. Pastor, can you baptize us?"

Pastor? I assured them I was nothing but a very new Christian. They didn't care. "Could you baptize us?"

Everyone else said, "Yeah, you should baptize them!" So, I reluctantly stood and led my newly acquired flock down toward the water. I felt like Moses Jr.!

I did not even know really how to technically baptize a person. I had been baptized myself but had never noticed the technique itself. *Do I hold the person's nose? What exactly do I say?*

I did the best I could and baptized those girls that day. Once again I was thankful but very relieved it was all over.

But I noticed that a rather large crowd had gathered as they observed these baptisms. Then it came to me as clear as day. The Lord spoke to my heart: "Proclaim My gospel to them!"

It was the moment I dreaded. It was what I had had nightmares about. But now that I was doing it by the leading of God's Holy Spirit, it was not a nightmare at all, but a dream come true. At the end of my mini-message I even offered an opportunity for those listening to come to Christ, and, as I recall, a few did. I baptized them as well. What a day.

God will give you the words when He wants you to speak. We may not all be called to be preachers, but we are all called to communicate His Word. You just take that step of faith.

3. "I Can't"

"Moses again pleaded, 'Lord, please! Send someone else'" (Ex. 4:13 NLT). In other words, "I am the wrong person for this. I stumble over my words. I just can't do it."

The Lord grew angry. He agreed to let Moses' brother, Aaron, do the talking. Moses liked that, but it was a big mistake. Aaron turned out to be a real albatross around Moses' neck. Don't forget that it was Aaron who had the bright idea of making a golden calf while Moses was away, receiving the Ten Commandments. Moses should have left Aaron at home and done what God had called him to do.

Don't tell the Lord, "I can't" when He knows you can—with His help. Paul reminds us that we "*can* do all things through Christ who strengthens" us (Phil.4:13, italics added).

The bottom line is that God can use anyone He wants to; even people who have made mistakes, even people who have sinned. It's all about His timing.

It's a fact that every runner in the race of life has sinned, has blown it in some way. Don't let appearances fool you: sin is an equal-opportunity sport. Run the track God assigns to you. Keep your excuses to yourself. If God is the One providing the power, how can you lose?

And if you're trying to run ahead of God's plan, slow down. Let Him start and stop the stopwatch. You'll never lose by letting the right Person control your pace. Let's see how Moses fared with the God of Abraham as his coach.

20
RUN WITH ALL YOU'VE GOT

Prior to knowing Jesus Christ, we perhaps thought we were the captains of our own ships, that we ran our own lives. But for all practical purposes, we were under the power of the prince of darkness. It was a big rip-off. He offered us life but gave us death. He promised us pleasure but gave us guilt. He promised us fun but brought us misery.

Then we discovered there was a God who loved us and had a plan for our lives. We took the plunge and gave our hearts to Jesus Christ. He forgave us of our sins and changed our eternal address from a place called hell to a place called heaven. It was a wonderful day that every Christian remembers vividly.

I hope that having done that, you weren't expecting a standing ovation in hell. You need to know that the devil was not happy about it—and still isn't. He lost one of his own. Consequently, the devil wants to bring you down. Satan knows that he cannot overpower God; therefore his objective is to draw you out through compromise.

Compromise has brought down more believers than has any other ploy the devil has in his toolbox. Through it he takes you down a bite at a time. It is so subtle you don't even realize it's happening.

In a race, compromise might mean skipping a lap, then saying you ran it...claiming to have run every day when you slept in instead...saying you were running to the end but quitting halfway there.

In our study of biblical characters and how they ran the race of life, we return now to our flawed hero, Moses. Compromise might have been a poison in his life that slowly ate away his purpose and power. Was it? Read on.

....

Nobody Said It Would Be Easy

We pick up the story where God had given Moses and Aaron their assignment, and they set off for Egypt.

> Moses and Aaron went in and told Pharaoh, "Thus says the LORD God of Israel: 'Let My people go, that they may hold a feast to Me in the wilderness.'" And Pharaoh said, "Who is the LORD, that I should obey His voice to let Israel go? I do not know the LORD, nor will I let Israel go."
> So they said, "The God of the Hebrews has met with us. Please, let us go three days' journey into the desert and sacrifice to the LORD our God, lest He fall upon us with pestilence or with the sword." (EXODUS 5:1–3)

Moses and Aaron were probably hoping Pharaoh would say, "No problem. God has been speaking to me about that as well. Go forth, and God bless you."

Not exactly.

You need to know that Moses and Aaron journeyed to Pharaoh with the support of Israel's elders. God had given Moses the power to perform certain wonders, to show Pharaoh he was on the side of the Israelites. Moses and Aaron showed these signs to the elders, and the elders believed their mission was from God.

But Pharaoh's response was less than enthusiastic: "Are you kidding? There is no way I am going to let that happen."

What does this show us? It reminds us that being in the will of God doesn't mean we will always have green lights and blue skies. Sometimes we think if the Lord has shown us to do something, it will be easy to do. Not necessarily. The devil will oppose you.

What did Moses and Aaron do? Did they say, "Forget it" and go back home? No. I love their tenacity and commitment. They refused to renege on their mission and went back for more.

> Moses and Aaron went in to Pharaoh, and they did so, just as the LORD commanded. And Aaron cast down his rod before Pharaoh and before his servants, and it became a serpent.
>
> But Pharaoh also called the wise men and the sorcerers; so the magicians of Egypt, they also did in like manner with their enchantments. For every man threw down his rod, and they became serpents. But Aaron's rod swallowed up their rods.
>
> And Pharaoh's heart grew hard, and he did not heed them, as the LORD had said. (EXODUS 7:10–13)

You may know that the serpent, specifically the cobra, was a respected symbol among the Egyptians. What was the first miracle Aaron did? He threw down his staff, and it turned into a serpent, which was probably a cobra. The pharaoh's magicians said, "We can do that too." Sure enough, their stick transformed into a snake as well. But the snake God produced through Aaron consumed the snake of the magicians. Still Pharaoh did not believe.

. . . .

Imitation and Infiltration

Who were Pharaoh's magicians? We read in 2 Timothy 3:8 that they were known as Jannes and Jambres: "These also resist the truth: men of corrupt minds, disapproved concerning the faith." They opposed Moses as people oppose the truth today; they were men with depraved minds.

We find in Jannes and Jambres one of Satan's most effective strategies: imitation and infiltration. He will try to stop a work altogether, but if that doesn't work, he will imitate. In these ways he seeks to minimize the power and glory of God and neutralize the impact of someone's life and testimony.

Let me illustrate. You know the story Jesus told of the wheat and the tares. A farmer sowed a field of wheat, and in the darkness of night his enemy sowed tares in the field. The tare is a plant almost identical to wheat in its initial stages of growth. To the undiscerning eye, it looks exactly like wheat. You can't tell the tare is there until it actually grows up and chokes out the wheat.

In the same way, the devil floods—infiltrates—the market with cheap imitations. How many times have you heard someone say, "The reason I am not a Christian is because there are so many hypocrites in the church"? That puts us in the very uncomfortable position of trying to defend people that don't practice what they preach.

Maybe, though, they aren't believers at all. Maybe they are tares among the wheat. Can you see how effective that ploy could be? Maybe Satan has placed those imitations there for the very purpose of keeping the nonbeliever from coming to faith.

Only the uncompromised life, such as the one Moses was then leading, can reveal God's glory and draw people to the Savior. The fakes can only do damage.

. . . .

Pharaoh's Strategy

Pharaoh was fooled by his fake magicians' trickery—or, at least, he chose to be. The result? Ten disastrous plagues sent from God.

He and his people faced nothing less than a river of blood, an abundance of frogs, dust turning to lice, relentless flies, wiped-out livestock, boils, hail, locusts, unending darkness, and finally, the death of every family's firstborn. During his weakest moments, Pharaoh actually began to relent.

But only a little.

In moments when the pharaoh realized he was outgunned, he tried to trick Moses through a series of compromises. As we watch Pharaoh try to manipulate Moses and drain him of his power, we see a picture of how the devil attempts to do the same to us.

Compromise #1: Go, But Stay

Scripture shows us that after the plague of flies, Pharaoh was beginning to soften.

> Pharaoh hastily called for Moses and Aaron. "All right! go ahead and offer sacrifices to your God," he said, "but do it here in this land. Don't go out into the wilderness."
>
> But Moses replied, "That won't do! The Egyptians would detest the sacrifices that we offer to the LORD our God. If we offer them here where they can see us, they will be sure to stone us. We must take a three-day trip into the wilderness to offer sacrifices to the LORD our God, just as he has commanded us."
>
> "All right, go ahead," Pharaoh replied. "I will let you go to offer sacrifices to the LORD your God in the wilderness. But don't go too far away. Now hurry, and pray for me."
>
> (EXODUS 8:25–28 NLT)

Pay careful attention. This is the anatomy of a compromise. What did God tell Moses and Aaron to do? Take the Jews three days' journey in the wilderness. Put three days' distance between them and Egypt, then sacrifice to the Lord. Pharaoh said, "Go sacrifice. Go call on your God—only do so here in Egypt."

Pharaoh was trying to get Moses to make some concessions. "Go ahead, if you don't want to worship the gods of Egypt and have to worship your God. Go do it. But don't go far. Stay around."

Then he added the little twist "Pray for me." That sounded promising. Moses might have said, "Look, Aaron, the Lord is opening Pharaoh's heart. He wants us to remember him in prayer. Maybe we should agree to his demands. After all, it's close enough to what God commanded."

No. Moses knew the Lord said to put significant distance between Egypt and Israel before making a sacrifice. It was a trick.

Have you ever seen this trick before? Perhaps after you gave your life to Christ, the devil whispered in your ear, "I didn't want you to do that, but I will concede that you have gone to the other side. Let's strike a deal. Don't be too fanatical here. Can we still have a little fun together? You don't have to give up all of your old friends or lifestyle. You can still believe in God, but be practical."

Essentially Satan says, "Go ahead and go, but don't go too far. You don't have to believe all of this stuff. You don't have to do everything the Bible says."

Some people have never fully repented. They have believed in Jesus but haven't moved very far from the old life. They stayed close enough that the enemy still has a foothold. Un-Godly friends still influence them. Persistent sins still drag them down.

Maybe that is what the devil is trying to pull off when he initiates a romantic relationship between a believer and a nonbeliever. I know sometimes Christians think they can reach the unsaved if they operate on their level: *I'll just lay low and be cool with them.* No one has ever been won to Christ by so called coolness. They are won by Godly living. They are won by a person's living a genuine, uncompromised life before God. And they are won as we lovingly and faithfully proclaim the gospel to them.

Sometimes we are trying so hard to be cool and relate that we forget about living a righteous life. We forget about standing up for what is right.

This is what the pharaoh was trying to do: "Sure, take a journey. But stay within the borders. Sure, offer a sacrifice. Just do it here. And while you're at it, pray for me." The pharaoh knew that if he could keep the Israelites near Egypt, he could keep them under his influence and reel them back again.

Compromise #2: Leave the Kids Here

After the plagues of boils and hail, Pharaoh again showed signs of cracking. Look at Exodus 10.

> So Moses and Aaron were brought back to Pharaoh. "All right, go and serve the LORD your God," he said. "But tell me, just whom do you want to take along?"
>
> "Young and old, all of us will go," Moses replied. "We will take our sons and daughters and flocks and herds. We must all join together in a festival to the LORD."
>
> Pharaoh retorted, "The LORD will certainly need to be along with you if you try to take your little ones along! I can see through your wicked intentions. Never! Only the men may go and serve the Lord, for that is what you requested." And Pharaoh threw them out of the palace. (VV. 8–11 NLT)

Pharaoh said to go but wanted to know Moses' roster.

"We are taking everyone," Moses responded. "Old people, young people, even our animals."

Pharaoh retorted "You think I am going to let you go with your kids? Forget about it. Go on and leave if you want. Leave your children here. I want them."

God's judgment once again came on Pharaoh for his resistant disobedience to release the Jews (Ex.10:12).

The devil wants you distracted. Do you see a spiritual lesson here? Do you think the devil wants your kids? How many generations of young people have been destroyed by drugs, sex, and rock and roll? It is amazing how each successive generation acts as though this is a new phenomenon. Kids get into the same things we got into when we were their age.

One of the ways the devil tries to get your children is by distracting you as a parent. How many children have been neglected as parents chased after success? Do any of these excuses sound familiar?

- "We do all this so we can give them a better life than we had."
- "We have to work the two jobs and put the kids in day care so they will have nicer toys at Christmas."
- "We focus on quality time with them instead of quantity of time."

You would be better off living in a smaller house and being home with your kids. The best thing you can spend on your children is time, and lots of it.

Face it: chasing success up the ladder rather than chasing your kids around the yard is a compromise of your job as parent. Now, I know that some parents, especially if they are single, do not have the luxury of staying home full-time to raise their children. But do whatever you can to spend as much time as possible with your little ones. Those days will pass so quickly.

The devil wants to divide and conquer you. Think of how many children have been destroyed as selfish husbands and wives have dissolved their marriages because of so called irreconcilable differences. What are irreconcilable differences, anyway? I have had irreconcilable differences with my wife for thirty-two years. She is neat, and I am messy. She is often late, and I am usually early. She is more kicked-back and relaxed, and I am more rushed all the time. I don't think we will ever completely agree. So what? Welcome to the real world.

If you want to spend life with someone who always agrees with you, marry yourself. Or better yet, stay single. Why were you initially attracted to your spouse? Because he or she was different from you. He or she had qualities that you admired or aspired to. That person balanced you, and you balanced him or her. You complemented one another.

Now those differences have turned into a wide chasm. Maybe you think that by dissolving your marriage and moving on to another, you won't have any more problems. In your mind, your mate is the source of all evil, and you are all good—is that it? Wake up and think about the children!

"They will be fine. Children are resilient. They will bounce back." They don't bounce back as quickly as you think they do. I know this as a child of divorce. I have experienced it firsthand. And I have seen it with so many others over thirty-one years of pastoring.

Roland Warren, president of the National Fatherhood Initiative, said, "There's a hole in the soul of every kid in the shape of their fathers, and for about forty years in social policy, we've been trying to fill that hole with lots of other things—money, quality time, mentors...They long for families and they mourn the fact they didn't have a family."[1]

Granted, there are other reasons marriages fall apart. There are even biblical allowances for divorce. But my experience is that many, if not most, of the marriages that have dissolved could have been saved if the husband and wife had made a greater effort to forgive and forget.

Parents, listen to me. Don't let the devil have your kids. Draw the line. You say to the enemy, "They belong to the Lord, and you can't have them."

Moses was digging in here. There would be no compromise.

Compromise #3: Leave a Little Livestock

Pharaoh had one more compromise up his sleeve. Exodus 10:24: "Then Pharaoh called to Moses and said, 'Go, serve the LORD; only let your flocks and your herds be kept back. Let your little ones also go with you.'"

The devil was fighting tooth and nail for Moses' character. Why did Pharaoh care about their animals? Because it would have been a victory, albeit a small one, to get something of the Israelites.

Imagine how tempting this must have been for Moses. "You want our animals? You will let the rest of us go? Good deal!" Aaron might have said, "Moses, this sounds doable!"

I love what Moses said: "Not a hoof shall be left behind" (v. 26). In other words, "Pharaoh, read my lips. You get zero, zip, nothing, nada. You don't even get an inch. You don't even get a sick animal. We are taking everyone and everything, and we are leaving, whether you like it or not."

That is what we need to say to the devil. The devil says, "If I can't have all of your life, let me have this one area. How about your fantasy life? A little fun with pornography. It won't go any further. How about this area? Just skim a little off the top."

Do you know why he wants something? Because little things will lead to big things. That's why you can't make deals with the devil. That's why you can't negotiate with Satan. That's why there can be no compromise.

If you are not prepared to go far away from him, you are never going to make it to what God has for you. If you are going to stay close to him and give him pieces of your life, he is going to manipulate you and kill your influence. It is time to break free.

Is there an area you know you need to deal with? Is there a situation in which you have been compromising? If something just jumped to the forefront of your mind—it feels like a raw nerve—the Lord brought that to your attention for a reason. It is not to drive you away in despair and guilt. It is a problem and a potential weakness. The Lord brought it to your mind so you can deal with it.

Take action. Right now, make a decision to dedicate that area of your life to God. Give it to Him. It is not too late. God can free you from it. He is still in the miracle-working business, but He needs your cooperation. Make a decision today that in giving your life to the Lord, *not a hoof will be left behind.*

Living an uncompromised life is how you get all your energies back in the race. Remember Moses and how he unflinchingly remained faithful to the task God set before him. He put his all into the race before him. You can do the same.

21
RUNNING *WITH* CHARACTER

Character counts

In fact, it may be the most important thing in a person's life. And it's not just what you say, but what you are. In fact, if you want to know who you really are, here is what it comes down to: when you are all alone, when no one is watching, when there is no one to impress— that is who you really are.

The measure of a man's real character is what he would do if he knew he would never be found out. A poll was taken of Americans asking, "Why do you not steal?" Here are the results:

- Reason #1: "I might get caught."
- Reason #2: "The other person might try to get even."
- Reason #3: "I might not need the item."

That strikes me as really missing the point. What about not stealing because it is wrong? More specifically, because God Himself has told us "You shall not steal" (Ex.20:15)?

If you were to take this flawed reasoning to other areas of life, you could say, "The reason I don't commit adultery or lie or whatever is fear of being caught." Then it is only a matter of time until you do one of these things, because there will, no doubt, come a situation where you may think you can indeed get away with one of these sins. Therefore, you will go ahead and do it.

There is a better deterrent. It's called integrity.

....

Who Are You When No One Is Watching?

I read an article in the paper about three men who stole some items from a home, including a DVD player, computer, TV, and other electronic gear. One of them realized that the owner of that house had a pet parrot and he might have heard one of the thieves refer to the name of one of the others.

So they decided to go back and get the bird, who, they feared, might turn out to be a stool pigeon! When they were loading the bird into their getaway car, police showed up. This ended up in a chase with the burglars and bird-thieves being arrested.

This reminds me of a statement by humorist Will Rogers: "So live that you would not mind selling your pet parrot to the town gossip."

Again, character or integrity is all about what you are when you are alone:

- What do you think about the most?
- What do you like to watch on TV?
- What Web sites do you visit?
- What saddens you?
- What makes you angry?
- What makes you laugh?

That is your character. As one German proverb says, "A man shows his character by what he laughs at."

Everyone has character of some kind. It is either good or bad. This personal integrity or character is something you develop on a daily basis. With every thought you think and deed you do, you are either building it up or tearing it down. It comes down to this: if you cheat in practice, you'll cheat in the game. If you cheat in your head, you'll cheat on the test. You'll cheat on the girl. You'll cheat in business. You'll cheat on your mate.

It's been said:

Sow a thought, and you reap an act;
Sow an act, and you reap a habit;
Sow a habit, and you reap a character;
Sow a character, and you reap a destiny.

I heard the story of a pastor who boarded a bus one Monday morning. He paid his fare and the bus driver gave him too much change. Even though he could have used the money, the pastor went up to the driver and said, "You must have made a mistake. You gave me too much change!"

The driver responded, "It was no mistake. I was in your church last night, and you spoke on honesty. I thought I would put you to the test!"

That's character.

. . . .
The Imperfect Moses

Moses was a man who had integrity, so much so that his personal godliness kept literally millions of Israelites from falling into idolatry. As long as Moses was around, his influence was so profound and significant that it kept a massive number of people from doing the wrong thing. He was such a good runner in the race that he inspired others to run as well as he did.

But even Moses wasn't perfect. Although he almost daily mirrored the personal character God desired in the Israelites, he had his moments of failure. And he paid for them. What's important is that he was constantly striving to be a man of integrity, in spite of his human shortcomings. He might have been temporarily barred from the track, but in the end he finished strong.

Let's pick up his story where we left off.

....
The People Weren't Perfect, Either

You'll remember that ten successive plagues fell upon Egypt, each growing in intensity, until finally and reluctantly the pharaoh relented and released the Israelites to Moses' care. Off they went from the bondage they had suffered for so many years.

God continued to look after the Israelites. As they were making their way out of Egypt, they came to an apparent impasse. Before them was the Red Sea. To the right and left was treacherous territory they could not enter. Behind them was Egypt. To make matters worse, Pharaoh had had second thoughts about releasing the Israelites, and his armies were in hot pursuit.

God's people cried out, "What is going to happen to us?" They went from being wildly ecstatic and thankful to Moses and God for their release to being wildly panicked.

The Lord told Moses, "Stand still, and see the salvation of the Lord" (Ex. 14:13). He opened up the Red Sea, and Moses led the Israelites through to dry ground. Then God released the waters, and the sea crashed down on and drowned the pursuing Egyptian army.

The Israelites sang a song of praise to God.

Then the Lord began to lead the Israelites in a very obvious way. In the daytime a big cloud served as their guide;

when the cloud moved, they were to move. When the cloud stopped, they were to stop. At night it was a pillar of fire. It was better then GPS! (What a great way to get around. For someone like me, who is clearly navigationally dysfunctional, this would be wonderful!)

The Lord provided for their physical needs as well. Every morning when they emerged from their tents, waiting for them was fresh manna. God faithfully provided this supernatural foodstuff. All they had to do was gather it up and enjoy it. You can imagine how the Israelites must have revered Moses at this point.

Then Moses went away to receive the Ten Commandments...and everything fell apart. Bickering, confusion, and idol worshiping became the rule of the day. Think about this: the Israelites were literally surrounded by miracles and the supernatural, yet in a relatively short period of time they turned to full-tilt idolatry. How could such a thing happen?

Because miracles do not necessarily guarantee Godly living. You might think if only there were miracles in your life, or more supernatural phenomena taking place, you would be stronger spiritually. Not always. Not if you're misplacing your thankfulness.

The Israelites' problem came down to one thing: the shallowness and superficiality of their faith. As we will discover, they bowed before a man-made golden calf. That clearly was idolatry. But their first idol was not the golden calf; it was *Moses.* They never seemed to develop their own relationship with God. It is as though their relationship with God was dependent upon Moses' presence. That's a wonderful tribute to the influence of a Godly man, but it is also a criticism of their lack of personal faith.

Let me illustrate. When you travel overseas, you need to take electrical adapters with you. Your American plugs won't fit their outlets, and your electrical currency needs might not match what is available. A number of years ago I was in Israel. I plugged my hair dryer into the wall and noticed that my hair was drying a little more quickly than normal. I discovered that 220 volts of electricity were pumping into that little hair dryer designed for 110. I also noticed that my hair dryer was on fire. The nozzle was literally melting. I needed an adapter.

Without an adapter, you cannot utilize the electricity that is available to you. In the same way, the Israelites needed an adapter. They could not relate to God on their own. If Moses wasn't there, whatever connection they had with the Lord seemed to fall apart. Their relationship with God depended upon Moses' relationship with God. This is never a healthy thing spiritually.

Case in point: God called Moses up to Mount Sinai to receive the Ten Commandments. Look at what happened:

> Now when the people saw that Moses delayed coming down from the mountain, the people gathered together to Aaron, and said to him, "Come, make us gods that shall go before us; for as for this Moses, the man who brought us up out of the land of Egypt, we do not know what has become of him." (EXODUS 32:1)

Moses was gone, and Israel needed something or someone to worship. Instead of recognizing it was the Lord through Moses who had led them out of Egypt, they credited Moses himself. As soon as Moses was gone, they wanted something to take his place.

Basically the Israelites were saying, "We need something tangible. It is hard for us to relate to an invisible, supernatural God. We want something we can reach out and take hold of."

So began the plans for the golden calf. This ultimately led to a pathetic scene of sexual immorality and idol worship. Moses was Israel's first idol, and the golden calf was their second.

. . . .

A Little Integrity Goes a Long Way

We can't blame Moses for this, because it was his personal godliness and integrity that had kept Israel in line up to that point. Consider this: one man had kept three million people from turning away to worship false gods.

It reminds us that God can do a lot with a little. Jesus said that we as His church are the salt of the earth; as you know, a little salt goes a long way. Just a pinch of salt in some oatmeal can enhance its flavor. Too much, and it's ruined.

In life, one "salty" person can go a long way. One Christian in a family, in a neighborhood, or in a workplace can influence many, many people. Often, though, we try to get out of those uncomfortable situations.

Perhaps, at your worksite, all of the other guys are nonbelievers. They laugh at you. You are the brunt of their jokes. You want to get a new job.

Maybe in your classroom, you are the one Christian who will disagree with the professor when he is promoting evolution or some other secular worldview. It is hard; you're definitely in the minority, and it makes you uncomfortable.

Perhaps you have some neighbors that like to stay up late and drink and party the night away.

You want to be in a Christian school, a Christian neighborhood, a Christian job. Life would then be easier. But did you ever stop to think maybe God put you where you are to be an influence?

That is what Moses was. Imagine how hard it was for him. Those people were so full of unbelief and whining and complaining. But through his integrity and personal holiness, Moses influenced them for the good. Oh, how we need more people like this who will make a difference in this world! You think things are bad in this country now—and they are, with our terrorism, immorality, epidemics of divorce and suicide. These are crazy times. But think: it is the presence of the church in the world today that is keeping it from getting even worse. Just wait until the Lord calls His church home. Imagine what will happen when we who are the salt of the earth are no longer here. We are God's representatives.

Moses was God's representative. In contrast to this man of integrity, there was Aaron his brother. Aaron made a mess of things. In the absence of Moses, the people sought a new leader, and, unfortunately, Aaron complied. When they demanded something to worship, Aaron told them to give him all their gold earrings. He took the gold, melted it, and fashioned it into a golden calf (Ex. 32:4). They stripped off their clothes and danced naked before it.

Let's look at some of the characteristics of integrity and how Moses and Aaron did or didn't represent it well.

1. A Man of Integrity Is an Intercessor

Down in the valley Aaron had allowed the Israelites to worship a golden idol. Up on Sinai, God alerted Moses to what was happening. What did Moses do when God told him?

> And the LORD said to Moses, "Go! Get down! For your people whom you brought out of the land of Egypt have corrupted themselves. They have turned aside quickly out of the way which I commanded them. They have made themselves a molded calf, and worshiped it and sacrificed to it, and said, 'This is your god, O Israel, that brought you out of the land of Egypt!'"
>
> And the LORD said to Moses, "I have seen this people, and indeed it is a stiff-necked people! Now therefore, let Me alone, that My wrath may burn hot against them and I may consume them. And I will make of you a great nation."
>
> Then Moses pleaded with the LORD his God, and said, "LORD, why does Your wrath burn hot against Your people whom You have brought out of the land of Egypt with great power and with a mighty hand? Why should the Egyptians

speak and say, 'He brought them out to harm them, to kill them in the mountains, and to consume them from the face of the earth'? Turn from Your fierce wrath, and relent from this harm to Your people.

"Remember Abraham, Isaac, and Israel, Your servants, to whom You swore by Your own self, and said to them, 'I will multiply your descendents as the stars of heaven; and all this land that I have spoken of I will give to your descendants, and they will inherit it forever.'"

So the LORD relented from the harm which He said He would do to His people. (EXODUS 32:7-14)

You might read these passages and think the Lord was really in the wrong, and Moses brought him around. That is not true at all. God wanted to see if Moses was learning anything.

Remember Jesus tested His disciples. We read of the multitudes that gathered. Jesus turned to His disciple Philip and asked, "Where are we going to find food to feed all of these people?" The Bible says, "This He said to test him" (John 6:6). He wanted to see if they had learned anything.

Moses faced such a test. When the Lord said, "I am going to destroy these people," Moses said, "Hold on now, Lord. These are Your people that You brought out of Egypt, and You made a covenant with Abraham, Isaac, and Jacob that You would multiply their descendants. If you kill them, then the Egyptians will say, 'Look at this God who delivers His people to death.' This is a bad move. Spare Your people."

The Lord answered, "I will spare them." God was always going to spare them. But he wanted Moses to be an intercessor.

That's what prayer is all about: it's seeing things the way God sees them and praying accordingly. It's standing in the gap. God wants you to care about lost people as He does, see them as sheep without a Shepherd, and pray for them.

We see how much Moses cared when in Exodus 32:32 he prayed, "Please forgive their sin—and if not, blot me out of the record you are keeping" (NLT). Do you understand what Moses was saying? "Lord, if this is what it takes, I am willing to go to hell that they could go to heaven." Fortunately God required no such thing, but it shows the heart of a true intercessor, one who really cares.

Paul said something similar when he wrote, "My heart is filled with bitter sorrow and unending grief for my people, my Jewish brothers and sisters. I would be willing to be forever cursed—cut off from Christ!—if that would save them" (Rom. 9:2–3 NLT). That is the heart for people we need to have.

2. A Man of Integrity Is Responsible for His Actions

Moses descended from the mountain holding the commandments God gave him in his arms. When he encountered Aaron, he heard perhaps the lamest excuse found in the pages of the Bible. Aaron's rationale for the Israelites' behavior was so absurd it should permanently be enshrined in the Excuse Hall of Fame, along with "My alarm didn't go off," "The dog ate my homework," and "The check is in the mail."

Upon seeing the people dancing before the golden calf:

> Moses said to Aaron, "What did this people do to you that you have brought so great a sin upon them?"
>
> So Aaron said, "Do not let the anger of my lord become hot. You know the people, that they are set on evil. For they said to me, 'Make us gods that shall go before us; as for this Moses, the man who brought us out of the land of Egypt, we do not know what has become of him.' And I said to them 'If you have any gold, let them break it off.' So they gave it to me, and I cast it into the fire, and this calf came out." (EXODUS 32:21–24)

How lame was that? He refused to take responsibility for his actions. Aaron should have drawn the line when Israel said, "Moses is gone, and we need something to worship." He should have said, "You just worship God, and wait until Moses gets back." Instead he caved in. Then when Moses confronted him, he passed the buck.

It reminds me of a substitute teacher. God bless you if that is what you do for a living. We used to abuse them horribly when I was in school. We knew we could get away with anything. They didn't know all of the rules, so we made them up. The substitute lacked the authority and knowledge of the teacher, so we tormented him or her to no end.

Aaron was sort of like a substitute teacher. He was the polar opposite of Moses. Moses had backbone. He thought clearly. He was decisive. He had integrity. Aaron had no backbone. His thinking was muddled. He had no integrity. He wanted to be popular. He didn't want to offend anybody. Not only did he go along with Israel's plan, he even facilitated it. He lacked the authority and steadfastness of Moses, Israel's true leader.

Many people are like Aaron today. When they are around committed Christians, they are temporarily strong. But when they get away from Christians, they blend into the woodwork. The story of Aaron's spiritual demise serves as a warning to the vacillating, compromising person who always wants to go along with public opinion and is more concerned with what people think than with what God thinks. (I dealt with this more in-depth in my book *The Great Compromise*, Allen David Publishers.)

Don't be an Aaron. Aarons reach no one. Be a Moses. Be a man or a woman who stands up for what is right. One person can make a big difference.

. . . .

Even the Best Runner Sometimes Stumbles

Fast-forward to the time when Moses and the Israelites had traveled through the wilderness for thirty-nine years. They were on the brink of entering the promised land. Moses had put up with years of whining, sniveling, complaining, ungratefulness, and outright sin. Finally, he was just about to blow his lid.

Numbers 20 records the incident:

Now there was no water for the congregation; so they gathered together against Moses and Aaron. And the people contended with Moses and spoke, saying: "If only we had died when our brethren died before the Lord! Why have you brought up the assembly of the Lord into this wilderness, that we and our animals should die here? And why have you made us come up out of Egypt, to bring us to this evil place? It is not a place of grain or figs or vines or pomegranates; nor is there any water to drink." (VV. 2–5)

Moses and Aaron entered the tabernacle and prayed. God was gracious and told Moses, "Take the rod; you and your brother Aaron gather the congregation together. Speak to the rock before their eyes, and it will yield its water; thus you shall bring water for them out of the rock, and give drink to the congregation and their animals" (Num. 20:8).

Notice that God said only to speak to the rock. When God tells us to do something, we need to do it. The problem is that sometimes we *selectively* hear and obey God. If God says to do something we like, we respond, "Yes, Lord." Then he tells us to stop doing something we personally enjoy, and the reception suddenly grows fuzzy. "God, you're breaking up!"

Jesus said, "You are My friends if you do whatever I command you" (John 15:14). He didn't say, "You are My friends if you do the things with which you personally agree."

God has told us how to live in His Word. It is not for us to pick and choose the parts of the Bible we like and throw the others aside. This is a package deal.

Back to Moses and the rock. Earlier in his travels with Israel, they had also run out of water. In that case, God told Moses to "strike the rock, and water will come out of it, that the people may drink" (Ex. 17:6). This time He said, "Speak to the rock."

It may seem like a small thing to us, but it was a big thing to God. He had his reasons for saying what he said. One may be that the rock is used in the Scripture as a picture of God. How many times do we read of God being compared to a rock? Psalm 31:3 says, "You are my rock and my fortress; / Therefore, for Your name's sake, / Lead me and guide me." In the New Testament we read in 1 Corinthians 10:4 that the Israelites "drank of that spiritual Rock that followed them, and that Rock was Christ."

When God told Moses to strike the first rock, it was a symbol of what happened to Jesus. The Rock was struck—He was crucified. Because of His death on the cross, we can be forgiven. Hence afterward all Moses had to do was speak to the rock.

The second time, though, Moses disobeyed the Lord's specific command:

Moses and Aaron gathered the assembly together before the rock; and he said to them, "Hear now, you rebels! Must we bring water for you out of this rock?" Then Moses lifted his hand and struck the rock twice with his rod; and water came out abundantly. (NUMBERS 20:20–11)

Whoops. God said, "Son, I want to speak with you. What did I tell you to do? I told you to speak to the rock. You struck it. Come back behind My woodshed for a moment." Then the

LORD spoke to Moses and Aaron and said, "Because you did not believe Me, to hallow Me in the eyes of the children of Israel, therefore you shall not bring this assembly into the land which I have given them" (Num. 20:12).

. . . .

How Moses Blew It

Think of how close they were to the promised land. For thirty-nine years, Moses had, with integrity, led, tolerated, and interceded for God's stubborn people, and yet he would not enjoy their reward. Why?

1. Moses Stole the Limelight

First of all, Moses took personal credit for what God had done. That is not a smart thing to do. What did he say? "You rebels! Must *we* bring water for you out of this rock?" Moses never got water out of any rock for Israel. God did.

It sounds as if Moses, instead of giving the glory to God, believed his own press. That is always a danger; when God uses you, you may start thinking you are indispensable. *It won't happen without me. I am God's man [or woman] of faith and power for this hour.* Be careful now. When God does something through your life, always give Him the glory.

2. Moses Disobeyed

Mistake number two was that Moses went against God's wishes. God told him to speak to the rock, and he struck it instead.

Have you ever done something in a rage that you were sure was right? But when the adrenaline wore off, you realized you had acted like a fool. That is what happened to Moses. He was so angry, he beat on the rock. He was out of control. He disobeyed God.

Leaders have an awesome responsibility. James reminded us, "Let not many of you become teachers, knowing that we shall receive a stricter judgment" (3:1). One day God will hold leaders accountable for what they have done. So we want to be very careful that everything we say and do is based on God's truth. When we stand to speak for God, we need to treat it as a serious responsibility.

We should prepare ourselves. We should make sure it is the real work of God. God does not like misrepresentation. Remember that Jesus saved His more scathing words for the religious hypocrites of the day, the Pharisees, because they misrepresented God to the people.

Moses misrepresented God and failed to honor Him. He lost entrance to the promised land. What a price to pay!

. . . .
Even if You Trip, Finish the Lap

You say, "That is overkill. Poor Moses. Look at all of the things he put up with!" I know. He was sort of like a runner who tripped in his final lap. In the end, though, he did do well. Moses was a winner in the spiritual race. How so? He eventually entered the promised land. Remember when Jesus was transfigured? Who stood on each side of him? Elijah and *Moses.*

In the end, Moses was still the man of God, the man of integrity.

How do you measure up? What if we were to interview people who know you well—your spouse, your children, your coworkers? What would they say about you? "He is a man of God"? "She lacks integrity"?

Are you seeking to be an influence on those around you? Are you living a life of integrity? Are you an intercessor caring enough to pray for those who are separated from God?

Let's remember to give God the glory for everything He does in our lives. Let's be careful that we do things the way the Lord tells us to. If we remember to do these things, who we are in private and who we are in public will be one and the same. We will finish the race well, whatever our stumbles along the way. We will be winners.

CONCLUSION:
THE GREATEST
WINNER *OF* ALL

We have looked together at some losers and winners, saints and sinners. Some have run and fallen, never to rise. Others have fallen and got back in the race. And some have started and finished well.

I think Hebrews 12 nicely summarizes all we have studied:

Therefore we also, since we are surrounded by so great a cloud of witnesses, let us lay aside every weight, and the sin which so easily ensnares us, and let us run with endurance the race that is set before us, looking unto Jesus, the author and finisher of our faith, who for the joy that was set before Him endured the cross, despising the shame, and has sat down at the right hand of the throne of God.

For consider Him who endured such hostility from sinners against Himself, lest you become weary and discouraged in your souls. You have not yet resisted to bloodshed, striving against sin. And you have forgotten the exhortation which speaks to you as to sons:

"My son, do not despise the chastening of the Lord,
   Nor be discouraged when you are rebuked by Him;

For whom the LORD loves He chastens,
    And scourges every son whom He receives."
(HEBREWS 12:1–6)

This passage gives us a few things we need to consider.

. . . .
Lessons from Hebrews 12

1. We Need to Consider the Winners

We are told there is "a great cloud of witnesses." Think of people in the grandstands at a sports event. This verse describes those people Hebrews 11 lists as being in the hall of fame of faith. These are men and women who lived Godly and obedient lives. They gave us an example to follow, a pace to keep, a template to apply.

2. We Need to Consider Ourselves

When the race is difficult, we tend to blame circumstances, other people, or even God. We need to remember that if we stumble or fall in the race of life, it is our own fault. The Bible says, "His divine power has given to us all things that pertain to life and godliness" (2 Pet. 1:3).

Hebrews tells us to "lay aside every weight, and the sin which so easily ensnares us." Do you see the distinction? Lay aside the *weight* and the *sin*. Sin is sin, no matter how you slice it or dice it. A weight may be something else.

I've mentioned this before, but it's worth repeating. Ask yourself about each thought, activity, idea, word: is it a wing, or is it a weight? Is it something that speeds you on your way? Or is it something that slows you down?

A great concert violinist was asked her secret. Her answer? "Planned neglect." She said, "Anything that would keep me from practicing and playing well must be neglected." Some of us could use some planned neglect in our lives. We carry around a lot more junk than we may realize. Periodically we need to jettison this excess weight and let it go.

Lay aside both sin *and* weight.

3. We Need to Consider the Race Itself

What race should we run? The race that is set before us. Remember that I am not competing with you. You are not competing with me. Our competition is the enemy—the world, the flesh, and the devil. Our goal is not to outrun each other. Our goal is to outrun those wicked influences that could bring us down.

You might justify your slow pace by saying a lot of people are still behind you on the track. True. But there are also probably a lot of people ahead of you. Don't concern yourself with who is behind or ahead of you. You are to run the race that is set before you. God has not called you to run my race, nor me yours. He calls each to run his own race.

Today, are you running the race of life as well as you ought to? Or are you just offering a half-effort?

The apostle Paul set an example for us in Philippians 3: "I am focusing all of my energies on this one thing... I strain to reach the end of the race and receive the prize" (vv. 13–14 NLT).

Keep your eyes on your own lane. Run your race.

4. We Need to Consider Jesus Christ

"Looking unto Jesus, the author and finisher of our faith, who for the joy that was set before Him endured the cross, despising the shame, and has sat down on the right hand of the throne of God." This is what will keep you going in the race of life.

We are running for an audience of one. Jesus is watching us, and He is rooting for us. He is even praying for us.

Remember, this is what gave young Stephen the courage to

face death when his audience's anger boiled. Just before they stoned him, he said, "Look! I see the heavens opened and the Son of Man is standing at the right hand of God!" (Acts 7:56). The sight of Jesus gave Stephen the ability to run the race and finish it.

Keep your eyes on Jesus; look unto the Author and Finisher of your faith. Why? Because circumstances will disappoint and at times devastate you. People will let you down. Feelings will come and go. But Jesus is there standing before you, holding your reward and saying, "Come on, you can do this! You can live this life. You can finish this race. I am here with you. Let's do it."

What do you want to be—a winner or a loser in this spiritual race?

. . . .

Did Jesus Have an Advantage?

Jesus was the greatest winner of all. You may say, "Of course. He was God. He had a definite advantage over the rest of us." But there's more to it than that.

We sometimes think that because Jesus was and is God, it was relatively easy for Him to run His race and finish His work on earth. It wasn't. He lived the same way you and I must: by faith in God and obedience to His Word. Hebrews 5:8 says, "Even though Jesus was God's Son, he learned obedience from the things he suffered" (NLT). Don't forget that Jesus experienced rejection…deep sorrow…intense loneliness. Jesus felt every human emotion.

Even when He resisted the devil's temptations in the wilderness, Jesus responded in a way we can. When the devil tempted Him, Jesus didn't say, "Back off, Satan. I am Jesus Christ, the only begotten Son of God. You can't touch Me." Nor did He airlift Himself out of the situation. He faced it as any human being could: He fought back with the Word of God.

Jesus has run before us. He is the ultimate winner. He is showing us how to do it. As Corrie ten Boom said years ago, "Look within and be depressed. Look without and be distressed. Look at Jesus and be at rest."

Are you looking to Jesus today? How are you doing in the race of life? Are weights slowing you down? Are sins tripping you up? If so, I urge you to follow the leader—Jesus. Keep to your own lane, hold a steady pace, and that finish line will be at your feet any minute. I know you can do it.

Be a saint, not a sinner. Be a winner.

NOTES

Introduction

1. Larry King, *Remember Me When I'm Gone* (New York: Nan A. Talese, 2004).

Chapter 1

1. "I Have Decided to Follow Jesus," Indian melody, writer unknown, public domain.

2. Adapted from Heather Stringer, "Faith on Flight 175," *New Man*, January/February 2002.

Chapter 5

1. Alan Redpath, *The Making of a Man of God* (Grand Rapids, MI: Revell, 1994).

2. Charles Swindoll, *David* (Nashville, TN: W Publishing Group, 1997).

Chapter 10

1. Adapted from Jeffrey Kluger, "Fear Not!" *Time*, April 2, 2001.

Chapter 20

1. Steve Beard, "Childhood Divorce Fuels Fire of New Rock," *Washington Times*, October 4, 2002.

Perfecting Your Purpose

40 Days to a More Meaningful Life

DAVID D. IRELAND, PHD

What a difference forty days can make. In fact, the Bible is filled with examples of monumental events that effected great change in just forty days; the great flood survived by Noah and his family is just one example.

Now, David Ireland offers "God's 40-day plan" to help readers create purposeful lives filled with meaning and direction. Dr. Ireland teaches readers to establish and adhere to a routine for forty days—thereby creating habits that will last a lifetime. Using illustrations from the Bible, along with specific examples of ordinary people who have successfully followed this method, Dr. Ireland shows readers how easy it can be to start over, discover their personal purpose, and start living according to God's plan—all in just forty days.

LaVergne, TN USA
15 November 2010
204987LV00001B/40/P